The Gaither Committee,
Eisenhower, and the
Cold War

The Gaither Committee, Eisenhower, and the

COLD WAR

David L. Snead

Ohio State University Press

Columbus

Library of Congress Cataloging-in-Publication Data

Snead, David L. (David Lindsey)
 The Gaither committee, Eisenhower, and the Cold War / David L. Snead.
  p.   cm.
 Includes bibliographical references and index.
 ISBN 0-8142-0805-3 (cloth : alk. paper).—ISBN 0-8142-5005-X (pbk. : alk. paper)
 1. Eisenhower, Dwight D. (Dwight David), 1890–1969. 2. National security—
United States—History—20th century. 3. United States—Military policy—History—
20th century. 4. United States—Foreign relations—1953–1961. 5. United States—
Politics and government—1953–1961. 6. Cold War. 7. Gaither, H. Rowan (Horace
Rowan), 1909–1961. I. Title.
 E835.S57   1998
 327.73'009'045—dc21   98-28163
                                                                                    CIP

Text and cover design by Ron Starbuck.
Type set in Galliard by G & S Typesetters, Inc.
Printed by Braun-Brumfield, Inc.

The paper used in this publication meets the minimum requirements of the American National
Standard for Information Sciences—Permanence of Paper for Printed Library Materials. ANSI
Z39.48–1992.

9 8 7 6 5 4 3 2 1

For Lori,
My Wife and Best Friend

CONTENTS

Acknowledgments

As with any study of this magnitude, I am deeply indebted to many individuals for their assistance. Sylvia Koner graciously allowed me to use the photograph of H. Rowan Gaither, Jr., taken by her husband, Marion Koner. The staffs of the Alderman Library at the University of Virginia, the Eisenhower Library, the Library of Congress, the George S. Marshall Foundation, the Massachusetts Institute of Technology Archives, the National Archives, and the U.S. Military Academy Archives provided invaluable assistance in my research visits. In particular, I would like to thank Tom Branigar, Dawn Crumpler, Marti Gansz, and Helen Samuels.

Various scholars provided assistance and support at various stages of this project. I owe a great deal to my close friend and compatriot Robert Hopkins for his great knowledge of intelligence operations in the 1950s. Robert Bowie, Richard Immerman, Burton Kaufman, and Robert Watson provided insight into specific areas of the manuscript. Brian Balogh, Nelson Lichtenstein, and Allen Lynch served as readers on my dissertation committee and offered invaluable advice that helped sharpen my arguments. Last, but not least, Melvyn Leffler guided this entire project with the precision and alacrity for which he is well known. I cannot begin to thank him enough.

I would also like to thank the Eisenhower Library for the award of a travel grant that allowed me to make an extra research trip to its wonderful facility in Abilene, Kansas.

I cannot begin to thank the staff at Ohio State University Press enough. Barbara Hanrahan offered unending encouragement from the first day she saw my manuscript. Ruth Melville, Beth Ina, and Colleen Romick, the freelance copyeditor, provided expert editorial advice.

ix

I would like to thank my family and friends who supported me throughout this study. Lynn and Parker Fretwell and Keith and Cindy Patterson provided unsurpassed friendships through many trying times. D.C. and Carolyn Hughes followed this project closely and offered tremendous encouragement. My brothers and sister—Rucker, Billy, Mac, and Lynne—constantly supported my efforts to complete this study. I cannot express the appreciation I have for my mom, Marilyn Snead, nearly enough. She provided financial support and, more important, love and encouragement.

Finally, my wife, Lori, endured many long years of study and research trips. She supported me on the many nights and weekends when I had to work. She provided financial support to our family as I pursued this study. She proved to be an invaluable critic of my work as she read page after page about the Gaither committee. For all of this assistance, I am deeply grateful. Without her love, support, and patience, this manuscript would never have been completed.

Introduction

Coming off a landslide victory over Adlai Stevenson in the November 1956 election, President Dwight D. Eisenhower began his second administration seemingly poised to continue the policies of his first term. Ironically, however, 1957 would become one of the longest and most difficult years of his presidency. Over the course of the year, he struggled with congressional cuts to his defense budget, faced a racial crisis over segregation in Little Rock, saw the Soviet Union launch the first satellite into space, and observed the economy sinking into a recession. The results were dramatic. In less than a year his popularity in the polls had fallen over twenty percentage points.[1]

The crises Eisenhower faced at the end of 1957 can be traced to both domestic and foreign policy issues. Without underemphasizing the widespread disenchantment with Eisenhower's handling of race relations and the economy, the concern of most Americans in late 1957 lay elsewhere. For the first time, the Soviet Union had made a significant technological advancement ahead of the United States. On October 4, 1957, the Soviet Union shocked the world with the launch of *Sputnik*. Coupled with the Kremlin's earlier claim of a successful test of an intercontinental ballistic missile (ICBM), the launch of *Sputnik II* on November 3, and the embarrassing failure of the U.S. Vanguard rocket in December, the Soviet satellite represented a clear challenge to U.S. technological superiority. More important, it raised the possibility that the Soviet Union might be able to launch a surprise nuclear attack against the United States using this new missile technology. Eisenhower's attempts to minimize the implications of the Soviet accomplishments only inflated fears, as many Americans assumed he was trying to conceal U.S. military weaknesses.[2]

1

In the midst of this uproar, Eisenhower received a top-secret report prepared by a blue-ribbon committee of leading scientific, engineering, economic, and military experts. The panel, called the Gaither committee in recognition of its first chairman, H. Rowan Gaither, Jr., emphasized both the inadequacy of U.S. defense measures designed to protect the civil population and the vulnerability of the country's strategic nuclear forces in the event of a Soviet attack. The Gaither committee members viewed these defense measures—ranging from a missile system to defend the continental United States to the construction of shelters to protect the population from radioactive fallout—and the maintenance of sufficient strategic forces to launch military strikes against Soviet targets as essential for the preservation of U.S. security. They concluded that in the case of a surprise Soviet nuclear attack, the United States would be unable to defend itself with any degree of success. The report emphasized the urgent need for the Eisenhower administration to strengthen the country's continental and civil defenses and to accelerate the development of its strategic striking power. It stressed that the United States either had to respond immediately to the expanding Soviet military capabilities or face potentially grave consequences.

The Gaither committee recommended that the United States reduce the vulnerability of its strategic forces, strengthen and enlarge its nuclear ballistic missile capabilities, improve the ability of the armed forces to wage limited military operations, reorganize the Department of Defense, and construct fallout shelters to protect the civilian population. These recommendations would cost $44.2 billion, spread between 1959 and 1963. The price was high, but the committee concluded that the costs for not instituting them would be higher yet—the possible subjugation of the United States to the Soviet Union. It emphasized, "The next two years seem to us critical. If we fail to act at once, the risk [of not preparing for a Soviet attack], in our opinion, will be unacceptable."[3] The committee accentuated that by the end of this two-year period the Soviet Union would possess sufficient nuclear forces to overwhelm U.S. defenses and to eliminate U.S. strategic nuclear capabilities. The only way the United States could avoid this "risk" was to adopt the recommendations advocated by the committee.

Eisenhower evaluated the Gaither report in the same manner as he studied most national security issues. He used the National Security Council (NSC) as the nexus for discussion of the committee's conclusions and recommendations. After receiving the report in November 1957, the NSC assigned to various government agencies the responsibility for analyzing specific parts of the report. By January 1958 the NSC was ready to discuss the report itself and the agencies' comments. For almost six months, the Gaither report or issues directly related to it dominated NSC discussions. During the remainder of the Eisenhower administration and throughout the Kennedy administration, these same issues reappeared periodically in discussions of U.S. national security policies.

The Gaither report significantly influenced Eisenhower's national security policies for the remainder of his presidency. Of all the Gaither committee recommendations, Eisenhower disagreed with only a few. While he opposed construction of fallout shelters and the expansion of military capabilities to wage limited war, he approved the implementation of most of the other recommendations, at least in part. His requests for supplementary appropriations to the FY 1958 defense budget and increases to the FY 1959 budget reveal the importance of the Gaither report. Between the two budgets, Eisenhower added nearly $4 billion in defense spending, an almost 10 percent increase in annual expenditures. He accelerated the development and deployment of ICBMs, intermediate-range ballistic missiles (IRBMs), and the Polaris submarine system for launching missiles. He ordered the reduction of Strategic Air Command (SAC) vulnerability through the construction of early warning radar, the dispersal of SAC forces to a larger number of airfields, and the implementation of alert programs. Furthermore, he sought and received congressional approval for the reorganization of the Defense Department.

The influence of the Gaither report did not end with these changes. As a senator and then as president, John F. Kennedy championed many of the same programs. After the contents of the report were leaked to the media in December 1957, many critics, including Kennedy, challenged Eisenhower's policies. The Massachusetts senator questioned why the United States was not doing more to overcome the apparent Soviet lead in military preparedness. While Eisenhower refused to expand military spending beyond certain levels, Kennedy did not show the same inhibitions. In the 1960 campaign and during his presidency, Kennedy received advice from at least a dozen Gaither committee members. His "flexible response" military strategy reflected much of the advice contained in the Gaither report. He accelerated ballistic missile developments, expanded limited war capabilities, and advocated civil defense programs.

Key Historiographical Debates

The Gaither committee's conclusions and recommendations had a clear influence on the Eisenhower and Kennedy administrations. The report itself, however, has been ignored or at least underemphasized by most scholars.[4] One of the main reasons for this slight is that scholars focused on *Sputnik* as the cause of the changes in Eisenhower's policies. While the satellite obviously magnified concerns about Soviet missile capabilities, the Gaither report provided specific recommendations to overcome any possible deficiencies in U.S. military preparedness. Only in the past decade, as the Eisenhower Library, the National Archives, and other depositories have begun to release previously classified documents, has the true importance of the Gaither report become apparent.

The historiography of the Gaither committee is very limited. Only four scholars—Morton Halperin, Fred Kaplan, Gregg Herken, and Peter Roman—have performed substantive research on this topic. With the exception of Roman, all of them have relied on the Gaither report itself, secondary sources, and/or interviews to obtain their evidence. Roman has tapped into some recently declassified documents to bolster his arguments. While they all examine some of the committee's findings, none of them analyze why it reached the conclusions that it did or exactly how influential it was in changing Eisenhower's policies.

Halperin's 1961 study remains the best published source of information on the Gaither committee. Halperin used primarily newspaper reports and congressional testimony as the basis for his analysis. He was chiefly concerned with how the presidential decision-making process worked and did not attempt to evaluate the bases for the committee's conclusions or its impact on the Eisenhower administration. In his study, he argues that the Gaither committee revealed both the strengths and weaknesses of the president acquiring advice from civilian experts. On the positive side, he states, an independent committee can supply "an additional source of information for the President, unencumbered by future and past policy responsibility."[5] However, on the negative side, the "fear of civilian expertise and the inability of the Gaither group to put any influence back of its recommendations combined with the motives discussed above [bureaucratic struggles between government agencies and military branches] to explain the failure of administration agencies to support the Gaither proposals."[6]

For over twenty years, Halperin's article represented the most comprehensive attempt to evaluate the Gaither committee. In the 1980s, both Kaplan and Herken added to Halperin's assessment in their analyses of the role of experts in decision making.[7] Kaplan examines the influence of the RAND Corporation in the development of U.S. nuclear strategy, arguing that its strategic analysts played a pivotal role in the Gaither committee's evaluation of Soviet military capabilities. He stresses in particular the influence of RAND experts Andrew Wohlstetter, Herman Kahn, and Spurgeon Keeny.[8] While Kaplan asserts that these experts influenced the conclusions of the Gaither committee, he concludes that Eisenhower accepted few of the committee's findings: "Eisenhower did not take [Robert] Sprague's comments enough to heart, did not take the Gaither Report so seriously, as to believe that their fears warranted spending tens of billions of dollars, on top of an already expanding budget, to shore up a deterrent that he thought was, for the time being, already quite adequate."[9]

Herken also explores the role of experts in developing U.S. nuclear policy. He argues that "American nuclear policy since 1945 has always been influenced, if not determined, by a small group of civilian experts— scientists, think-tank theorists, and academics."[10] He stresses that while Eisenhower rejected most of the Gaither recommendations, the report did stimulate the president and other experts to reexamine the importance of arms control. He points to the experiences of three Gaither committee members—Herbert York, Jerome Wiesner, and Spurgeon Keeny—as examples of experts who began to realize, after their work on the Gaither committee, the impossibility of constructing an effective missile defense system. Herken concludes that "the report would seem in retrospect the beginning of a fundamental change in attitude of scientists toward the arms race."[11]

While Halperin, Kaplan, and Herken focus on the role of experts, they perform only a cursory examination of the committee's conclusions and recommendations and spend even less time analyzing how and why it developed the findings that it did. Roman takes a different approach. He is concerned with Eisenhower's role in nuclear force planning from the launch of *Sputnik* to the Kennedy inauguration. He argues that "Eisenhower was an active participant in force planning who succeeded in manipulating the decision process, enabling him to impress his policy objectives on the outcomes."[12] While stressing the impact of the Gaither committee on the nuclear debate during 1958, he criticizes it for failing "to resolve four aspects of nuclear deterrence. These were: the credibility of nuclear deterrence, reaction time for nuclear forces, reliance on nuclear weapons in the U.S.

defense posture, and whether strategic systems should be designed to disarm the Soviet Union or to retaliate."[13] In making his arguments, Roman was the first scholar to use newly declassified documents to show the influence of the Gaither committee.

This brief overview of the arguments of four scholars is not meant to imply that the Gaither committee has not been discussed elsewhere. However, most other analyses rely on these authors for their evidence.[14] A common feature of all the literature is a lack of discussion of the Gaither committee itself. Who were its members? What were their backgrounds? How did they approach their study? Why did they devise the conclusions and recommendations that they did? The limited historiography now available provides glimpses at some very compelling issues. Halperin's use of the Gaither committee as a case study on decision making sheds much light on the benefits and drawbacks of using civilian committees. Both Kaplan and Herken reveal the important role of experts in advising the Eisenhower administration. Finally, Roman makes it clear that the Gaither committee had a significant influence on the development of Eisenhower's national security policies in the late 1950s.

Yet despite these studies, much of the Gaither committee's history is still obscure. Until recently, scholars faced severe hardships in studying the committee. Although its report was declassified in the early 1970s, other information related to the committee has been restricted. The release of documents over the past few years, however, allows scholars to examine the Gaither committee in much greater detail. The new information provides an opportunity to acquire a greater understanding of the Gaither committee's significance in the development of national security policies, Eisenhower's decision-making system, the president's use of civilian experts to gain policy advice, and the debates over civil defense.

Scholars over the past two decades have reversed initial assessments of Eisenhower as a do-nothing president who spent more time on the golf course than at the White House. While critical evaluations of Eisenhower's handling of important issues, in particular civil rights and the developing nations, are becoming more prevalent, most scholars rank Eisenhower as a very good president.[15] While this study does not attempt to minimize the failures and weaknesses of the Eisenhower presidency, it does show that Eisenhower established a distinct decision-making system, followed a consistent set of values, and actively participated in decision making during his presidency. Although the leak of its report caused him to regret having created the Gaither committee, that did not stop him from carefully evaluating the committee's findings to determine which ones would enhance U.S. security.

Eisenhower based his decisions on an established set of values and a highly organized decision-making system. In addressing national security issues, Eisenhower analyzed the impact that a decision would have on both the country's military security and its economic strength.[16] In an impassioned plea to the NSC in 1955, he told his advisers:

> Budget-Making time is always difficult and expenses are mounting. Nevertheless, no official of the Government is truly performing his duty unless he clearly realizes that he is engaged in defending a way of life over a prolonged period and unless he is constantly aware of the weight of financial burden that our citizens are willing and able to bear. Our Government could force upon our citizens defense and other spending at much higher levels, and our abundant economy could stand it—for a while; but you cannot do it for the long pull without destroying incentives, inflating the currency, and increasing government controls. This would require an authoritarian system of government, and destroy the health of our free society.
>
> We must, of course, do what we must do to defend ourselves. We must not put dollars above the security of the United States. But we must prove, if we are to demonstrate the superiority of our system, that in times of unprecedented prosperity we can pay as we go without passing on intolerable burdens to coming generations.
>
> Consequently, every official of this Government must search out places where we can save a dollar which could be used somewhere else where its contribution would be vital. This issue is critical. This doctrine should be remembered and preached in every waking hour by every official in this administration.[17]

Almost four years after leaving the White House, Eisenhower described his belief system in a letter to his brother. At the time, he was trying to provide direction to the Republican Party after it had been soundly defeated in the 1964 presidential election. His advice for his party reflected the values and principles that guided his decision making. In the letter to his brother, he summarized his basic convictions:

A. Americans, individually and collectively, should strive constantly for greater excellence in the moral, intellectual and material structure of the nation.

B. The individual is of supreme importance. The rights guaranteed to him and the states by the Constitution and the "Bill of Rights" must be jealously guarded by government at all levels. The purpose of government is to serve, never to dominate.

C. The spirit of the people is the strength of our nation; human liberty and the American system of self-government with equal rights for all are the mainspring of that spirit. . . .

D. To be secure and stay free we must be strong morally, economically and militarily. This combination of strength must be used prudently, carefully and firmly to preserve peace and protect the nation's vital interests abroad.

E. Political power resides in the people; elected officials are expected to direct that power wisely and only as prescribed by the Constitution.

F. Government must have a heart as well as a head. Republicans . . . insist that solutions must conform to common sense and recognize the right and duty of local and state government normally to attack these at their roots before the Federal Government acts.

G. America cannot truly prosper unless all major areas and groupments [*sic*] in our society prosper. Labor, capital and management must learn to cooperate as a productive team, and reject any notion of "class warfare" bringing about maximum prosperity.

H. To protect all our citizens, and particularly workers and all those who are, or will be, dependent on pensions, savings and insurance in their declining years, we strive always to prevent deterioration of the currency. In the constant fight against inflation we believe that, except in emergencies, we should pay-as-we-go, avoiding deficit spending and adverse balance-of-payments.

I. Under God we espouse the cause of freedom and justice and peace for all people.[18]

These values and convictions provided the cornerstones for Eisenhower's decision making. His creation of the Gaither committee and later analysis of its report reflect these concerns. Eisenhower sought the best advice possible so that he could make the most informed decisions about U.S. national security needs. After receiving the committee's advice in November 1957, he carefully considered how its recommendations, if implemented, would affect the way of life he sought to preserve. He accepted the recommendations that he believed were necessary to guarantee U.S. security without undermining individual freedom or economic solvency.

Eisenhower's use of the Gaither committee represents one way he ob-

tained counsel. When he entered office in 1953, he believed he could improve the organization of the White House and the entire decision-making
process. As far as decisions affecting national security, he viewed the NSC
as the natural vehicle for obtaining advice. One of his first directives was to
have Robert Cutler study ways to make the NSC more efficient and better
able to provide guidance to his presidency. Cutler recommended significant changes in the operations of the NSC. He suggested that the president
attend as many NSC meetings as possible, that the council meet regularly
each week, and that a new planning board be established to prepare study
papers for the full council. While Eisenhower did not normally call for the
NSC to make decisions, he did use it to obtain advice, as a forum for vigorous discussions, and as a means to disseminate policy to his key advisers.[19]

Seldom did Eisenhower make decisions involving national security issues without at least consulting the NSC. It must be stressed, however, that
the NSC always remained an advisory body, not a decision-making one.
When a reporter suggested in 1957 that the NSC made decisions, Eisenhower responded, "The National Security Council is set up to do one
thing: advise the president. I make the decisions, and there is no use trying
to put any responsibility on the National Security Council—it's mine."[20]
He also used it as a channel to acquire advice from civilian experts. While
Halperin, Kaplan, and Herken persuasively argue that Eisenhower used experts on several occasions, no scholar has systematically examined their use.
The Gaither committee is a prime example of Eisenhower's use of a group
of civilian experts to obtain policy advice.

Critics of the effectiveness of Eisenhower's NSC have often relied on the
conclusions reached by the Senate Committee on Government Operations
in 1961. The committee stressed that Eisenhower's NSC was plagued by
bureaucratic conflicts, compromised too often, and failed to challenge already established strategies.[21] However, most scholars who have had access
to internal NSC documents have raised serious questions about these assessments. They argue that Eisenhower's NSC fostered vigorous debate,
facilitated long-term planning, and provided valuable advice.[22] This study
of the Gaither committee supports the conclusion that the NSC played a
pivotal and effective advisory role in Eisenhower's decision-making system.

Eisenhower established the Gaither committee to obtain advice that he
hoped would be untainted by bureaucratic interests. This approach had
worked for him previously, when he created the Solarium task forces in
1953 and the Killian committee in 1954. He established Project Solarium

during the first year of his presidency to evaluate different national security policies. After the Soviet Union tested a hydrogen bomb and demonstrated increasing capabilities to deliver nuclear weapons against the United States, he created the Killian committee to analyze the ability of the Kremlin to launch a surprise attack against the United States. After the groups completed their studies, Eisenhower incorporated many of their recommendations into his national security programs.

Eisenhower's use of experts to acquire advice demonstrates the cooperation of the federal government with leading scientific, engineering, business, and educational professionals that had developed in World War II and increased during the first fifteen years of the Cold War.[23] The government's use of experts continued during the Truman administration. It was Eisenhower, however, who brought experts to central areas of policy making. Herken eloquently concludes, "During the fifteen years since the dawn of the atomic age this nucleus of experts had for the most part merely witnessed the making of strategy and policy on the bomb. They had remained on the sidelines of the great national debate over defense. . . . Henceforth, they would be at its center."[24]

In creating the Gaither committee, Eisenhower turned to leading experts who were either specialists in particular disciplines or possessed a broad understanding of national security issues. He asked the committee to evaluate whether the United States should embark on an expensive program of constructing active and passive defenses, including anti-aircraft and antimissile weapons, early warning radar, and fallout shelters. Based on his desire to maintain a balance between economic and military security in his national security planning, Eisenhower believed a committee of experts would avoid making recommendations that benefited a particular government department or military service but not necessarily the nation. He failed to recognize, however, that the Gaither committee members entered the study with preconceived beliefs based on previous experiences or affiliations that would color their interpretations and analyses. Furthermore, he never acknowledged or fully realized the contradiction between using a committee of experts that was removed from public scrutiny, on the one hand, and his emphasis on the individual's right to self-government, on the other.[25]

The Gaither committee was composed of a group of experts with diverse backgrounds. Its initial director, Rowan Gaither, was well known for leading nonprofit research organizations such as the RAND Corporation and the Ford Foundation. William Foster and Robert Sprague, who codirected the committee after Gaither became ill, built their reputations in the chemical and electrical industries, respectively. James Killian and James Baxter were the respective presidents of Massachusetts Institute of Technology (MIT) and Williams College. Generals James Doolittle and James McCormack had illustrious military backgrounds and close ties to the business community. Other members of the committee were equally noteworthy. As a group they did not enter the Gaither study with a set agenda, political objective, or financial motive. However, they did share a concern for U.S. national security that went beyond their support for Eisenhower or his policies.

Significance of This Study

Eisenhower's second term proved to be a watershed period in the Cold War. At the time of the president's inauguration in January 1957, Soviet leader Nikita Khrushchev was just consolidating his power in the Soviet Union. Over the next four years, the Cold War solidified and accelerated a technological arms race that dramatically raised the stakes of potential future conflicts. The Gaither committee stood at the forefront of the whirlwind of debates concerning U.S. national security policies and U.S.-Soviet relations. Its recommendations precipitated increases in U.S. defense spending and the nuclear arsenal; led to cultural debates about fallout shelters and the future of mankind in a nuclear world; raised questions about the right balance between domestic, foreign, and defense spending; and challenged traditional ways of decision making.

Eisenhower's handling of the Gaither committee raises several questions about his effectiveness as president. While he made decisions based on established convictions and the counsel of a well-organized advisory system, his failure to provide careful oversight of the Gaither committee allowed it to expand the scope of its study and challenge some of his fundamental principles. Eisenhower adamantly believed that U.S. strength rested on a careful balance of economic, military, and political power. He further emphasized the importance of protecting individual rights and democratic principles. Eisenhower foresaw the problem of reconciling the Gaither committee's recommendations with maintaining the balance of power that he saw as so important. However, he never successfully persuaded the American people that his program for meeting the challenges of the late

1950s was indeed the best strategy for the United States; therefore, it took almost every ounce of Eisenhower's energy to restrain the forces for change unleashed by the Gaither report and the Soviet launch of *Sputnik*.

Eisenhower had good intentions and brought a dignity to the White House that has been lacking ever since. His mistake in his second term was to rely too much on his own reputation and sense of right and wrong when the nation wanted strong, dynamic leadership. Eisenhower failed to offer the reassurance and confidence that the people needed when their way of life seemed to be in question. Whether any president could have provided the necessary leadership in the late 1950s is open to question. It is clear, however, that Eisenhower never fully realized the depths of apprehension the populace felt.

1 | Eisenhower's Core Values and Decision-Making Systems

Dwight D. Eisenhower won the 1952 presidential election against Democratic candidate Adlai Stevenson despite having never previously held an elective office. While both parties had asked him to serve as their candidate in the 1948 election, he had constantly rebuffed any political overtures.[1] It was only in early 1952 that he felt duty-bound to accept the Republican nomination for president. After Eisenhower's victory, retiring President Harry S. Truman questioned Eisenhower's ability to make the transition from military officer to president. Truman doubted whether Eisenhower could adjust to the political arena, where orders were often questioned and sometimes not followed.[2] Truman's assessment proved shortsighted. As George Reedy, a key aide to then Senator Lyndon Johnson in the 1950s, recalled, Eisenhower's "most important attribute . . . was that he had held a number of political positions that the public did not regard as political."[3] While Eisenhower had only limited experience with Washington politics, he had dealt successfully with politics within the U.S. Army, at Columbia University, and as a commander of multinational military forces. This experience and training provided significant preparation for his time as president.

Before World War II, Eisenhower had pursued a successful, yet relatively undistinguished, career in the Army. After a quarter-century of service, he had risen to the rank of colonel but had little chance of advancing much further in the peacetime Army. Because of the limited size of the military, promotions were rare and far between.[4] U.S. involvement in World War II dramatically altered Eisenhower's career. From working for General George Marshall's War Plans Division in Washington, D.C., to commanding Allied forces in North Africa, to planning and implementing the defeat of

13

President Dwight D. Eisenhower. Eisenhower is shown speaking at a White House ceremony in January 1958. (National Park Service/Dwight D. Eisenhower Library)

Germany in Western Europe, Eisenhower quickly rose in rank from an obscure colonel to a five-star general whose name was recognized and praised around the world.

After the war, Eisenhower served as the Army chief of staff from 1945 to 1948. He then retired in order to become president of Columbia University, where he remained from 1948 to 1951. However, his service to the nation did not end while he was there. From December 1948 to the late summer of 1949, he spent several days a week in Washington serving as the unofficial chairman of the Joint Chiefs of Staff (JCS). Upon Truman's request, in late 1950 he left Columbia to become the first supreme commander of NATO's military forces. He remained in this position until he announced his candidacy for the Republican nomination in the late spring of 1952.[5] His experiences during the war and afterward reinforced and clarified his basic system of values and beliefs. Conservative by nature, Eisenhower learned to cherish the American system of government and the freedoms it represented, to value the importance of a balanced budget for a sound economy, and to make decisions based upon a carefully organized and structured decision-making system.

Eisenhower's Basic Values

Specific values, based on a strong faith in the American democratic system of government and in the freedoms guaranteed by the Constitution, guided almost all of Eisenhower's decisions.[6] While he contemplated Columbia University's offer of its presidency in June 1947, he reminisced about his military career. In a letter to longtime friend Everett "Swede" Hazlett, Eisenhower described how he had developed his beliefs: "I had absorbed several simple conceptions and observations that would remain with me until the end of my days." He then emphatically explained:

> I believe fanatically in the American form of democracy—a system that recognizes and protects the rights of the individual and that ascribes to the individual a dignity accruing to him because of his creation in the image of a supreme being and which rests upon the conviction that only through a system of free enterprise can this type of democracy be preserved. Beyond this I believe that world order can be established only by the practice of true cooperation among the sovereign nations and that American leadership toward this goal depends upon her strength—her strength of will, her moral, social and economic strength and, until an effective world order is achieved, upon her military strength.[7]

Eisenhower's firmly held beliefs originated in a childhood characterized by rugged individualism, strict discipline, and moral piety. His parents instilled in him and his brothers the principles of hard work, equality, and individual responsibility.[8] While these values provided the core of Eisenhower's belief system, he never systematically examined the concept of democracy before World War II.[9] However, after the United States joined the Allies, he emphasized the importance of understanding exactly why the war was being fought. He argued, "Belief in an underlying cause is fully as important to success in war as any local esprit or discipline induced or produced by whatever kind of command or leadership action."[10] In a letter to his son, Eisenhower identified this underlying cause. He explained that "no other war in history has so definitely lined up the forces of arbitrary oppression and dictatorship against those of human rights and individual liberty."[11] In an order to his commanders in 1942, he added that each American soldier needed to recognize that "the privileged life he has led . . . is under direct threat. His rights to speak his own mind, to engage in any profession of his own choosing, to belong to any religious denomination, to live in any locality where he can support himself and his family, and to be sure of fair treatment when he might be accused of any crime— all of these would disappear" if Hitler's armies prevailed.[12]

In his memoirs of his World War II experiences, Eisenhower further illustrated these beliefs as he reflected on past, present, and future U.S.-Soviet relations. At a meeting in Berlin in late 1945, he met and developed a friendship with Marshall Grigori Zhukov, one of the Soviet Union's most successful military commanders.[13] Sharing a common bond from the war, Eisenhower and Zhukov reminisced about their experiences. During these conversations, they discussed a variety of topics ranging from military strategy to the philosophical differences between democracy and communism. From these conversations, Eisenhower gained a greater understanding and appreciation of the principles he supported "fanatically."

As they discussed the use of infantry during the war, Eisenhower quickly realized that he placed a much greater emphasis on the life of the individual soldier than did Zhukov and other Soviet leaders. For instance, Zhukov indicated that when confronting German positions that were protected by land mines, it was standard Soviet military practice to send their infantry straight through the minefield rather than to stop and try to clear it.[14] While Eisenhower found the willingness of Russians to die for their country commendable, he was appalled that the Soviet leaders were so willing to sacrifice their soldiers to clear a minefield. Furthermore, Zhukov's sincere dedication to communism, a system of government that Eisenhower saw as inherently evil, demonstrated how powerful and persuasive the communist message could be.

Eisenhower's abhorrence of communism did not stem from any systematic study of that system of government.[15] Rather, it developed from what he saw as communism's rejection of basic individual freedoms. He explained how Zhukov had asked him to try "to understand a system [of government] in which the attempt was made to substitute for such motivations [individual aspirations] the devotion of a man to the great national complex of which he formed a part."[16] For Eisenhower, such a government placed the nation's welfare above the individual's welfare. He believed that while communism's appeal to the common good represented an admirable goal, in reality it resulted in "dictatorial rule."[17] He later elaborated this belief by explaining, "The main issue [between the United States and the Soviet Union] is dictatorship versus a form of government only by the consent of the governed, observance of a bill of rights versus arbitrary power of a ruler or ruling group."[18]

These conversations with Zhukov in many ways helped shape Eisenhower's views of the Soviet Union. While gaining a deep respect for Zhukov as a military leader and for the willingness of the Soviet people to accept sacrifices for their nation, Eisenhower left Berlin with an even greater loathing of the Communist system and the lack of compassion the Soviet government seemed to have for its own people. After recounting these conversations, he concluded his memoirs with a strident defense of democracy and a rebuke of communism. "We [the democracies of the world]," Eisenhower emphasized, "believe individual liberty rooted in human dignity, is man's greatest treasure. We believe that men, given free expression of their will, prefer freedom and self-dependence to dictatorship and collectivism."[19]

Before his election in 1952, Eisenhower never clearly articulated how he would translate these beliefs concerning democracy, individual freedoms, and human dignity into specific policies. However, he did provide, on occasion, glimpses into how these guiding principles should be defended. Eisenhower believed that the fundamental role of any U.S. president was to defend these principles with unflinching determination. In performing this task, he recognized that preservation of the American way of life had to consider much more than military defense. Specifically, the defense of the United States involved the protection of its territorial boundaries and its citizens, while at the same time maintaining an economy that would allow the country to prosper.[20] These goals—preserving a way of life, building a strong military, and overseeing a prosperous economy—came to guide Eisenhower's defense policies in the 1950s.

In testimony before the Military Subcommittee of the Senate Appropriations Committee in 1950, Eisenhower attempted to describe the balance that the United States needed in its national security programs. While a strong military was obviously necessary, he resisted increases in defense spending that he thought might undermine the very way of life that it sought to protect. "If we should deem war imminent," Eisenhower testified, "there would be no expense too great and no preparation too elaborate to meet what we would see as an impending crisis." However, he cautioned the subcommittee that this was not the case. He continued by arguing, "Since the purpose is to defend a way of life at the heart of which is the guaranteed freedom of the individual, we must not so over-burden or tax the resources of the country that we practically enslave or regiment people in the effort to keep them free from foreign aggression." He concluded, "To wreck our economy, would be as great a victory for the Soviets as they could remotely hope for in a war."[21]

In January 1952 President Truman presented to Congress an $85 billion budget that included approximately $65 billion in spending for national security programs. As submitted, the budget would have created a $14 billion deficit. Eisenhower was shocked at such spending levels and believed they represented the height of irresponsibility. In one of his clearest statements of the philosophy that guided his decision making, he articulated the dangers of high budgets and deficit spending. He recorded in his diary: "I am greatly afraid that certain basic truths are being forgotten or ignored in our public life of today. The first of these is that a democracy undertakes military preparedness only on a defensive, which means a long-term basis. You do not attempt to build up to a D-day because, having no intention of our own to attack, we must devise and follow a system that we can carry as long as there appears to be a threat in the world capable of endangering our national safety."[22]

He then explained that "it is necessary to recognize that the purpose of America is to defend a way of life rather than merely to defend property, territory, homes, or lives. As a consequence of this purpose, everything done to develop a defense against external threat, except under conditions readily recognizable as emergency, must be weighed and gauged in the light of probable long-term, internal, effect."[23] This theme consistently appears in Eisenhower's public and private life. He stressed that U.S. strength resided in a way of life represented by a combination of "devotion to democracy," "free enterprise," "industrial and economic strength," "moral probity in all dealings," and "military strength."[24] Together these qualities set the United States apart from the rest of the world, especially the Soviet Union. Eisenhower believed that as long as the United States emphasized and protected these values, it would prevail in the Cold War.

In Eisenhower's mind, the budget Truman had submitted failed to take adequate cognizance of the dangers inherent in deficit spending. He was especially concerned that the proposed national security programs were designed to meet a specific period of danger in the future. Eisenhower believed the fallacy of such planning was that policy planners could never predict with any accuracy the future actions of a potential adversary. The Truman budget reflected the contention that 1954 was the year of maximum danger. Eisenhower disagreed. He stressed that national security programs should be based on what the country could afford over an indefinite period. He viewed the Truman budget as contrary to that guideline. It emphasized a maximum year of danger without seriously considering the financial burdens that would be experienced by the United States in the years that followed.

After critiquing the dangers of the Truman program, Eisenhower identified the defense philosophy that he would follow in his presidency. He explained that, as Army chief of staff and then as the unofficial chairman of the JCS, he had learned that planning for the long term was essential, since "one of the most expensive practices in the maintenance of military force is unevenness in the scale of preparedness and in yearly appropriations. Peaks in one year or a series of years, followed by unwise reductions in a period when economy is the sole watchword, tend to demand extraordinary expenditures with no return."[25] Eisenhower saw the proposed Truman budget as a fiscal drain on the economy, because it produced large budget deficits without really increasing long-term U.S. security. He then added that he and Secretary of Defense James Forrestal had "very greatly hoped to produce a plan and budget that would be, in effect, an element of bipartisan policy and which would be as free as possible of the defects and costs brought about by yearly cuts or increases, usually due to impulses or aberrations of the moment."[26] Although it had not yet been developed, Eisenhower was articulating the basic premise of his New Look policy.

Eisenhower concluded his diary entry with a statement that exemplified the essence of his national security philosophy: "We can say only that properly balanced strength will promote a probability of avoiding war. In this sense, we need the strength soon—but it must be balanced between moral power, economic power, and purely military power."[27] The goal of preserving and magnifying these trilateral "powers" guided Eisenhower in the development of his administration's economic and national security policies.

During the 1952 presidential campaign, Eisenhower championed similar beliefs. He questioned the increased defense spending resulting from the Korean War and, more important, from National Security Council 68.[28] Between June 1950 and the 1952 election, spending for national security programs increased by more than 200 percent.[29] Eisenhower challenged the efficacy of such high spending and openly wondered whether the United States could continue to afford such defense programs. In a campaign speech in September 1952, he eloquently expressed these doubts. He argued that increasing spending on defense would not necessarily augment U.S. security. The key was to develop a defense strategy that the nation could afford for the indefinite future. "The real problem," he explained, "is to build the defense with wisdom and efficiency. We must achieve both security and solvency. In fact, the foundation of military strength is economic strength. A bankrupt America is more the Soviet goal than an America conquered on the field of battle."[30]

Eisenhower's Cabinet advisers reinforced his economic advisers. During his two terms in office, Eisenhower relied heavily on his secretaries of the treasury, George Humphrey and Robert Anderson; the chairmen of the Council of Economic Advisers (CEA); and the various directors of the Bureau of the Budget. Although differing on certain economic points, they were all fiscal conservatives who despised budget deficits, abhorred inflation, and supported a smaller role for the federal government in society. These advisers assisted Eisenhower in developing a moderate conservative economic policy that emphasized balanced budgets and low inflation while preserving and expanding New Deal legislation such as social security, unemployment insurance, and bank deposit insurance.[31] One recent scholar of Eisenhower's economic philosophy and policies persuasively concludes that the president "was more dependent on his economic advisers than on his national security advisers."[32]

After Eisenhower accepted the Republican nomination, the outcome of the November election was a foregone conclusion. He had tremendous advantages over the Democratic nominee, Adlai Stevenson. First, retiring Democratic president Truman was unpopular. Second, the Democratic Party had been in power for two decades, and people were looking for a change. Finally, Eisenhower was a military hero who Americans believed could end the Korean War. Together, this fame and the widespread disenchantment with the Truman administration formed the basis of Eisenhower's resounding victory. As he entered the White House, Eisenhower viewed the election as a mandate for his political and economic philosophy and endeavored to create a presidential administration that propagated his values.[33]

On several occasions as the Army chief of staff and the unofficial chairman of the Joint Chiefs of Staff, Eisenhower had visited President Truman at the White House. While conceding that the visits did not allow him to acquire a full understanding of how the presidency operated, they left an impression that he did not like. In his memoirs, Eisenhower explained how he saw the reorganization of the White House as one of the priorities of his new administration: "With my training in problems involving organization, it was inconceivable to me that the work of the White House could not be better systemized [*sic*] than had been the case during the years I observed it."[34] Eisenhower's military experience had led him to conclude that the best decisions were made only after careful consideration by all of those involved.[35] The reorganization of the White House along the lines of a military staff system enabled Eisenhower to make careful decisions in a manner that reflected his basic political and economic philosophy.

Contrary to the claims of some critics, Eisenhower did not see organization as an end in itself.[36] He viewed it as an effective means of acquiring, analyzing, and synthesizing the vast information created by large administrative bodies. Eisenhower elucidated why developing and maintaining an efficient organizational system was critical for effective government: "Organization cannot make a genius out of an incompetent, even less can it, of itself, make the decisions which are required to trigger necessary action. On the other hand, disorganization can scarcely fail to result in inefficiency and can easily lead to disaster. Organization makes more efficient the gathering and analysis of facts, and the arranging of the findings of experts in logical fashion. Therefore organization helps the responsible individual make the necessary decision, and helps assure that it is satisfactorily carried out."[37]

Eisenhower carefully organized the White House to produce maximum efficiency.[38] "Because of his long experience with military organization," Chester Pach concludes, "Eisenhower believed that clear lines of authority radiating from the Oval Office would ensure the smooth workings of his presidency." [39] One of Eisenhower's greatest criticisms of other presidential administrations was the lack of effective coordination within the White House. To overcome this problem, Eisenhower appointed Sherman Adams as his special assistant. Adams supervised the White House staff and prepared the president's schedule. Additionally, Eisenhower appointed other subordinates to supervise specific areas of presidential policy such as congressional liaison (General Wilton B. "Jerry" Persons), racial minority issues (Maxwell Rabb), and top-secret national security matters (first General Paul T. "Pete" Carroll and then Colonel Andrew J. Goodpaster). [40] By delegating authority within a well-designed organization, Eisenhower achieved a degree of efficiency that previous presidents had rarely experienced. [41]

The Reorganization of the NSC

The NSC structure that Eisenhower inherited in 1953 was still relatively new. It had been in existence only since 1947, when Congress established it as part of the National Security Act. As with any new organization, the NSC experienced its own share of growing pains. Before the outbreak of the Korean War in 1950, Truman rarely attended the NSC meetings. However, after the outbreak of the war and his acceptance of NSC 68, Truman turned more and more to the NSC for policy advice. [42] For the remainder of his administration, NSC 68 guided many of Truman's national security policies. [43]

Along with the Korean War, NSC 68 led the Truman administration to increase spending for national security programs from the programmed $13.5 billion for FY 1951 (July 1, 1950, through June 30, 1951) to more than $48 billion by December 1950. These spending levels continued for the remainder of the Truman administration and reflected a growing perception of the Soviet threat. The important point is that only approximately 10 percent of the spending increase went toward the cost of the Korean War. [44] It was the other 90 percent that raised Eisenhower's concern. He did not believe that the Truman administration had carefully analyzed the long-term impact of such increases on the U.S. economy.

When Eisenhower assumed the presidency, he was determined to reduce defense spending. In order to do this, he wanted to examine policy alternatives, ranging from containment to rollback, that might lead to a more efficient and effective defense policy. He anticipated that the NSC would analyze these alternatives. One of Eisenhower's most important advisers recalled that the president used the NSC to obtain "an integration of views which would be the product of continuous association between skilled representatives of all elements germane to national security."[45] However, Eisenhower did not believe that the NSC structure he inherited from the Truman administration was capable of performing such a study. Before he could assign the NSC this responsibility, he had to restructure it into the organization that he wanted.[46]

Eisenhower turned to Robert Cutler, a key campaign aide and influential Boston banker, for advice concerning the reorganization of the NSC. After a brief study, Cutler recommended several changes to the NSC's structure. After the National Security Act had been revised in 1949, the NSC had only five statutory members: the president, the vice president, the secretary of state, the secretary of defense, and the chairman of the National Security Resources Board (NSRB). The chairman of the JCS and the director of the Central Intelligence Agency (CIA) acted as advisers. Three other groups—the CIA, the senior NSC staff, and the Interdepartmental Intelligence Committee—served in a variety of capacities. While the National Security Act had established this membership structure, it provided no specific guidance as to how the NSC should operate. Before the Eisenhower administration, the NSC did not operate in either a consistent or a particularly systematic manner.[47]

Cutler asked several government officials, including the former head of the State Department's Policy Planning Staff, Paul Nitze, how the NSC could operate more efficiently and effectively. Nitze recommended several specific changes in the NSC's operations. He stressed the need to create an advisory committee to formulate policy papers for consideration before the NSC. This committee would replace the NSC senior staff. The policy papers would contain both majority and minority opinions if no consensus could be reached, to ensure that the NSC discussed the issues that could not be resolved by the advisory committee. Finally, he concluded that the statutory membership of the NSC should remain the same.[48]

Cutler incorporated many of Nitze's recommendations in his proposal to Eisenhower, including major changes in the NSC's structure. He proposed that the president attend and serve as chairman of as many NSC meetings as possible. Cutler believed that one of the weaknesses of the Truman NSC was the failure of the president to take an active role in its meetings. He argued that the president had to be an integral part of the meetings for it to operate most effectively. The original senior staff should be replaced by the newly created planning board, whose purpose would be to develop policy papers for NSC discussions. The planning board would consist of representatives from each of the statutory agencies of the NSC. The policy papers created would reflect a consensus opinion of its members, but the board would submit any dissenting views to the NSC. Finally, Cutler recommended the appointment of a new adviser, a special assistant for national security affairs, to coordinate the activities of the planning board and the NSC.[49]

A few days after he approved Cutler's recommendations, Eisenhower publicly announced plans for the restructured NSC. He appointed Cutler as his new special assistant for national security affairs. He expanded the NSC's membership to include the secretary of the treasury, the director of the Mutual Security Administration, and the director of the Office of Defense Mobilization (who replaced the NSRB chairman).[50] As Cutler had recommended, Eisenhower established the planning board to develop papers for NSC discussions. Finally, he announced that the NSC would periodically seek civilian consultants "to bring to Council deliberations a fresh point of view, not burdened with departmental responsibilities."[51]

Eisenhower's revamping of the NSC clearly shows how he desired to incorporate his philosophy and organizational beliefs into his decision making. First, he expanded the NSC's membership to obtain a more balanced examination of national security issues. By including the secretary of the treasury and the budget director, Eisenhower emphasized the importance of analyzing the economic implications of any national security policies. Second, by appointing Cutler and by creating the planning board, he revealed his desire for an organization that would examine policy options more systematically. Finally, by occasionally turning to civilian consultants, he recognized the significance of obtaining advice independent of the government bureaucracy.[52]

Project Solarium, NSC 162/2, and the New Look

Having completed the reorganization of the NSC, Eisenhower turned to the federal budget deficit that he inherited from the Truman administration. Forecasts for Truman's FY 1954 budget predicted a shortfall of approximately $10 billion. To eliminate this deficit, Eisenhower knew he would have to cut military spending—over 66 percent of the total budget.[53] Although Eisenhower had questioned Truman's refusal to increase spending beyond $15 billion in the late 1940s, he was very reluctant to accept budgets for national security programs that had tripled in three years to exceed $50 billion.[54] As with his reorganization of the White House and the NSC, Eisenhower believed that his national security programs could be developed and implemented in a cheaper and more efficient manner.

In September 1952 the NSC asked Secretary of State Dean G. Acheson, Secretary of Defense Robert Lovett, and Director of Mutual Security Averell Harriman to prepare a report analyzing the status of U.S. national security policies. This small committee presented its report, NSC 141, to Truman as he prepared to leave office in January 1953. It recommended the continuation of existing policies and the appropriation of additional funds to improve continental defenses.[55] This report served as the starting point for changes Eisenhower wanted to make in U.S. national security programs.

At one of the NSC's first meetings under the new administration, Cutler recommended that this report be used as the basis for the study and development of new national security policies.[56] During the spring, Eisenhower and his top advisers discussed ways to cut spending on national security policies while at the same time preserving U.S. military strength. In May, Eisenhower ordered the NSC to create three panels to review national security policy alternatives. The NSC turned to outside consultants to staff these groups. Operating under the code name Project Solarium, the panels launched a six-week investigation of current and future U.S. policies.[57] The NSC's use of experts outside the government established a precedent that would be repeated several times in the Eisenhower presidency, as when he subsequently established the Gaither committee.

The NSC appointed the directing panel of Project Solarium to develop guidelines for the study.[58] The panel established three task forces—A, B, and C.[59] The panel ordered task force A to assume the position advocated by NSC 141—the continuation of Truman's containment policies—and to recommend a national security policy based on that alternative. The panel assigned task force B the responsibility for developing a national security policy based on an explicit statement of the areas that the United States would automatically defend against a Soviet attack. Finally, the panel ordered task force C to develop a policy based on "rolling back" communism.[60] As Glenn Snyder succinctly argues, Eisenhower's goal in creating these task forces "was to highlight three dramatically different policy lines and to develop thoroughly the implications of each."[61]

The directing panel, with Eisenhower's approval, selected seven members for each task force. George Kennan, General James McCormack, and Admiral Richard Conolly served as the chairmen of task forces A, B, and C, respectively.[62] The panels convened in June at the National War College in Washington, D.C., for a six-week study of their respective alternatives. The details of Project Solarium were of the highest confidentiality. George Kennan stated years later, "It was all highly secret—you have no idea how well this was protected; nobody knew [about Project Solarium] the whole summer despite the fact that fifty to a hundred people were involved in it."[63]

The directing panel ordered each task force to consider three possible courses of Soviet action before making their recommendations. First, the Soviet Union might decide to launch a war to achieve its policy objectives or to preempt a perceived military attack from the United States. Second, it might pursue an aggressive policy, having only a slight risk of war, of trying to weaken free world alliances. Finally, it might adopt a defensive posture to consolidate its current positions and place only a limited pressure on the free world.[64] These alternatives represented the generally accepted views of U.S. policymakers as to possible future Soviet actions.

On June 26 the three task forces made preliminary presentations to the NSC. Cutler wanted to familiarize the council with the task forces' general arguments and to acquaint each task force with what the others were doing. Not surprisingly, the recommendations followed the basic arguments assigned earlier to each task force. However, a common theme permeated their reports. The theme, best stated in task force A's report, was, "On the question of the relation of our defense effort to domestic economic problems, the position will be stressed that the U.S. economy can stand for a considerable length of time a higher level of defense expenditures than the currently operative ones."[65]

On July 16 each task force presented its final report to the NSC. Under the direction of George Kennan, task force A recommended continuing the policies advocated by the Truman administration, making slight increases in spending to improve continental defenses.[66] The task force believed that the Soviet Union posed a threat in three broad areas: its maintenance of a strong and dangerous military establishment, its control of Eastern and Central Europe, and its ability to subvert democracy throughout the world.[67] In light of these threats, Kennan's panel stressed the need for flexibility in U.S. policy planning, as the directions of Soviet policy could never be predicted with great accuracy. It concluded that the United States needed "to recapture essential flexibility, to effect better integration and cohesion within our strategy, and to improve its implementation" (15–16).

Task force A criticized the rapid demobilization of American forces after World War II and warned that a similar policy at the conclusion of the Korean War would provide "the most likely invitation to aggression" (22). It therefore advocated a policy of maintaining military forces at a level sufficient to fight either limited or general wars. Military force and equipment levels, the task force stressed, should be based on analyses of Soviet military capabilities, not on "the zigzags of Soviet political policy" (23). It argued that the United States needed to maintain adequate military capabilities to achieve its objectives and to resist any possible Soviet aggression. Flexibility was task force A's military strategy. The United States needed the capability to meet any Soviet aggressive move with an appropriate military response.

Task force A identified the second objective of U.S. national security policy as rallying both Americans and non-Americans to the strategy of containing the Soviet Union. It believed that the public had to understand what was being done to counter the Soviet threat. Only a well-informed public would support the policies necessary to wage the Cold War. It placed considerable importance on maintaining European support for U.S. policies. Although the authors of the report believed that Americans would support increased defense spending and a greater reliance on nuclear weapons, they expressed reservations that Europeans would do so. "A strong, vitalized and cohesive free Europe, orientated towards the same general objectives of the United States," the task force emphasized, "would be most important, if not decisive, factor in the successful resolution of the Soviet threat" (83).

The last issue addressed by task force A concerned a topic of special interest to Eisenhower. He wanted to balance the budget as soon as possible and knew that defense spending had to be cut. He had therefore asked each task force to predict the probable costs of its policy recommendations assuming the Korean War would end in 1953.[68] Task force A indicated that under its proposals, defense programs would cost between $43 billion and $44 billion for FYs 1954 and 1955 and would then gradually decline to approximately $35 billion per year. The task force believed that the U.S. economy was capable of meeting this burden of defense spending without raising taxes. However, it supported the imposition of a new defense tax if additional revenue was needed to offset the increased costs. In the final analysis, it argued, "The United States can afford to survive." [69]

The directing panel assigned task force B the alternative of drawing a line beyond which any move by the Soviet Union would precipitate a general war with the United States. Under this strategy, the United States would explicitly state what Soviet actions would automatically lead to general war. Supporters of this strategy assumed that if Soviet leaders knew the consequences of their actions, they would be more reluctant to act aggressively. Task force B criticized the strategy of task force A as too ambiguous, and it strongly opposed continuing the policies of the Truman administration. It concluded that such a strategy "may be beyond the economic capabilities of the United States, will deprive the nation of the initiative, and will certainly divert the American people from the task of making the best possible use of their power and resources to be prepared to inflict decisive defeat on the Soviet Union if it imperils the vital security of this nation by continuing an active policy of expansion." [70] Instead, the task force recommended developing a strategy based on waging a general war if Soviet bloc military forces advanced beyond their current borders.

To facilitate the implementation of its strategy, task force B stressed that the United States needed to expand its offensive nuclear power. "Our policy," it concluded, "will bring into focus the central fact that U.S. strategic power is the ultimate military deterrent to Soviet aggression" (13). The task force proposed that by relying on nuclear weapons, the United States would be able to avoid the costly expense of maintaining sufficient military forces to wage both limited and general wars. In addressing the costs of alternative B, the task force assumed a position similar to that of task force A. It emphasized that, regardless of the cost, the United States had to address the Soviet threat. "Whatever the evils of inflation, whatever the economic problems involved in efforts to control it," the task force argued, "these cannot be weighed in the same scales with the grave danger to our national survival" (20). It concluded, "Alternative B is in effect an announcement that the United States and the Free World will accept the risk of annihilation before they accept Soviet domination" (I-4).

The directing panel ordered task force C to develop a national security policy based on the alternative of "rolling back" communism. This alternative proposed using every means available, except military force, to undermine communist-controlled countries. Task force C stated its broad

objectives as "ending Soviet domination outside its traditional boundaries, destroying the communist apparatus in the Free World, curtailing Soviet power for an aggressive war, ending the Iron Curtain, and cutting
down the strength of any Bolshevik elements left in Soviet Russia."[71] It
believed that the only way to achieve these goals was to take the foreign
policy initiative away from the Soviet Union. Alternative C required the
United States to assume a much more aggressive policy. Believing that
the United States had forfeited the initiative by only reacting to Soviet
moves, it argued that the only way to regain the advantage in the Cold War
was "by waging a political offensive." The task force stated more explicitly
that "we must proceed to bring about the political subversion and liqui-
dation of the conspiracy against us" (9).

To regain the initiative, task force C proposed two strategies—sub-
verting communism and continuing a military buildup. Subversion was
the policy of action, and military buildup was the insurance if subversion
failed. Task force C recommended: "In carrying out this policy [of sub-
version], we recommend that this Government aggressively, both overtly
and covertly, attack the Communist apparatus wherever it be found in
the world. . . . What we seek to do is to harass and hound every conceivable Communist activity using all available political, legal, financial and
economic devices in our possession" (22). The task force placed few limitations on possible U.S. subversive policies. It argued, "All means of action . . .—short of preventive war—are available under the Alternative"
(85). It recognized that this policy embodied a greater risk of war but argued that the only way to win the Cold War was to be aggressive.

Task force C's evaluation of the expense of its policy revealed a greater
initial cost than either alternative A or B but a smaller amount in the long
term because the Cold War would have ended in victory. It called for
$60 billion annual defense budgets for FYs 1954 and 1955 and $45 billion
for each year thereafter until the United States won the Cold War (62). It
argued that the cost was worth the benefits of victory. By assuming this
policy, the United States would prevail in any type of conflict with the Soviet Union.

After receiving the task force presentations, the NSC ordered the Planning Board to analyze the reports and to develop a policy paper incorporating the best features of each one. The Planning Board established an ad
hoc committee of representatives from each of the statutory members of
the NSC. For three weeks the committee studied the three reports. Robert

Bowie, director of the Policy Planning staff and the State Department representative on the Planning Board, stated that "the planning board worked on this . . . and attempted to build on what had been in the task force reports, particularly Task Force A which was pretty much recognized as the principal basis on which the president had come down."[72] The Planning Board presented the draft of its policy paper to the NSC on September 30. This policy paper evolved through three broad stages: NSC 162, 162/1, and 162/2.[73]

In the final version, the NSC established the basic goal of having the United States meet the perceived Soviet threat while avoiding economic ruin.[74] Not surprisingly, it incorporated recommendations from each of the Solarium task forces. While it viewed the world through the spectrum of an East-West struggle, as did the task forces, it placed a much greater emphasis on economic security than any of them did. To achieve its national security goals, it established three requirements:

    a. Development and maintenance of:
      1. A strong military posture with emphasis on the capability of inflicting massive retaliatory damage by offensive striking power;
      2. U.S. and allied forces in readiness to move rapidly initially to counter aggression by Soviet bloc forces and to hold vital areas and lines of communication; and
      3. A mobilization base, and its protection against crippling damage, adequate to insure victory in a general war.
    b. Maintenance of a sound, strong and growing economy.
    c. Maintenance of morale and free institutions and the willingness of the U.S. people to support the measures necessary for national security.[75]

These requirements embodied most of task force A's recommendations.[76] The differences arose in NSC 162/2's emphasis on both economic and military strength.

The NSC also adopted the principle that both tactical and strategic atomic weapons would be used in wartime.[77] To differing degrees, each task force had recommended a greater reliance on these weapons in case of a military conflict. Accepting this premise, the NSC argued: "The major deterrent to aggression against Western Europe is the manifest determination of the United States to use its atomic capability and massive retaliatory striking power if the area is attacked."[78] The true meaning of "massive retaliatory striking power" became much clearer when the NSC emphasized the important role of nuclear weapons in any type of conflict. "In the event of hostilities," it stated, "the United States will consider nuclear weapons to be as available for use as other munitions" (593).

While the NSC recognized that the efficacy of atomic deterrence could be limited, even so it believed that reliance on nuclear weapons provided the most cost-efficient strategy for successfully waging the Cold War. It concluded that if Soviet leaders knew there were certain actions that would lead automatically to a U.S. nuclear counterattack, then they would pursue a more cautious policy. This concept of clearly declaring specific responses to possible Soviet actions is reminiscent of task force B's "drawing the line" (581). The idea in NSC 162/2 was not to define an entire policy around this concept but to warn the Kremlin leaders of the possible consequences of their actions. The NSC believed that if the United States explicitly stated its position regarding Soviet aggressive moves, then U.S. military officials would be able to develop plans based on more clearly defined policies.

In addressing the policy of "rolling back" communism, NSC 162/2 concluded that there was little likelihood of detaching a country from the Soviet bloc. However, it did recommend that the United States "take overt and covert measures to discredit Soviet prestige and ideology as effective instruments of Soviet power" (595). NSC 162/2 accepted task force C's premise that communism could be thwarted in countries not firmly aligned in the Soviet bloc. The idea was to undermine the governments of countries that had communist leanings but at the same time were not directly tied to the Soviet Union. The Eisenhower administration clearly adopted this position in its later policies toward such countries as Iran and Guatemala.[79]

NSC 162/2 represented the Eisenhower administration's clearest expression of its "New Look" national security policy. It emphasized that military plans would be developed under the assumption that atomic weapons would be used in future conflicts, it authorized the use of both overt and covert operations to achieve U.S. goals, and it recognized the importance of economic strength to U.S. security. The paper also stressed the importance of the rest of the world to the United States. It stated, "The assumption by the United States, as the leader of the free world, of a substantial degree of responsibility for the freedom and security of the free nations is a direct and essential contribution to the maintenance of its own freedom and security."[80]

The development of NSC 162/2 clearly reveals the importance Eisenhower assigned to examining policy alternatives thoroughly within a tightly organized decision-making system. By stressing his economic and political philosophies to the participants in this system, he provided guidance for the development of his policies. General Andrew Goodpaster, a member of task force C and later Eisenhower's staff secretary, recalled that in the NSC meetings the president wanted to bring together all of the people involved with an issue. Eisenhower "had what amounted to a tacit rule that there could be no non-concurrence through silence. If somebody didn't agree, he was obliged to speak his mind and get it all out on the table . . . and then in light of all of that, the President would come to a line of action, he wanted everybody to hear it, everybody to participate in it, and then he wanted everybody to be guided by it."[81] This approach allowed Eisenhower to select his preferred national security policy alternatives.

The Threat of Surprise Attack and the Killian Committee

In early 1954 Eisenhower again turned to the NSC and outside consultants to examine a problem that had been bothering him for many months. Recent technological advances, including the successful Russian test of the H-bomb and the development of long-range aircraft, raised the question of whether the Soviet Union could launch a successful surprise attack against the United States.[82] The lack of concrete intelligence concerning Soviet military capabilities or intentions accentuated the concern. In March, Eisenhower turned to the Science Advisory Committee of the Office of Defense Mobilization to study whether the Soviet Union had the capability or intention of launching an attack against North America and what the United States could do to prepare for that possibility.

Eisenhower's fears mirrored the concerns of many earlier U.S. policymakers. In the immediate aftermath of World War II, U.S. officials recognized the preponderance of U.S. world power.[83] However, after the Soviet detonation of the atomic bomb in 1949, U.S. superiority became less certain, and accurate assessments of Soviet intentions became even more paramount. Ever since Pearl Harbor, Americans had experienced a forbidding sense of vulnerability. The Soviet atomic test then raised the specter that the Kremlin leaders might one day acquire the capability to attack the United States. In assessing the significance of Soviet possession of the bomb less than two months later, Air Force Chief of Staff Hoyt Vandenberg revealed, "There are strong reasons to believe that a sudden surprise attack by Soviet atom bombers would result in not only inflicting unthinkable mortalities on our people and our industry, but also might cripple our strategic air forces, thereby denying us the means to redress the balance through retaliation."[84] In a separate memorandum on the same day, Vandenberg discussed the inadequacies of U.S. air defenses and asserted that "almost any number of Soviet bombers could cross our borders and fly to most of the targets in the United States without a shot being fired at them and without even being challenged in any way."[85]

During the early 1950s, a Soviet surprise attack was not expected, but the possibility could not be ignored. Most intelligence estimates from this time period, including National Intelligence Estimate (NIE) 3, NIE 48, and NIE 64, concluded that the Soviet Union would not deliberately initiate war.[86] Retired Air Force General Idwal Edwards chaired a committee for the NSC that examined the capability of the Soviet Union to injure the United States and concluded that if the Soviet leaders launched an attack, it "would be an act of desperation and not an exercise in military judgment."[87] However, while Edwards's committee and the other NIEs did not expect an attack, they would not eliminate that possibility. For example, after arguing that the Soviet Union would probably not initiate a general war against the United States, NIE 48 quickly equivocated and stressed that "Soviet courses of action can never be predicted with confidence. In particular the possibility of deliberate initiation of general war cannot be excluded at any time merely because such initiation would contradict past Soviet political strategy."[88]

Eisenhower also received a steady stream of conflicting reports concerning Soviet capabilities and U.S. vulnerabilities. A notable deficiency in most of these reports was the lack of a detailed analysis of Soviet intentions. In 1953 the Strategic Air Command (SAC) initiated Operation Tailwind to discover "How well could SAC survive a Pearl Harbor type of attack?"[89] Simulating one possible Soviet attack scenario, SAC launched ninety-nine bomber sorties against targets in the United States during a forty-eight-hour period when the Air Defense Command (ADC) was on alert for an attack. Despite the attack warning and its alert status, the ADC intercepted only six bombers.[90] This dismal performance supported SAC's contention that "it is extremely difficult to effectively prevent penetration of coordinated heavy bomber attacks which hit the early warning screen from many directions simultaneously."[91]

Influenced in part by Operation Tailwind, the NSC examined U.S. continental defenses during the summer of 1953. It emphasized, "The present continental defense programs are not now adequate to prevent, neutralize or seriously deter the military or covert attacks which the USSR is capable of launching, nor are they adequate to ensure the continuity of government, the continuity of production, or the protection of the industrial mobilization base and millions of citizens in our great and exposed metropolitan centers." It then concluded, "This condition constitutes an unacceptable risk to our nation's survival."[92] The NSC therefore recommended improving intelligence-gathering capabilities, expanding radar coverage, increasing fighter-interceptor and anti-aircraft forces, developing plans for government continuity after an attack, and adopting new civil defense programs.[93] These recommendations closely mirrored the views of the JCS at the same time.[94]

While these reports made it clear that U.S. defenses were inadequate to stop a Soviet attack, the question remained whether the Soviet Union intended to take such actions or even whether it could do so. In a striking report, "Magnitude and Imminence of the Soviet Air Threat to the United States," neither the Air Force, the Navy, nor the JCS expected the Soviet Union to launch an attack before the end of 1957.[95] The Navy representative summarized this position by arguing, "The preservation of the security of the USSR under the worst possible contingencies of war will loom large in their estimate of the situation. In the Soviet mind, overwhelming strength will be required. It is not believed that the Soviets are likely to conclude, between now and 1957, that they have such strength."[96]

However, Soviet advances in both atomic weapons technology and long-range bomber capabilities clouded these conclusions. While it would have been difficult for the Soviet Union to launch an attack, its testing of the H-bomb in 1953 and its introduction of new medium- and long-range bombers in 1954 indicated that it was acquiring the capability to do so.[97] More important, the destructive power of nuclear weapons gave an aggressor the potential capability to win a war through a carefully planned first strike.[98] At this stage, the perception among U.S. policymakers that the Soviet Union sought world domination became widespread. Charles Bohlen, the State Department representative on Truman's NSC senior staff, concluded that "there is no important disagreement [among policymakers] that if matters reach the point where the Soviets attain the capability of delivering a 'decisive' initial blow on the United States without serious risk to their own regime, they would do so."[99]

The question of whether the Soviet Union would launch an attack if it could was further complicated by American memories of Pearl Harbor.

The Japanese had caught the United States by surprise and had mounted a devastating attack against U.S. naval and air forces. The introduction of nuclear weapons raised the stakes if a similar attack was used to start a new war. Jack Nunn, in a pioneering study of the importance of Soviet first-strike capability, carefully articulates how this capability, when tied to the memories of Pearl Harbor, changed U.S. perceptions of its vulnerability. "The Japanese attack," he argues, "was etched on the collective U.S. consciousness, the name linked with a vision of a surprise attack—pitting a calculating aggressor against an unaware and unwarlike democracy." [100]

One of Eisenhower's greatest problems was that he did not know what the Soviet Union planned to do.[101] While he did not expect the Kremlin to order an attack, he could not rule out that possibility. If the Soviet Union possessed the capability to attack the United States with nuclear weapons and U.S. defenses remained vulnerable to such an attack, the enemy posed a potentially deadly threat. This cruel dilemma bedeviled Eisenhower. While he did not expect an attack, the assumption that the Soviet Union might attack, if it believed it could do so without suffering devastating retaliation, formed the basis of U.S. policies.[102] In essence, Eisenhower had to base his policies on a strategic alternative that he did not expect to happen.

In 1954 Eisenhower continued to view U.S. strength with confidence. However, technological advances in both weaponry and delivery capabilities raised the possibility that the Soviet Union might soon be able to launch a devastating surprise attack against the United States. In March 1954 he expressed this concern to his Science Advisory Committee and asked its members whether technological means existed to obtain early warning of a Soviet surprise attack and to defend the United States if such an attack did occur.[103] His concerns led to the creation of a special committee to address these technological questions.[104]

In July 1954 Lee Dubridge, the chairman of the Science Advisory Committee, proposed a study that would analyze Soviet capabilities and explore possible scientific and technological means to meet any threat. Upon Eisenhower's request, James Killian, president of the Massachusetts Institute of Technology (MIT) and a member of the Science Advisory Committee, agreed to serve as chairman of the soon-to-be-created Technical Capabilities Panel (TCP). From September 1954 to February 1955, this panel, known as the Killian committee, assessed the Soviet Union's strengths and weaknesses, the vulnerability of the United States to surprise attack, and the measures needed to improve U.S. offensive and defensive capabilities. The committee presented its 190-page report to the NSC in February 1955.[105]

The TCP's activities, conclusions, and recommendations are of striking importance to understanding the Gaither committee. As later chapters will show, many of the Gaither committee's conclusions and recommendations reflected the influence of the TCP. Considering their respective memberships, this is not surprising. Of the nine members of the TCP's steering committee, five—James Killian, James Fisk, James Baxter, James Doolittle, and Robert Sprague—would later serve on the Gaither committee in significant capacities.[106] In addition, five consultants served on both the TCP and the Gaither committee.[107]

In the preface to its study, the TCP's steering committee stated that its objective was to examine "the present vulnerability of the United States to surprise attack and ways whereby science and technology can strengthen our offense and defense to reduce this hazard."[108] To address this problem fully, Killian asked outside consultants to sit on three panels that would examine specific problems related to technological changes. Panel 1, chaired by Marshall Holloway, examined U.S. offensive capabilities. Panel 2, headed by Leland Haworth, studied U.S. continental defense. Panel 3, directed by Edwin Land, studied U.S. intelligence capabilities. The creation of these three panels reflected key assumptions that guided the steering committee. First, it viewed offensive and defensive weapons as integrated components in the defense of the United States. Second, it believed that continental defenses, ranging from early warning to anti-aircraft weapons, were inadequate. Finally, it recognized that the acceleration of Soviet technological developments increased U.S. vulnerability.[109]

The TCP concluded that U.S. offensive forces, comprising at that time primarily the Strategic Air Command, were essential to reduce U.S. vulnerability to a surprise attack. In reaching these conclusions, it operated under the assumption that "both 'offensive' and 'defensive' forces are essential to accomplish the general mission of defending the United States. Both are deterrents to surprise and, should war begin, both contribute to the destruction of the enemy power. Neither one alone is adequate to defend the United States."[110] The panel concluded that aircraft, and later missiles, would provide the United States with a deterrent capability that might force Soviet leaders to reevaluate any plans to launch a first strike. If the Soviets did order an attack, the survival of an offensive striking capability would allow the United States to retaliate through a devastating counterstrike. Finally, the existence of an offensive striking force gave the United States the option of launching a first strike if it so chose.[111] While never the official policy of the United States, this option was still being seriously considered in different crisis situations in the 1950s.[112]

In evaluating the threat of a surprise attack against the United States, the committee gave no real consideration to Soviet intentions. The Killian committee readily acknowledged that it based its conclusions on technological changes rather than on any reevaluation of Soviet intentions. It simply accepted the assumption that the Soviet Union's ultimate goal was world domination and that Soviet leaders would be willing to use any means to achieve it. Technological advances in weaponry and delivery systems magnified the threat. The committee was particularly concerned with the Soviet development of a hydrogen bomb and its research into ballistic missiles. "This evolution of nuclear bombs and the means to deliver them," the committee stressed, "has given warfare a potential for swift, complete destruction and sudden decisiveness that is revolutionizing our concepts of offense and defense."[113]

The Killian committee concluded that advances in delivery capabilities posed a greater threat than improvements in nuclear weaponry. While it did not rule out further advances in warhead design and/or yield, it stressed that such advances would be relatively minimal. Equally important, it noted that the United States would not be able to maintain its lead in warhead technology for long, since present "technology is already near the upper limit of yield per ton of bomb allowed by nature" (7). With the imminent emergence of virtual equality in the field of nuclear weaponry, advances in delivery systems became pivotal in the military balance of power between the Soviet Union and the United States (14).

The committee examined the effectiveness of two types of delivery systems: bombers and ballistic missiles. It argued that "attack by manned bombers will continue to be a threat long after the advent of the intercontinental missiles" (76). However, it did emphasize the potential strategic and psychological consequences of the development of the ICBM. It concluded, "In the hands of the Soviets such a weapon [the ICBM] would represent an even greater jump in capability since it would to a considerable extent wipe out the present geographical advantage enjoyed by the U.S." It further stressed, "With such a capability the Soviets could put pressure on much of the world outside of the U.S., either by direct threat to them or by threat against the U.S. It, therefore, appears urgent to achieve this type of capability before the Soviets, in order to at least match threat with threat" (64).

The defense problems raised by both long-range bombers and ballistic missiles brought into focus the issues before panels 2 and 3. Offensive striking forces would be useless if they could be destroyed before the United States could launch a retaliatory strike. This dilemma forced the panels to determine the impact of technological advances in several areas. Panel 2 had to analyze whether the threat raised by these advances could be countered by improving U.S. defenses. Panel 3 had to determine how technological advances could strengthen U.S. intelligence-gathering capabilities. For both panels, technology could either undermine or strengthen U.S. security.

In a scathing critique of U.S. continental defenses, the Killian committee concluded that "the United States is at present unacceptably vulnerable to surprise attack. Our military defenses are as yet numerically deficient and have serious qualitative weaknesses. The defenses could be avoided or overwhelmed and might even be unaware of an attack until the first bomb exploded. Under these circumstances our cities could suffer millions of casualties and crippling damage, and enough SAC bombers and bases could be destroyed to reduce drastically our ability to retaliate" (18). More specifically, the committee argued that if the Soviet Union launched an attack, the United States would receive little or no warning because of the weaknesses in its intelligence-gathering capabilities and the gaps in radar coverage at both high and low altitudes (75–76, 96–97, 101–2). These deficiencies opened the United States to a surprise attack if the Soviet Union decided to launch one.

Because of the existing and expected advances in delivery capabilities and the deficiencies in continental defense, Edwin Land's panel examined how effectively technology was being used to acquire intelligence of the Soviet Union. In the mid-1950s the United States lacked a clear knowledge of Soviet capabilities. The various U.S. intelligence agencies, including the CIA and the intelligence departments within each branch of the military, based their estimates of Soviet capabilities on limited firsthand evidence, extrapolations from known U.S. weapons capabilities, estimates of Soviet manufacturing capabilities, and sightings of Soviet military hardware (often at military parades and air shows).[114] The Killian committee aptly concluded that "estimates of the *specific capabilities* and *immediate intentions* of the Soviets have, at their center, only a very small core of hard facts" (emphasis in original).[115] Quite obviously, intelligence estimates based on such evidence could not be totally reliable and might lead to incorrect or at least ambiguous conclusions and recommendations.

Although most of the section of the Killian report dealing specifically with the acquisition and interpretation of intelligence remains classified, enough evidence is available to indicate the committee's basic conclusions and recommendations. It emphasized that "there is a good possibility that an enemy's preparations for a massive surprise attack on the United States would be detected. However, this possibility is not a certainty" (24). Accordingly, it stressed, "Because we are unable to conclude that the United States surely will, or surely will not, have useful strategic warning in the event of a surprise attack, we recommend that our planning take serious account of both possibilities" (25). The committee stated that the United States "*must* find ways to increase the number of hard facts upon which our intelligence estimates are based, to provide better strategic warning, to minimize surprise in the kind of attack, and to reduce the danger of gross overestimation or gross underestimation of the threat" (44; emphasis in original).

An important question is whether the committee believed that the United States should launch either a preventive or a preemptive war against the Soviet Union. While the committee never explicitly made either recommendation, evidence suggests that it supported maintaining a first-strike capability.[116] For example, it stated, "Our striking forces must blunt the attack at its source."[117] In a more extensive analysis, it concluded, "The importance to the defense of the U.S. of an offensive air striking force stems from its ability to attack the Soviet long-range air force on the ground."[118] By being able to strike at the "source" or "on the ground," the United States would be capable of preventive war or, at a minimum, preemptive war.[119]

The final Killian report made several specific recommendations to limit the vulnerability of the United States to a surprise attack by the Soviet Union. The committee called for the acceleration of ballistic missile development, the acquisition of additional bases for the Strategic Air Command, the completion of a comprehensive review of both U.S. and Soviet target systems, the construction of the Distant Early Warning Line, the addition of gap-filler radar, the use of atomic weapons in defense against attacking bombers and/or missiles, and the study of ways to reduce civilian casualties in the event of an attack.[120]

The Killian committee's findings had a tremendous influence on Eisenhower and his administration, especially in the areas of accelerating missile development and intelligence gathering. David Rosenberg argues that "the TCP . . . provided an important benchmark in the evolution of Eisenhower's thinking about nuclear strategy."[121] Eisenhower acknowledged in his memoirs how he accelerated the development of both the IRBM and the ICBM after receiving the Killian report.[122] However, Land's intelligence panel probably had the most important influence. It recommended the construction of an airplane capable of photographing the Soviet Union from high altitudes. The recommendation to build such a spy plane was so sensitive that it was presented to Eisenhower directly, instead of to the full NSC.[123] Eisenhower accepted this recommendation and immediately initiated the U-2 program. In the view of retired CIA historian Donald Welzenbach, after the meeting of the TCP, "Killian and Land virtually controlled the development of the nation's technical intelligence collections agencies."[124]

The recommendations of the Killian committee that Eisenhower incorporated into his national security policies were tremendously influential. They laid the foundation for the acceleration of U.S. intelligence gathering and ballistic missile programs. The TCP exercise is a clear example of how Eisenhower sought advice from outside consultants who were experts in specific fields. Through the filter of his national security decision-making structure, Eisenhower ordered, received, and evaluated this advice. He accepted parts of it, modified others, and rejected some. The result of the entire process was a policy that reflected Eisenhower's desire to wage the Cold War based on a combination of political, military, and economic strength.

Conclusions

Eisenhower succeeded admirably in achieving his objectives during his first term as president. Starting with a systematic review of U.S. national security programs in 1953, Eisenhower devised a military strategy based on his country's overwhelming superiority in atomic weapons and delivery capabilities. He decided that, rather than react to every world crisis by deploying troops or by increasing the defense budget, the United States would emphasize the deterrent power of atomic weapons. In so doing, he was able to cut overall defense expenditures by reducing the size of U.S. conventional—nonnuclear—forces. This New Look strategy, as it was called, allowed Eisenhower to balance two of his first four annual budgets and to maintain the military capability necessary to launch a devastating counterstrike if the Soviet Union decided to attack the United States.

In all of his decisions, Eisenhower attempted to preserve what he viewed as the twin foundations of American society: democratic government and a viable capitalist economic system. When making decisions concerning national security matters, he believed these principles could be protected only by maintaining a careful balance between a sound economy—meaning low inflation and a balanced budget—and defense spending. An overemphasis on one would lead only to weakness in the other. Throughout his first term in office, Eisenhower struggled to maintain these twin goals while resisting almost constant calls for more spending.[125]

To ensure the integration of his political and economic philosophies into his national security policies, Eisenhower employed a decision-making process that he had carefully designed at the inception of his presidency. Drawing on a complex system of committees and advisory groups and reviewing a problem or issue step by step, from the lowest to the highest levels of policy making, he believed, would facilitate the development of the best possible policy alternatives. Through this process, Eisenhower expected to obtain advice and guidance based on careful study and discussion.[126] On matters of national security, the NSC stood at the center of this process. Following the advice of Robert Cutler, Eisenhower streamlined the process for developing policy papers, established a standardized procedure for presentations at NSC meetings, set the precedent for using outside consultants, and expanded the NSC membership to include both the secretary of the treasury and director of the budget.

Eisenhower used these new procedures to analyze national security issues. On two occasions during his first term, the NSC turned to outside consultants to examine specific national security problems. In 1953 it created three task forces as part of Project Solarium to examine policy alternatives. Eisenhower incorporated many of their final recommendations in his new national security policy—NSC 162/2. This policy emphasized the maintenance of an overwhelming offensive striking power, the use of tactical nuclear weapons as well as conventional arms in future conflicts, and the employment of covert operations to undermine communism. In 1954 Eisenhower again turned to outside consultants when he ordered the creation of the Killian committee to analyze the vulnerability of the United States to a Soviet surprise attack. After receiving the committee's conclusions, Eisenhower accelerated the development of both IRBMs and ICBMs and implemented the U-2 program to acquire intelligence of Soviet military capabilities and possible intentions.

Scholars such as H. W. Brands, I. M. Destler, Samuel Huntington, and Jeremi Suri have questioned the effectiveness of Eisenhower's organizational structure. They argue that rather than requiring policy advisers to make clear decisions on controversial issues, the NSC developed recommendations based on compromise and consensus building. Eisenhower's critics claim that these recommendations were more often than not too broad or ambiguous. In either case, they provided only minimal guidance in developing specific policies.[127]

While this may have been true in some cases, the examples presented in this chapter reveal an organizational system that produced the type of advice that Eisenhower sought.[128] Eisenhower turned to the NSC and outside consultants to acquire the assistance he needed to make decisions. He utilized the recommendations he received from Project Solarium and the Killian committee to help formulate his policies. The committees and the NSC served Eisenhower as a means to explore different policy options in an environment conducive to open discussion and debate. From these alternatives, Eisenhower was able to develop and augment his New Look policies.

The examples of Project Solarium and the Killian committee reveal the reliance that Eisenhower placed on his decision-making system. He used outside consultants to obtain fresh appraisals concerning specific problems and the NSC as a forum for thorough discussion and debate. Through this system, he was able to develop policies that reflected his economic, military, and political philosophies. Although not without its faults, the organizational structure that Eisenhower constructed and used in making decisions concerning national security policies during his first term provided clear and effective guidance for waging the Cold War.

2 | The Establishment and Background of the Gaither Committee

$\mathbf{T}$he New Look policies that Eisenhower adopted in 1953 and 1954 remained the centerpieces of U.S. strategy throughout his presidency as he relied on nuclear weapons and continued technological improvements to deter the Soviet Union, as well as covert and psychological operations to wage the Cold War against communism. The experts involved in both Project Solarium and the Killian committee helped devise the administration's policies. The results seemed positive. After a brief economic downturn in 1954, the economy prospered. Furthermore, while the Soviet Union continued to strengthen its military forces, the United States augmented its own capabilities by placing greater emphasis on strategic nuclear power.

Eisenhower's policies won acclaim from the American population. Without sacrificing security, defense spending was at its lowest since before the Korean War. In addition, the economy was experiencing steady growth with little inflation—one of Eisenhower's most important goals. After defeating the Democratic candidate, Adlai Stevenson, in the 1956 presidential election, he began his second term with hope and confidence. Unfortunately, the promising beginning to 1957 proved short-lived. By the end of the year, his administration was under attack from all directions. In late November 1957 he wrote to a friend, "Since July 25th of 1956, when Nasser announced the nationalization of the Suez, I cannot remember a day that has not brought its major or minor crisis." [1]

Of all the controversies that plagued Eisenhower in 1957, the question of civil defense had the greatest influence on the establishment of the Gaither committee. Debates raged over the implications of radioactive fallout, the correct balance between shelters and evacuation, and the requirements for stockpiling emergency materials. [2] These controversies were not

43

new. Ever since the Soviet Union had acquired the capability of attacking the United States, the president and his advisers had recognized the potential consequences of a nuclear exchange for the civilian population, the country's infrastructure, and the government's ability to continue to function.[3] Months before the establishment of the Gaither committee, Eisenhower told the NSC "that the picture of the terrific destruction resulting from a nuclear attack warranted taking a look at the whole matter in terms of determining how much destruction the United States and its people can absorb and still survive."[4]

The question about civil defense that most concerned Eisenhower was how to develop a plan that would "avoid hysteria on one side and complacency on the other."[5] He recognized that U.S. civil defense programs were important to U.S. security, yet he did not want to adopt a plan that would undermine the way of life he sought to protect. He desired a middle ground between regimenting society in preparation for an attack and accepting the destruction of urban centers as unpreventable.[6] In January 1957 the Federal Civil Defense Administration (FCDA) recommended that the United States build a $32 billion shelter system. Eisenhower and his advisers had to decide whether to accept such a major undertaking.

As he had in 1953 and again in 1954, Eisenhower turned to a group of experts to study the relationship between active defenses (interceptor aircraft, anti-aircraft guns, and air defense missiles) and passive defenses (early warning radar, evacuation plans, and shelters). With the assistance of the Science Advisory Committee of the Office of Defense Mobilization (ODM), Eisenhower asked H. Rowan Gaither in May 1957 to establish a committee of experts, formally called the Security Resources Panel but better known as the Gaither committee. Over the course of the summer and early fall, the committee examined U.S. national security programs. When it completed its final report in November, it made recommendations that reflected the preconceived biases and years of study of its expert members.

Plans for Civil Defense

The impetus for the creation of the Gaither committee came from growing pressures on the Eisenhower administration to reevaluate U.S. civil defense policies and to institute a nationwide shelter program. From January to June of 1956, Representative Chet Holifield (D-CA) chaired hearings before the House Military Operations Subcommittee of the House Committee on Government Operations concerning the adequacy of U.S. civil defense planning. Holifield believed that the administration was placing too much emphasis on offensive striking power at the expense of continental and civil defense. He subjected the FCDA, headed by former Nebraska governor Val Peterson, to the most vigorous criticism. Holifield believed that the FCDA placed too much emphasis on evacuating the population after receiving warning of a Soviet nuclear attack rather than on providing shelters for the majority of the urban population who would be unable to leave. He emphasized, "The FCDA's policy of reliance on evacuation as the key civil defense measure is weak and ineffective and indeed dangerously shortsighted."[7] Instead of evacuation, Holifield stressed the importance of shelters in protecting the population and deterring the Soviet Union.[8]

In January 1957 Holifield's committee submitted legislation, H.R. 2125, which if passed would have greatly expanded the importance of civil defense. In particular, it would have forced the federal government to assume control of civil defense planning whether it wanted to or not. The committee proposed the creation of a Department of Civil Defense, the development of a national plan for civil defense, and the construction of shelters in predetermined target areas.[9] More specifically, the legislation called for the construction of fallout shelters that would provide some protection to the entire American population of 170 million. The proposed shelter system would cost approximately $20 billion.[10] The House of Representatives rejected most of Holifield's legislation during the spring of 1957, but it did shift the burden for civil defense planning from the localities to the federal government.

Despite the criticism, Peterson and his assistants from the FCDA supported many of the Holifield committee's recommendations. Although they had originally emphasized evacuation, the advent of more powerful weapons and advanced delivery systems led them to develop a policy balanced between shelters and evacuation. In particular, the FCDA reevaluated its civil defense plans after the March 1954 Bravo nuclear test fanned the fears of radioactive fallout. This explosion yielded twice the expected power and produced fallout that covered nearly 7,000 square miles.[11] After the deadly results of the test became known, the FCDA placed even more emphasis on shelters because of the "greatly increased radiation hazard from fall-out."[12]

In December 1956 Peterson reported that the Soviet Union had the capability to launch a nuclear attack against the United States using bombers and submarine-launched missiles. After the advent of the ICBM, the warning time of such an attack could be as little as fifteen minutes.[13] Because of this potential threat, Peterson submitted an FCDA proposal in January 1957 to build a nationwide system of shelters that would be used in conjunction with preestablished evacuation plans.[14] The report, which became known as NSC 5709, accepted the conclusions of the Net Evaluation Subcommittee (NES), which argued that 80 percent of the casualties in a nuclear attack would result from radioactive fallout.[15] Concerned about the impact of this fallout and influenced by Holifield's call for shelters, the FCDA concluded, "Most of the fallout casualties could be prevented by adequate shelter."[16] It recommended spending $32 billion over the following eight years to build sufficient shelters to protect the entire population.[17]

Despite the report's dire warnings, neither Eisenhower nor his top advisers were willing to spend such a large sum of money on an unproven method of protection. Robert Cutler, Eisenhower's assistant for national security affairs, argued that while shelters may have been necessary, without knowledge of their impact on the economy and on domestic and foreign opinion a massive construction program could not be immediately implemented.[18] Nonetheless, administration officials, alarmed by the magnitude of the anticipated destruction from a Soviet attack, requested further examinations of the problem. They launched new studies to examine the likely casualties in a nuclear exchange, the effectiveness of passive defense measures in preventing casualties, the capability of active defenses to destroy Soviet forces before they reached their targets, and the economic consequences of these defense programs.[19]

The Establishment of the Gaither Committee

Eisenhower used the NSC to examine these issues. From January to March 1957, the planning board discussed the FCDA's report on shelters and recommended that the NSC perform another study that would answer a series of questions, the most important being, "What is the optimum balance between active and passive defense measures for protection of the civil population?"[20] On April 4, 1957, the NSC ordered four studies to answer the planning board's questions:

1. A study of different shelter programs by an interdepartmental committee composed of representatives from the FCDA, ODM, the Atomic Energy Commission (AEC), and the Department of Defense.
2. A study by the Science Advisory Committee of the ODM of active and passive defense measures for the protection of the civil population.
3. A study by the Council of Economic Advisers of the economic costs of various shelter programs.
4. A study by the Department of the Treasury of providing financial assistance to individuals and industries to stimulate private shelter construction.[21]

The study by the Science Advisory Committee proved the most important, as it eventually incorporated the findings of the other three in reaching its final conclusions. To perform this study, the NSC turned to the decision-making system it had used so successfully in the cases of Project Solarium and the Killian committee. It requested that the Science Advisory Committee appoint a panel of experts to study U.S. active and passive defense measures.[22]

The Science Advisory Committee gave James Killian, one of its members, the responsibility for selecting the project director. He recommended that the committee appoint Gaither, a longtime friend from their days at the World War II Radiation Laboratory, to oversee the study.[23] Based on this recommendation, Eisenhower asked Gaither to serve as the director of the soon-to-be-created Security Resources Panel.[24] Through the early summer, Gaither and the ODM selected individuals to serve on this panel, aptly called the Gaither committee. Gaither divided the committee into two principal groups: the steering committee and the advisory panel. After he was diagnosed with arterial thrombosis, he stepped down as the committee's director in September, to be replaced by Robert Sprague and William Foster. Sprague and Foster directed the steering committee, which also included James Baxter, Robert Calkins, John Corson, James Perkins, Robert Prim, Hector Skifter, William Webster, Jerome Wiesner, and technical adviser Edward Oliver. The advisory panel included Gaither (after his illness), Admiral Robert Carney, General James Doolittle, General John Hull, Mervin Kelly, Ernest Lawrence, Robert Lovett, John McCloy, and Frank Stanton. Two other groups played important advisory roles: a subcommittee of the Science Advisory Committee, whose members were James Fisk, James Killian, and Isidor Rabi, and a committee from the

Institute for Defense Analyses, composed of General James McCormack and Albert Hill.

In addition to its permanent members, the Gaither committee recruited nearly seventy expert consultants from leading scientific organizations, engineering firms, strategic think tanks, and business institutions to provide advice and make recommendations.[25] These consultants provided invaluable background material and technical support to the committee. In fact, some scholars have argued that several of these advisers actually played much larger roles than their titles as technical consultants would indicate. In particular, Colonel George Lincoln and Paul Nitze seem to have had great influence on the final report.[26]

The high caliber of this committee was without question. A sample of the qualifications of some of the members of the steering committee and advisory panel is ample evidence of the committee's expertise. Killian and Baxter served as the respective presidents of MIT and Williams College. For his research on molecular beams at the Radiation Laboratory, Rabi won the 1944 Nobel Prize for physics. During the last years of the Truman administration, Lovett and Foster acted as the secretary and the deputy secretary of defense, respectively. These men and the rest of the Gaither committee represented some of the best minds in the country.

The Gaither committee members were the type of experts that Eisenhower and his NSC used to acquire policy advice. The president wanted the assistance of consultants who were specialists in particular fields or who possessed a broad understanding of U.S. national security issues. Eisenhower's belief that experts could provide invaluable advice dated to his experiences in World War II. While serving as the Army chief of staff immediately after the war, he implored his key subordinates to recognize the essential contributions that scientists, business leaders, and other experts had made to the war effort. As he explained:

> The lessons of the last war are clear. The military effort required for victory threw upon the Army an unprecedented range of responsibilities, many of which were effectively discharged only through the invaluable assistance supplied by our cumulative resources in the natural and social sciences and the talents and experience furnished by management and labor. The armed forces could not have won the war alone. Scientists and business men contributed techniques and weapons which enabled us to outwit and overwhelm the enemy. Their understanding of the Army's needs made possible the highest degree of cooperation. This pattern of integration must be translated into a

peacetime counterpart which will not merely familiarize the Army with the progress made in science and industry, but draw into our planning for national security all the civilian resources which can contribute to the defense of the country.[27]

He concluded, "The association of military and civilians in educational institutions and industry will level barriers, engender mutual understanding, and lead to the cultivation of friendships invaluable for future cooperation."[28]

Background of Key Gaither Committee Members

More than a decade later, Eisenhower took his own advice to heart when he ordered the establishment of the Gaither committee. Its members were well known and widely respected within the Eisenhower administration. Most had either advised the administration earlier or had published their views on matters related to active and passive defenses. Without exception, the Gaither committee members viewed the expansion of Soviet military capabilities with great concern. They did not question the assumption that if the Soviet Union acquired the capability to launch a devastating attack on the United States without suffering a massive counterstrike, it would not hesitate to do so.[29] Most important, they believed that advances in Soviet nuclear weaponry and delivery capabilities raised the specter of a growing Soviet threat that had to be confronted with stronger U.S. strategic retaliatory forces, expanded continental defenses, and improved civil defenses.[30]

The Directors

As director of the new panel, Gaither assumed a position with which he was quite familiar. Throughout his career, he had repeatedly served the government, industry, and research institutions as an adviser in a variety of capacities, and on several occasions he had supervised the activities of groups of experts. While practicing law in California during World War II, Gaither was asked by the Radiation Laboratory at MIT to become the associate director in charge of administration. "His job," Dwight Macdonald explains, "was to coordinate the work of the scientific staff and to act as liaison officer between the Laboratory and the armed services."[31] While at MIT, he became acquainted with leading scientists, engineers, and social

H. Rowan Gaither, Jr. Gaither served as the director of the Gaither committee until he was forced to resign because of illness. (Photo by Marvin Koner, Ford Foundation)

thinkers, including Killian, Rabi, and Hill. Gaither's activities at the Radiation Laboratory earned him a reputation for efficient administration and leadership.[32]

After the war Gaither returned to California to teach law at the University of California Law School.[33] His tenure there was short, however, as the RAND Corporation asked him to assist in its transition to a nonprofit organization. RAND had been created during World War II as part of the Douglas Aircraft Company to perform research and development for the Army air forces. After the war, questions arose as to whether the military and a specific company should be tied so closely together. The Air Force and Douglas Aircraft agreed to spin off RAND as an independent, nonprofit corporation. Beginning in late 1947, Gaither joined RAND's board of trustees to lead it through this transition. From 1948 to his death in 1961, with the exception of only one year, Gaither served as the chairman of RAND's board of trustees.[34]

Gaither's leadership at RAND led to opportunities in other areas. One of Gaither's responsibilities was to arrange financing for RAND's operations. Through his contacts with former MIT president Karl Compton, he obtained a meeting with Henry Ford II to discuss a possible grant for RAND. Gaither's presentation so impressed Ford that the automotive heir not only gave RAND a $1 million grant but also asked Gaither to join the Ford Foundation and write a report proposing the objectives of that organization.[35] Gaither promptly accepted.

In his final report for Ford, Gaither reached several conclusions that are relevant to his later work on the Gaither committee. He saw the Ford Foundation as an organization that could provide financial support for "studies and analyses by special committees, individuals, or research institutes" in an environment unhampered by political pressures.[36] He believed it essential that the U.S. government avoid overly defensive or negative policies. He stressed, "If such a defensive attitude is allowed to control our planning and thinking, our national effort will be diverted unduly to expedient and temporary measures from the more important tasks ahead, and we may grow like the thing we fight."[37] Gaither's work on this report led to his appointment in 1951 as the Ford Foundation's associate director and in 1953 as its president.[38]

After Gaither fell ill in August 1957, he was unable to continue his duties as the director of the committee. He was succeeded by William Foster and Robert Sprague, who had equally illustrious backgrounds. Foster had served the Truman administration in a variety of capacities and was currently vice president of the Olin Mathieson Chemical Corporation. Sprague, the president of Sprague Electric Company, had advised the Eisenhower administration on continental defense questions on several occasions prior to 1957. Together, they completed the task that Gaither began.

Foster rose to prominence in the manufactured steel industry during World War II. Because of his position as president of the Pressed and Welded Steel Products Company, during the war he served on several government committees that were concerned with small-business manufacturing. After the war, Secretary of Commerce Averell Harriman asked President Truman to appoint Foster undersecretary of commerce. Foster served in that position from January 1947 to the summer of 1948. When Harriman was appointed ambassador-at-large to Western Europe to supervise the operations of the Economic Cooperation Administration (ECA), he asked Foster to join him as his assistant. From this position, Foster rose to become the deputy administrator of the ECA in 1949 and administrator in 1950. While serving in the ECA, he helped integrate Greece into the Marshall Plan, briefed Congress on European economic needs, and after the start of the Korean War, negotiated loans with European countries to encourage their participation in the war.[39]

In 1951 Truman appointed Foster deputy secretary of defense. From this position, Foster became acquainted with the most controversial military issues and learned a great deal about the formulation and implementation of Defense Department policies.[40] Two of his most important assignments during his tenure as the deputy secretary were briefing Congress on the efficiency of the Defense Department's organization and heading a panel of experts that made a comparative study of U.S. and Soviet military strength.[41] Of particular importance to his later work on the Gaither committee, he became aware of the strengths and weaknesses of the Strategic Air Command.[42]

When Eisenhower took office, Foster resigned from the Defense Department to become the first paid president of the Manufacturing Chemists Association. In 1955 he became executive vice president of the Olin Mathieson Chemical Corporation.[43] This company was very active in developing and maintaining ties with government agencies responsible for the defense of the United States.[44]

Sprague maintained much closer ties to the Eisenhower administration than did Foster. Sprague was Eisenhower's first choice for the position of under secretary of the Air Force in 1953. However, Sprague was unable to

William Foster. William Foster served with Robert Sprague as codirector of the committee. (George C. Marshall Foundation)

accept the appointment because he could not relinquish his stock holdings in his own Massachusetts electric company.[45] This problem did not long impede his opportunities for government service.[46] In October 1953 Senator Leverett Saltonstall (R-MA) requested Sprague's assistance in examining U.S. continental defenses.[47] Sprague traveled to SAC headquarters and received a two-day briefing from General Curtis LeMay concerning the

Robert Sprague. Sprague served as the codirector of the Gaither committee after Gaither resigned. (Fabian Bachrach/the Sprague estate)

relationship of SAC forces to continental defense.[48] He also gained access to numerous top-secret studies and reports from the Department of Defense, Army, Air Force, Navy, Atomic Energy Commission, NSC, and CIA.[49] Finally, JCS chairman Admiral Arthur Radford briefed him on the ability of the Soviet Union to prevent a retaliatory strike, the impact of such a strike on that country, and the vulnerability of the United States to a surprise attack.[50]

Sprague presented his report to the Senate Armed Services Committee in March 1954 and later also briefed the Joint Atomic Energy Committee and the House Armed Services Committee.[51] He recommended expanding early warning radar coverage, increasing the number and quality of interceptor airplanes, and strengthening anti-aircraft defenses around SAC bases.[52] He concluded that the problems of continental defense "will never be static" and that the United States would have "to face up to the fact that the threat of an air-atomic attack introduces a new factor in our way of life. Living with it may not be so comfortable as before, but it is a burden which the country can abide, still remaining free. It means doing the things which must be done, paying the bills which must be paid, and running the risks which must be run."[53]

Sprague reached even more alarming conclusions three months later, after Soviet scientists tested a one-megaton nuclear device and the United States completed a series of tests on thermonuclear weapons. The tests, which indicated that the Soviet Union was not far behind the United States in nuclear weapons technology, highlighted the gradual decline of U.S. military power relative to the Soviet Union. Sprague believed that the United States was more vulnerable to an atomic attack than the Soviet Union. He also stressed that the initiative in a conflict would remain with the Kremlin leaders, and "the moral character of the Soviet rulers is such that the thought of wide-spread death and destruction in an atomic war is of no significance [to them] in deterring such a war."[54] He then identified three possible policy alternatives. First, the United States could construct a defensive system capable of withstanding any possible Soviet attack. Second, it could "strike the first blow." Third, it could "Live with the USSR in a state of equilibrium brought about by mutual fear of atomic attack."[55]

After becoming a consultant to the NSC on continental defenses in June 1954, Sprague reported that the danger from a Soviet surprise attack had grown. He argued that since the United States had tested new thermonuclear weapons, the Soviet Union could not be far behind. Furthermore, these new weapons produced so much radioactive fallout that each nuclear explosion was now much more dangerous. Finally, the Soviet development of the Type 39 jet bomber signaled a potential Soviet capability to launch a surprise attack against the United States. Sprague concluded, "These three new elements of danger enormously increase the threat to our national survival in the event of a Soviet surprise attack against the continental United States."[56]

Less than a year later, Sprague presented a new report to the NSC. While making an obvious reference to the recently completed Killian report, Sprague argued that the years from 1958 to 1960 represented the "period of greatest danger—when Russia will have a large enough stockpile of multi-megaton weapons and the means for delivering them on continental U.S. targets."[57] When the NSC examined this report, Eisenhower said he believed that Sprague may have overestimated Soviet delivery capabilities, but he did not question the great value of Sprague's report. Its importance "lay in making us reassess our programs . . . for the purpose of seeing if we were placing proper emphasis on the right programs."[58]

Committee Members and Advisers

While Sprague worked extensively as a consultant with the Eisenhower administration, many other Gaither committee members had served in advisory roles. Several of them had developed close professional relationships with one another while working at the Radiation Laboratory during World War II. This was particularly true for Killian and Hill. Killian had served as vice president of MIT during the war.[59] In this capacity, he worked closely with the Radiation Laboratory. Hill, a physics professor, directed the laboratory's Division Five, dealing with transmitter components.[60] After the war, Killian and Hill collaborated closely on many problems involving MIT and defense issues.

In 1953 they coauthored an article for *Atlantic* magazine in which they argued that the United States "must achieve a stronger defense without weakening or subordinating our offensive power."[61] They were concerned that if the United States continued to neglect continental defenses while emphasizing offensive capabilities, the Soviet Union might acquire the ability to attack North America.[62] They identified five military priorities: controlling the seas, defending the continent, maintaining a nuclear counterstrike capability, protecting Western Europe, and preventing small wars from becoming larger ones.[63] They stressed that the United States needed to develop a reliable early warning system, anti-aircraft and antimissile defenses, and the ability to destroy enemy forces at long range.[64]

As MIT's president, Killian played a pivotal role in establishing the Lincoln Laboratory in February 1951. By this time there was a growing concern within the Air Force that the Soviet Union might acquire the capability to attack the United States. Because the chief of staff of the Air Force, General Hoyt Vandenberg, did not believe that the Air Force itself could analyze U.S. air defenses effectively, he approached Killian about establishing an independent research and development organization similar to the Radiation Laboratory. After months of negotiations, MIT accepted a tri-service contract from the Army, Navy, and Air Force to establish a military research laboratory. With Killian's approval, Hill directed the new laboratory until 1955.[65] Its main responsibility was to develop the Semi-Automatic Ground Environment (SAGE) air defense system.[66]

In addition to its involvement with the Lincoln Laboratory, MIT provided support facilities for several studies of U.S. defense issues.[67] In 1950 MIT physics professor Jerrold Zacharias, a future Gaither committee member, developed the concept of the summer study program when he directed Project Hartwell, a Navy-sponsored examination of undersea warfare. In 1951 and 1952, Hill supervised Project Charles and Project Lincoln—two separate studies of U.S. air defenses. In these same years, fifteen scientists participated in Project Beacon Hill, a study of Air Force intelligence and reconnaissance capabilities.[68] Together, these summer studies emphasized the need for "measures to reduce the vulnerability to surprise of our strategic air power, to keep the sea lanes open, to improve our military communications and gathering of hard intelligence, [and] to accelerate our ICBM programs."[69]

Of these studies, Project Charles and Project Lincoln were the most important in shaping Killian's and Hill's views concerning continental defenses. Project Charles vividly described the problems faced by the United States in planning air defenses. It found, "The problem of the defense of the United States against air attack is characterized above all by a lack of knowledge of what we have to defend against." The study concluded, "The enemy has the initiative. Our intelligence tells us essentially nothing about his plans; informs us only partially about his present capabilities; and as to his future capabilities leaves us essentially dependent on assumptions that he can, if he chooses, do about as well in any aspect as we expect to do ourselves."[70] Project Lincoln addressed these problems by recommending the extension of the Distant Early Warning (DEW) Line to provide earlier warning of a Soviet attack. The study also called for the development of an effective interceptor force and suggested that plans be devised to meet the threat posed by the ICBMs.[71]

After their 1953 article, Killian and Hill continued their involvement in studies of U.S. continental defenses. Killian directed the extremely influential 1954 Technical Capabilities Panel. This group, which included many future Gaither committee members, perceived a potentially significant threat as the Soviet Union acquired advanced nuclear weapons and delivery capabilities. It recommended the development of an intercontinental ballistic missile, the reduction of SAC vulnerability, and the strengthening of continental defenses. More specifically, it advised that the United States needed to construct additional SAC bases, institute an emergency dispersal plan for SAC forces, and develop active defenses surrounding SAC bases.[72]

As a member of the Science Advisory Committee, Killian's influence on Eisenhower did not stop with the panel's final report. In a meeting with Eisenhower in 1956, Killian and James Fisk, another member of the Science Advisory Committee and later of the Gaither committee, reiterated the need for strengthening U.S. continental defenses. They argued that the United States had to accelerate "the development of high altitude radar, SAC dispersal, and quicker reaction time for SAC in case of attack."[73] Without these improvements, they feared the Soviet Union would be able to launch a successful attack against the United States.

Demonstrating his confidence in Killian, Eisenhower asked him to chair a new committee, the President's Board of Consultants on Foreign Intelligence, that would examine the effectiveness of the CIA in performing its responsibilities. In addition to Killian, the committee included future Gaither committee members General James Doolittle and Robert Lovett, as well as Admiral Richard Conolly, Benjamin Fairless, General John Hull, Joseph Kennedy, and Edward Ryerson.[74] Eisenhower gave the board broad discretion in its investigations so that it could determine if the "policies and programs pursued by the CIA and other elements of the intelligence community are sound, effective, and economically operated."[75] While most of its activities remain classified, the committee did meet with Eisenhower five times and held nineteen other meetings between 1956 and 1961.[76] One of the most important conclusions that the committee reached was: "Quality of foreign intelligence—Both National and Departmental Intelligence with respect to the Soviets is seriously inadequate in all fields and at all levels."[77]

Hill served the Eisenhower administration more indirectly than did Killian. In addition to acting as the director of the Lincoln Laboratory until 1955, he also served as director of the Weapons Systems Evaluation Group (WSEG) and as vice president of the Institute for Defense Analyses (IDA). The JCS created WSEG in 1948 and assigned it three broad objectives:

1. To bring scientific and technical as well as operational military expertise to bear in evaluating weapons systems.
2. To employ advanced techniques of scientific analysis and operations research in the process.
3. To approach its tasks from an impartial, supra-Service perspective.[78]

In this capacity, WSEG studied numerous defense issues, including an examination of continental defenses in 1955 under Hill's direction.[79] While it did not reach any new conclusions, it enabled Hill to become acquainted with General LeMay and to learn about SAC.[80]

In 1956 both SAC and CIA intelligence estimates indicated that the Soviet Union could acquire the capability to launch missiles with nuclear warheads from submarines.[81] If the Soviets possessed this capability, they could have possibly launched an attack against the United States without warning. Accordingly, JCS chairman Admiral Radford asked Hill to lead a new ad hoc committee to study U.S. air defenses.[82] Hill's committee identified "the goal for the defense of North America against air attack" as "the achievement and maintenance of a level of air defense effectiveness sufficient to give a reasonable chance of defending approximately 80 percent of the vital target areas of the nation."[83] It found that the United States was falling dangerously short of these capabilities.

Hill's involvement in the IDA stemmed from his close association with Killian. One of Killian's overriding goals as the president of MIT was to foster close cooperation among scientists, academic institutions, and the government. In 1956 Killian worked with the Department of Defense to establish a university consortium to support WSEG. He organized five universities—MIT, California Institute for Technology, Case Institute, Stanford, and Tulane—into the nonprofit IDA. He hoped that the IDA would be "a means of lending scientific prestige to the enterprise [WSEG], facilitating access to the scholarly research community, and promoting a working climate that would appeal to civilian research analysts."[84] Hill became the IDA's vice president. The IDA later proved instrumental in the development of the Gaither report. Both Hill and General James McCormack,

MIT's vice president for industrial relations and a former participant in Project Solarium, served as the IDA's advisers to the Gaither committee.[85] "The [Gaither] Committee," one scholar concludes, "called on IDA as its prime contractor to help support the panel participants with technical assistance, research and fact-finding, managerial and administrative services, editorial and publication support, security, and the like."[86]

As an expert on continental defense issues, Hill also studied civil defense problems. In the 1950s he served on two committees concerned with these issues: the 1952 Project East River and the 1955 Review of Project East River. These committees included several future Gaither committee members, including General Otto Nelson and Lloyd Berkner. The 1952 study, named after the river that flows through New York City, laid the foundation for most civil defense plans developed in the Eisenhower administration.[87] In its six-volume final report, the initial Project East River committee reached several conclusions that were of direct relevance to the Gaither committee. The report stressed that the United States had to improve both its air defenses and civil defenses.[88] It then emphasized that continental and civil defenses were interchangeable components in the security of the United States. An air defense system must "be devised that aims at destroying substantially all of the airborne attackers prior to the time that they reach the United States. If this is not achieved, Civil Defense becomes unmanageable and largely futile."[89] In the area of civil defense, the committee called for achieving the earliest possible warning of an attack, constructing shelters, and educating the public to the dangers of radioactive fallout.[90]

In 1955 Secretary of Defense Charles Wilson, FCDA Director Peterson, and ODM Director Arthur Fleming requested that Nelson, Berkner, and Hill create a group to review the findings from the 1952 report and determine whether the United States had strengthened its continental and civil defenses in the intervening years. Wilson, Peterson, and Fleming told the group, "Most of all we need the thinking of those of you who are away from the day to day activities of the Federal Government, but who are still thoroughly concerned with the basic problems."[91] After their review, Nelson's committee concluded, "Despite the efforts made [between 1952 and 1955], it is necessary to report that the nation's preparations and progress in non-military defense are still far from what they should be."[92] They attributed the deficiencies to rapid technological advances and the lack of positive leadership in developing nonmilitary defenses. Without improvements in these areas, they believed, the United States was in serious danger.

The review committee of civilian experts was particularly influenced by the potential implications of the rapid advances in nuclear weapons technology. "The most important consequence of the rapid progress in making much more powerful and cheaper nuclear weapons and the resulting increasingly serious problem of radioactive fallout," it concluded, "is that the potential disaster area will be larger than any city boundary and will frequently overlap several state boundaries."[93] They recommended the strengthening of U.S. nonmilitary defenses, especially the protection of the civil population. They believed the best way to achieve these results was to create an intelligence-gathering apparatus that would provide the maximum strategic warning of a Soviet attack and to design plans for both the evacuation and sheltering of the civil population if such an attack was to occur.[94]

Testimony before the 1956 Holifield committee on civil defense echoed the findings of both the 1952 and 1955 Project East River committees. Representative Holifield invited many experts, including Hill, Berkner, Killian, and Nelson, to come before his committee. They all emphasized the inadequacies of U.S. civil defense programs and the need to recognize the close relationship between offensive and defensive capabilities in deterring the Soviet Union. Hill argued that "it is impossible to defend our offensive strength without defending the civilian population as well."[95] In evaluating the relationship between offensive and defensive capabilities, Berkner explained, "By remaining an easy and inviting target, we encourage an uncompromising enemy to believe that war against us is an easy and feasible way to succeed in his objectives."[96] In his testimony, Killian stressed, "While our main deterrent to war and to an attack against the United States is our capacity to inflict terrible damage on the enemy, this deterrent needs to be augmented and accompanied by the deterrent strength of an adequate defense against atomic attack and an adequate civil defense to reduce the damage of an atomic attack should it come."[97] Finally, Nelson argued that U.S. civil defenses "could become the critical, determining factor that might persuade the Soviets, in even a period of great rashness and madness, that they should not risk an atomic war."[98]

Other future Gaither committee members corroborated these findings in separate studies. Mervin Kelly, vice president of Bell Telephone Laboratories, and James Baxter, president of Williams College, participated in studies in 1952 and 1953 that examined U.S. air defenses. In 1952

Truman's secretary of defense, Robert Lovett, also a future Gaither committee member, asked Kelly to chair a panel that would study U.S. air defenses.[99] Although Kelly's committee concluded that an absolute defense network could not be built and that offensive capabilities had to be emphasized, it nevertheless called for the development of "a comprehensive plan for air defense," the extension of the early warning radar network "as far as possible from US borders," and the implementation of "a vigorous civil defense program."[100]

The Kelly report prompted Eisenhower to appoint two new committees to study U.S. continental defenses. The first, headed by retired General Harold Bull, presented its report in July and provided the foundation for the Eisenhower administration's first policy statement concerning continental defenses—NSC 159. The Bull report reached conclusions similar to those of the Kelly committee.[101] In evaluating the Bull committee's findings, Eisenhower turned to a second committee of outside consultants, including Baxter, for its opinions.[102] At a September 1953 NSC meeting, this committee supported NSC 159 but stressed the importance of continuing the administration's emphasis on reducing the budget.[103]

While various experts were lamenting the inadequacies of U.S. civil and continental defense plans, Eisenhower was growing concerned about the inability of the United States to acquire accurate intelligence assessments of the Soviet Union. His creation of the Killian committee reveals just how disturbed he was about the possibility of the Soviet Union being in a position to launch a surprise attack against the United States. His concern stemmed from the changing technological environment and the secrecy that enveloped the Soviet Union. Eisenhower attempted to identify and rectify some of the difficulties in intelligence gathering by asking General James Doolittle, a trusted adviser and World War II hero, to examine the effectiveness of the CIA's operations.

Doolittle became a national hero after leading a surprise air raid on Tokyo four months after the Japanese attack on Pearl Harbor. His expertise went beyond this accomplishment. Before the war he was a Rhodes scholar and earned a Ph.D. in aeronautical engineering from MIT. After the war, he became vice president of Shell Oil Company. In addition to working at Shell, Doolittle continued to advise the Air Force. From 1950 to 1958, he served on the Air Force Science Advisory Board and acted as its chairman from 1955 to 1958.[104] While this position may not seem illustrious, it provided Doolittle personal access to the Air Force chief of staff. One of his contemporaries recalled that "Jimmy [Doolittle] carried much more weight in Air Force affairs after he retired than the titles he held would indicate, and the reasons . . . were his reliability and his credibility."[105]

It was not surprising that Eisenhower turned to Doolittle in 1954. Not only was Doolittle already serving on the steering committee of the Technical Capabilities Panel but he also held a philosophy that comported with Eisenhower's. Doolittle recognized the importance of both economic security and technological advancement. In a 1949 speech, he emphasized, "Economy should be the watchword in our military thinking. Waste plays directly into Russia's hands. Balance between the services must be achieved with national, not individual service, welfare in mind. The course is clear: The first step in avoiding war with Russia is to avoid waste and to remain technologically ahead of her."[106] At an Air Force Science Advisory Board meeting during the same year, Doolittle discussed the importance of maintaining technological superiority over the Soviet Union. He explained that "the only thing that is going to keep us out of war is our technological advantage. It is far better to keep out of war than to win a war. If we permit a potential enemy to get ahead of us technologically . . . that is the surest way to start a war."[107]

When Eisenhower turned to Doolittle in 1954, he wanted to obtain "some indication of the over-all adequacy of our National Intelligence Program and the manner of its implementation." He added that "we should briefly review the activities of all agencies of government charged with the collection, interpretation and dissemination of intelligence dealing with the plans, capabilities and intentions of potential enemies."[108] For three months, Doolittle and the other committee members, William Frank, Morris Hadley, and William Pawley, examined U.S. intelligence operations. In their examination they had access to all available information concerning U.S. intelligence activities, including covert operations.[109]

Eisenhower treated the committee's report with the utmost sensitivity. He ordered CIA Director Allen Dulles "to show it to no one else" when he analyzed its recommendations and conclusions.[110] The White House press release describing the committee's findings said little more than that the committee had found a few areas that needed improvement but that, on the whole, the CIA was in good shape.[111] It is now clear that this press release understated the problems in U.S. intelligence operations. The study called for a new policy in waging the Cold War. "It is now clear," Doolittle's committee pronounced, that we are facing an implacable enemy whose avowed objective is world domination by whatever means and at whatever cost. There are no rules in such a game. Hitherto acceptable norms of human conduct do not apply. If the United States is to survive, long-standing concepts of "fair play" must be reconsidered. We must develop effective espionage and counter-espionage services and must learn to subvert, sabotage, and destroy our enemies by more clever, more sophisticated, and more effective methods than those used against us. It may become necessary that the American people be made acquainted with, understand, and support this fundamentally repugnant philosophy.[112]

As with his views on technology and the economy, Doolittle advocated intelligence policies that Eisenhower liked. The president had already followed such policies in Iran and Guatemala.

The Writers

The last two Gaither committee members who must be examined in some detail are Paul Nitze and Colonel George Lincoln. In his memoirs, Nitze claims that "Abe [Lincoln] and I were mentioned as 'project members' at the back of the [Gaither] report, which masked the fact that we shared importantly in shaping the substance of the final version."[113] While Nitze may have overstated their importance, the two certainly did influence the final report. Their earlier writings adumbrated the recommendations and conclusions of the subsequent Gaither report.

Although Paul Nitze is the more famous of the two men, his reputation should not overshadow Lincoln's accomplishments. Nitze himself wrote that Lincoln was his "most reliable mentor and advisor."[114] Lincoln acquired his reputation as a strategic planner while working on the staff of General George Marshall's Operations Division (OPD) during World War II. He served as chief of the OPD's Strategy and Policy Group, a role that "included, not only military planning, but also meshing the military side of international statecraft with the political side of strategy."[115] As part of this job, Lincoln served as a member of the Joint Planning Staff.[116] He also acted as a military adviser to Assistant Secretary of War and future Gaither committee member John J. McCloy on issues involving the State-War-Navy Coordinating Committee.[117] He described his work with McCloy as trying to arrange the "official marriage of political and military policy of the State Department and the War Department."[118]

Colonel George Lincoln. Lincoln cowrote the final Gaither report with Paul Nitze. (U.S. Military Academy Archives)

After the war, Lincoln continued to serve on the OPD in the military's transition from wartime to peacetime status.[119] Despite his prominent position and his bright future in the Army, he decided in 1947 to retire from active service and to teach at the United States Military Academy. When he announced his retirement, Eisenhower, the Army chief of staff, attempted to persuade Lincoln to reconsider. More than sixteen years later, Eisenhower recalled, "I used every pressure I could bring to bear on him to persuade him to stay in the Pentagon because of the high value I placed upon his knowledge, thoroughness and good sense."[120] After reluctantly accepting his resignation, Eisenhower wrote Lincoln, "I attribute in very great part to you a noticeable growth in the soundness and clarity of military policy pertaining to U.S. security. . . . I personally have leaned heavily on your advice since my arrival here, confident that your solutions would be the best that hard work, outstanding intelligence, integrity and devotion to duty could provide."[121]

Lincoln's contributions to military planning did not end with his retirement from the Army. He periodically returned to Washington to provide advice. In 1950 Ambassador Averell Harriman asked Lincoln to be his military adviser on the Temporary Council Committee for NATO. The committee examined the military, political, and economic capabilities of each NATO country to determine a practical strategy for the defense of Western Europe. Harriman later recalled, "I looked to Abe [Lincoln] to help me reconcile every factor."[122]

Lincoln's publications proved even more important. In 1954 he revised a compilation of essays, *Economics and National Security*. In this work, Lincoln addressed three issues of particular importance to the later Gaither committee. First, he outlined what he saw as the potential threat posed by the Soviet Union. Second, he discussed the importance of maintaining a high level of economic mobilization. Finally, he emphasized the significance of technological changes to national security programs.

Lincoln believed that the only way to coexist peacefully with the Soviet Union was to create an armistice "made by power and preserved by power." He further explained that "Soviet communism is committed to world conquest, and we cannot rely on it changing this policy in our time."[123] Lincoln did not expect the Soviet Union to initiate a war, but he believed a war could happen at any time due to miscalculation. He stressed that the successors to Stalin were not likely "to be tempted to rash actions gravely imperiling the Soviet base of communism. On the other hand

continual pressure and struggle are basic tenets of communism, and failure to take advantage of an opportunity for advance is a cardinal sin in
the communism code. The movement has a discipline usually described as
'Prussian.' It is versatile and resourceful. It is continually at war with the
remainder of the world and uses a strategy that understands the weaknesses
and appreciates the tactics in the fields of politics, economics, and psychol-
ogy" (24).

Because he saw the Soviet threat as "world-wide," "total," and "of indefinite duration," Lincoln argued that the United States had to maintain
an economy based on preparedness and government control (25, 44–45).
Until the Soviet Union recanted its philosophy or accepted defeat in the
Cold War, Lincoln believed that the United States had little choice but to
prepare for war. He argued that "the choice must be made between the
hazards of greater and lesser evils. . . . When the greater evil is the threat to
survival, the choice should fall on the lesser evil—which is a considerable
expenditure of resources for a sustained level of preparedness, an all-out
effort in case of war, and adequate measures to keep the economy strong
and healthy meanwhile" (43). He later added that if the threat of war became probable, then concern over the strain of defense spending on the
economy should become second to survival (85).

Lincoln also addressed the relationship of science and technology to
national security. Reminiscent of Eisenhower's memorandum to his subordinates at the end of World War II, Lincoln viewed the war as providing important precedents for sustaining cooperation between the scientific
community and the military establishment. He believed that:

1. Science must be integrated with military strategy in the future.
2. Military research and development are of the same order of importance
   as industrial preparedness and manpower reserves.
3. Timing of technological advances has become all important. The race for
   technological advantage is a major part of the race for survival in a power
   struggle. (364)

Lincoln feared that if the Soviet Union achieved some technological break-
through before the United States, it might use that advantage to move
against U.S. interests oppressively.

When Lincoln finished revising his book in 1954, the United States and
the Soviet Union were in the midst of an accelerating technological race.
The new thermonuclear weapons were a thousand times more powerful

than the atomic bombs dropped on Hiroshima and Nagasaki. The introduction of intercontinental bombers and the anticipated development of ICBMs raised the possibility that an aggressor could win a war in the initial strike. Lincoln stressed the importance of the United States maintaining its technological lead over the Soviet Union. He argued, "The time *element* . . . has been magnified by modern technology in at least three ways. First, the race for technological advantage is decided before hostilities. Second, the aggressor has an increasing advantage paralleling the upward slant of technological change. Third, and related to the preceding point, the surprise aggression becomes more attractive and harder to meet" (378; emphasis in original).

Lincoln's work did not go unnoticed in Washington. Eisenhower repeatedly asked Lincoln to serve as an adviser to the administration. In 1953 Lincoln worked on task force A of Project Solarium. In 1956 he participated in a committee that examined the psychological aspects of U.S. strategy for Eisenhower's adviser Nelson Rockefeller.[124] In that same year, Eisenhower and Secretary of State John Foster Dulles asked Lincoln to direct the State Department's Policy Planning Staff. Although Lincoln could not take the job, the offer reveals Eisenhower's continued interest and respect for the West Point professor.[125]

In addition to serving on the Gaither committee in 1957, Lincoln wrote an influential essay that discussed U.S. capabilities to wage limited military operations. In this paper, he asked, "Are we of the Western World so committed to deterrent nuclear force, and so fearful of the slightest nuclear threat that we lack the means, or wit, or both, to deal with local and limited situations?"[126] In raising this penetrating question, Lincoln was in essence challenging the reliance of the Eisenhower administration on massive retaliation.

Lincoln presented ten propositions to elaborate his philosophy concerning the relationship among technology, politics, and war. He emphasized that while the United States had to prepare for a general, atomic war with the Soviet Union, the most likely future conflicts would be limited in nature. He stressed that the United States had to maintain the capability to wage either general or limited wars and to be able to use either conventional or nuclear weapons. The key was maintaining a level of flexibility in military capabilities. Lincoln believed that technological changes widened the political and military options available to states, yet raised the stakes of waging war. "The hazards arising from the opportunities and temptations for rash, desperate, or just uninformed leadership," Lincoln concluded, "are increasing."[127]

Lincoln's close friend and sometime professional collaborator, Paul Nitze, played an active role in government affairs during the Truman administration. He participated in the assessment of the effects of the atomic bombs on Hiroshima and Nagasaki.[128] He subsequently joined the State Department and then directed its Policy Planning Staff from 1950 to 1952. He was the principal author of NSC 68, calling for much larger military expenditures.[129]

Nitze's tenure at the State Department came to an abrupt end after Eisenhower took office in 1953. Although Eisenhower's new defense secretary, Charles Wilson, offered Nitze a new position in his department, he met fierce resistance from congressional Republicans, especially Senate Majority Leader William Knowland, who believed that Nitze was tied too closely to the previous administration. Secretary of State Dulles found Nitze's continued presence in the administration appalling and demanded his dismissal. Bowing to pressure, Wilson asked for and received Nitze's resignation. Nitze was embittered and thereafter despised Dulles.[130]

Before he left the State Department, Nitze set forth his opinions concerning continental defense. Although he wanted a considerable increase in U.S. offensive capabilities, he did not believe they alone could preserve U.S. security. He believed that the United States also needed to construct civil and continental defenses. In one of his last memoranda while still at the State Department, Nitze explained, "In dealing with the problem of continental defense it is important to recognize the inter-relationship of military defense, offensive striking power, and the civil defense program. These three elements are complementary and mutually supporting."[131] Four years later, when he helped write the Gaither report, these views remained paramount.

In 1954 Nitze became an outspoken critic of the Eisenhower administration and in particular the policies articulated by Secretary of State Dulles. After listening to Dulles's speech about massive retaliation to the Council on Foreign Relations, Nitze privately circulated a dissenting paper. He argued that by placing primary reliance on atomic weapons, the United States was guaranteeing that any future conflicts would involve the use of these weapons. He argued, "If we are to obtain victory, or peace with justice and without defeat, we must attain it with non-atomic means while deterring an atomic war."[132] With this paper, Nitze began a campaign, which would last until the Kennedy administration, to force the government to recognize the importance of maintaining sufficient conventional forces to supplement U.S. nuclear capabilities.

Years later, Nitze described in his memoirs how he viewed the strategic situation in the 1950s. He explained:

> In the event of a crisis involving a serious possibility of war with the United States, how might the problem be seen from the Kremlin? Being careful planners, the Soviets undoubtedly would have carefully prepared war plans for a variety of contingencies. One could therefore theorize with some confidence that Soviet plans would include a disarming first strike, if we responded with the remains of the Strategic Air Command (SAC) by attacking Soviet base structure and nuclear attack facilities, the exchange ratios would go against us very quickly. In two, three, four, or at most five exchanges, the United States would be down to a woefully low level of capability while the Soviet Union could still be at a relatively high one. We could then be at their mercy. If we choose to attack their populations, we would invite almost total annihilation in the United States.[133]

Nitze's explanation clearly indicates his preoccupation with the Soviet Union's capabilities while giving little thought to its goals or intentions.[134]

In an article in *Foreign Affairs* in 1956, Nitze expounded an alternative strategy to massive retaliation. He argued that Eisenhower's policies were inconsistent because the U.S. military did not possess the ability, beyond atomic weapons, to wage the war against communism.[135] He explained that the country needed to acquire the capability to raise the stakes in a conflict gradually, rather than immediately resorting to massive retaliation. He emphasized that "it is to the interest of the West that the means employed in warfare and the area of engagement be restricted to the minimum level which still permits us to achieve our objectives. Our basic action policy must therefore be one of 'graduated deterrence'" (188). By responding in kind to an aggressive act, Nitze believed the United States could limit the scope of the conflict and the area affected by the military engagements. But, in 1956, Nitze did not think that the United States possessed the necessary capabilities.

Nitze stressed that the United States needed to expand its offensive retaliatory capabilities, build defenses against a surprise attack, and prepare to wage limited wars. Recent developments in nuclear weaponry and delivery technology particularly concerned him. "The side which has lost effective control of the intercontinental air spaces will face a truly agonizing decision. It may still have the capability of destroying a few of the enemy's cities. But the damage it could inflict would be indecisive and out of all proportion to the annihilation which its own cities could expect to receive in return." Accordingly, he stressed, "It is important that the West maintain indefinitely a position of nuclear attack-defense superiority versus the Soviet Union and its satellites" (196). Consequently, the United States needed to "develop an air defense system which makes full use of the West's geographic advantages" (197).

While not satisfied with either U.S. offensive retaliatory or defense capabilities, Nitze felt particular concern about the Eisenhower administration's cuts in conventional forces. He believed U.S. commitments exceeded its military capabilities. He emphasized that the United States needed the ability to wage limited wars both with and without atomic weapons. The United States should be able to meet aggression initially without atomic weapons. It should expand hostilities only if no other alternative existed to rectify the situation. If it decided to use atomic weapons, it should use them only against military targets. Nonatomic capabilities, therefore, were needed to lower its dependence on atomic forces (196). These policies would enable the United States to institute his strategy of "graduated deterrence."

Two months prior to the presentation of the Gaither report to the NSC, Nitze published another article that denounced the Eisenhower administration's reliance on massive retaliation. "Secretary Dulles' massive retaliation statement," Nitze wrote, "did not announce a new doctrine but a return to a pre-1950 doctrine [pre–NSC 68]. It is not a step forward; it was a step backward—a step back dictated not by new strategic considerations but by domestic political and budgetary considerations. Ever since, the rationale of our military-political doctrine has been a shambles of inconsistencies, inadequacies, and reappraisals."[136] Nitze stressed the need for a full range of military capabilities that would later be included in the Gaither report. "I see little purpose," Nitze concluded, "in making every war, even a limited war, a nuclear one."[137]

Conclusions

As he had on previous occasions, Eisenhower established a committee of experts in 1957 to examine a vexing national security problem. When the

FCDA proposed a $32 billion shelter system in January, the president had to decide whether such a program would sufficiently improve the country's security to justify its cost. While he was satisfied with the status of U.S. military strength and his national security programs, he recognized that others were justly concerned about the consequences of a nuclear war.[138] Eisenhower believed that the Gaither committee would provide answers to at least one key question. Should the United States attempt to reduce the vulnerability of its population through an elaborate system of continental and civil defenses?

The creation of the Gaither committee to address this very question represented Eisenhower's reliance on a decision-making system that he used throughout his presidency. Eisenhower wanted advice from those who were the most qualified. While he respected and valued the advice of his official advisers, he realized that they were not always experts in particular fields. He therefore turned to consultants outside the government. Eisenhower explained in his memoirs that the Gaither committee "had been formed to bring new minds and background experience to bear on major problems of government. It was empowered to receive information from government agencies and departments and to come up with an independent appraisal. With no vested interest in a particular department, and no federal jobs to protect, the panel was a means of obtaining independent judgments."[139]

The Gaither committee was composed of experts whom Eisenhower respected and admired. They came from a variety of backgrounds. Some, such as Rabi, Berkner, and Hill, were specialists in the fields of nuclear weaponry, radar, and radiation. Others, like Sprague, Fisk, Lincoln, Nitze, and Doolittle, had built their reputations in studies of U.S. continental defense, fallout shelters, intelligence operations, and military forces. Finally, there were consultants, such as Gaither, Foster, and Killian, who were known for supervising and coordinating diverse groups in the development of advisory reports.

These men shared many of the president's basic beliefs. Most were concerned with balancing economic and military strength. Almost all of them viewed the rapid technological changes of the 1950s with a sense of both accomplishment and dread. They saw U.S. security as dependent on the interplay of offensive and defensive military capabilities, a strong economy, and continued close relations with its allies in Europe and around the world. Eisenhower believed that their advice could help him comprehend and make decisions concerning questions that went beyond his expertise.

Eisenhower's use of experts raises several historiographical issues that transcend the importance of the Gaither committee itself. World War II had transformed the relationship between scientists, engineers, and other experts, on the one hand, and the federal government, on the other. Before the war, there was little close cooperation. While experts worried about the possible restrictions resulting from government involvement in their work, political leaders questioned spending money on projects that did not guarantee some direct benefit to the public. World War II forced both groups to work together. The government needed experts to develop new technologies that would help the war effort, and the experts sought funding that only the federal government could provide. Whether in the development of the atomic bomb, radar, or some other technology, this relationship proved relatively congenial.[140]

After the war, the quickening pace of scientific and technological advances precluded any layman from keeping abreast of all the changes. Furthermore, the exorbitant costs of research forced scientists and engineers to look for funding from different sources. As a result, the continued cooperation of experts and the government was only natural. Through expanded funding for research and development, the federal government maintained a pool of experts to call upon when it needed assistance in making decisions concerning highly technical issues. On the other hand, with the available funding scientists and engineers were in a position to perform research that they could not have afforded on their own.[141]

The Gaither committee represents one example of the federal government utilizing experts during the early Cold War to acquire scientific and technical advice. Before World War II, this type of committee would have been unnecessary. However, given the expansion of knowledge during and after the war, political leaders needed some means to understand the complicated technological and scientific problems they faced. To acquire assistance in these areas, Eisenhower readily cultivated a close relationship of the federal government with business, the academic community, and research institutions. Yet he never reconciled his growing reliance on experts who obtained their influential positions outside of normal democratic processes with his emphasis on the importance of the individual to the American system of government. Although surely inadvertently, Eisenhower introduced an advisory system that at times impeded the citizen's ability to supervise and influence the decision making of the government.

By the end of his administration, Eisenhower recognized the transformation that had occurred in decision making since 1945, and he lamented the possible repercussions. In his now famous farewell address, he warned the American people:

> This conjunction of an immense military establishment and a large arms industry is new in the American experience. . . .
>
> In the councils of government, we must guard against the acquisition of unwarranted influence, whether sought or unsought, by the military-industrial complex. The potential for the disastrous rise of misplaced power exists and will persist.
>
> We must never let the weight of this combination endanger our liberties or democratic process. . . .
>
> The prospect of domination of the nation's scholars by Federal employment, project allocations, and the power of money is ever present—and is gravely to be regarded.
>
> Yet, in holding scientific research and discovery in respect, as we should, we must also be alert to the equal and opposite danger that public policy could itself become the captive of a scientific-technological elite.[142]

Despite these warnings, it was Eisenhower who expanded the role of experts in presidential decision making and left a precedent for their use in future administrations. As Gregg Herken persuasively concludes, "The culminating irony of Eisenhower's presidency was the fact that he himself had done more than anyone else to raise the role of experts and expertise to prominence in the government."[143]

3 | 1957: A Year of Turmoil

The question of civil defense was only one of many problems that Eisenhower faced in 1957. Although the year began with Eisenhower's popularity at its height, he soon faced a sequence of serious problems. Legislatively, he was at loggerheads with a Democratic Congress. Politically, new civil rights legislation and the confrontation in Little Rock, Arkansas, polarized the nation. Economically, the country slowly slipped into a recession. Technologically and militarily, the Soviet Union's launch of *Sputnik* and the continued disappointments in U.S. space programs engendered soul-searching about the superiority of American science and the military security of the United States.[1]

It was in this atmosphere that Eisenhower received and evaluated the Gaither committee's final report. Although only the president's struggles with Congress over the FY 1958 defense budget and the controversy over *Sputnik* were directly related to the issues examined by the Gaither committee, the magnitude of all of the problems endured by Eisenhower limited his ability to evaluate the report. Without doubt, the Soviet launch of *Sputnik* alone would have caused headaches for Eisenhower, but when that development combined with other problems, he faced the most difficult period of his presidency.

Politics of the Defense Budget and a New Recession

Iwan Morgan argues that when Eisenhower entered office in 1953 he believed that "the nation faced economic ruin unless fiscal responsibility was quickly re-established as the guiding principle of budgetary policy."[2] By the end of 1956 Eisenhower thought that he was restoring fiscal prudence. He had lowered annual defense spending from $43.8 billion in FY 1953 to

$35.5 billion in FY 1956 and had produced budget surpluses of $3.2 billion and $4.1 billion for FY 1956 and FY 1957, respectively.[3] These figures were in sharp contrast to the $5.3 billion deficit Eisenhower inherited in the FY 1954 budget.[4]

Despite his success in limiting government spending, in January 1957 Eisenhower presented Congress with the largest peacetime budget in U.S. history—$73.3 billion for FY 1958. Although he expressed concern that further increases in spending could lead to higher taxes and greater inflation, he believed that this budget reflected a careful analysis of the domestic needs and international responsibilities of the United States. In particular, Eisenhower recognized that as long as the United States and the Soviet Union remained locked in the Cold War, there were limits to how much overall spending could be cut. In this budget, he requested $43.3 billion for major national security programs. The president regretted the need for such high spending levels, but he felt "the size of the national budget largely reflected the size of the national danger."[5]

Even with the increases in the budget, Eisenhower expected Congress to increase the defense budget and believed he would have to fight to hold the line on defense spending.[6] He was surprised when the Democrats "inexplicably became economy-minded."[7] Public opinion seemed to be demanding budget cuts and Democrats wanted to get on the bandwagon.[8] Even worse for the president, many conservative Republicans, including Senators William Knowland, Styles Bridges, and Barry Goldwater, advocated a smaller role for the federal government, limited involvement of the United States in international organizations, and more aggressive policies against communism. They did not criticize Eisenhower's defense policies, but they concluded that he was spending too much on social programs and foreign aid.[9]

The Democrats welcomed the fissures in the Republican Party as an opportunity to gain political support for their programs.[10] Led by Senate Majority Leader Lyndon Johnson (D-TX) and Speaker of the House Sam Rayburn (D-TX), the Democrats argued that the budget could be reduced without cutting existing domestic programs. In particular, they saw the budgets for the Defense Department and the Mutual Security Administration as good areas to find savings. With bipartisan support, Congress passed a defense budget in July that reduced Army spending from $8.465 to $7.265 billion, Navy spending from $10.487 to $9.866 billion, and Air Force spending from $16.471 to $15.930 billion.[11] With an additional

$1.7 billion in cuts from the rest of the budget, including $1 billion from the Mutual Security program, Congress was able to reduce the president's spending plans by nearly $4.0 billion.[12]

The spring 1957 budget crisis represented a new problem for Eisenhower and his advisers. In his first term, he had to protect the economy against demands for additional spending. In 1957 he found himself defending the military budget against the calls for more cuts. He sent a letter to Speaker of the House Rayburn requesting that Congress reconsider its reductions: "I most solemnly advise the House that in these times a cut of any appreciable consequence in current expenditures for national security and related programs would endanger our country and the peace of the world."[13] He added that "a multibillion-dollar reduction in 1958 expenditures can be accomplished only at the expense of the national safety and interest."[14] His request went unheeded.

As debate over the FY 1958 budget came to a close, economic indicators revealed the economy was slipping into a recession.[15] William McChesney Martin, the chairman of the Federal Reserve Board, believed the economic problems were tied to inflation and raised the discount rate from 3 to 3½ percent. Instead of stimulating the economy, the increase stymied economic growth.[16] In late 1957 and early 1958, exports declined precipitously, industrial production fell 14 percent, corporate profits declined 25 percent, and unemployment rose to 7.5 percent. It was only in May 1958 that the economy began to recover.[17]

Eisenhower reacted to the new economic situation with his usual caution. Other than reducing the discount rate to 3 percent in November 1957 and releasing $177 million for the housing industry in December, Eisenhower and his advisers did little to combat the recession.[18] In particular, he resisted calls for a tax cut and emergency public works programs. He explained to his former CEA chairman, Arthur Burns, "I trust that I am not getting stubborn in my attitude about logical federal action in this business slump, but I am bound to say that I cannot help but feel that precipitate, and therefore largely unwise, action would be the worst thing that we could now do." He then stressed that "my honest conviction is that the greatest service we can now do for our country is to oppose wild-eyed schemes of every kind. I am against vast and unwise public works programs . . . as well as the slash-bang kinds of tax-cutting from which the proponents want nothing so much as immediate political advantage."[19] While Eisenhower held true to his principles to limit the role of the federal government in the economy and to avoid deficit spending, his popularity and effectiveness suffered another blow.[20]

Civil Rights and Preserving the American Constitutional System

Eisenhower's struggles in 1957 were not limited to his disagreements with Congress over the budget and the economic recession. He also faced major civil rights controversies. While these problems did not directly impact his handling of the Gaither committee or other defense questions, they provided additional distractions that hampered the president's decision making and established doubts about his ability to lead the nation. For the first time since Reconstruction, Congress passed civil rights legislation, and the president used military force to support the integration of southern schools.[21] While these civil rights issues illuminated Eisenhower's desire to limit the role of the federal government yet guarantee individual rights, they raised concerns about how the United States would be seen around the world. Eisenhower decried how the country's racial problems continued "to feed the mill of Soviet propagandists who by word and picture were telling the world of the 'racial terror' in the United States."[22]

In 1957 Eisenhower asked Congress to pass a civil rights act that protected the voting rights of black Americans.[23] Eisenhower's call for civil rights legislation met a fairly positive response. Congress produced a bill that contained most of the provisions Eisenhower requested. While the president was not completely satisfied with the bill, he decided that minimal civil rights legislation was better than none at all.[24]

Almost immediately after signing the bill, Eisenhower faced a new and potentially violent crisis in Little Rock, Arkansas. Despite the Supreme Court's decision in *Brown* v. *Topeka Board of Education,* most schools in the South remained segregated in 1957.[25] The court's ruling in 1955 that it was the responsibility of the states and localities to integrate schools "with all deliberate speed" allowed the southern states to establish a slow pace for desegregation.[26] In Little Rock, the school board implemented an eight-year plan in May 1955 to integrate schools gradually, and on several occasions courts ruled that the plan represented a legitimate means of achieving the objective of integration. With its emphasis on slow and incremental change, this plan represented what Eisenhower saw as an appropriate, noninflammatory way to educate the population.

As the 1957 school year began, Central High School in Little Rock was earmarked to be integrated under the local school board's plan. In an act of open resistance, Arkansas Governor Orville Faubus ordered the National Guard to prevent the attendance of black students. He argued that their presence could provoke violence. Eisenhower faced a delicate crisis: a state governor was blatantly challenging the Supreme Court's right to judicial review and the federal government's authority to enforce the laws of the land.[27] The stalemate between Faubus and the federal government continued until September 20, when Faubus ordered the National Guard to withdraw. Although the crisis seemed over, an important question remained. Without the National Guard present, would anybody try to stop the black students from attending school on Monday, September 23? On that day nine black students entered the high school relatively uneventfully. However, as the day progressed a mob grew outside. By midday the police asked that the black students be sent home for their own safety.[28]

The mob violence forced Eisenhower's hand. He believed that the federal government had the responsibility to preserve public order and to enforce laws when the states could not or would not do so. The president called the occurrences in Little Rock "disgraceful" and explained that he would "use the full power of the United States including whatever force may be necessary to prevent any obstruction of the law and to carry out the orders of the Federal Court."[29] He authorized the dispatch of troops from the Army's 101st Airborne Division to Little Rock to restore peace and guarantee respect for the law.[30]

While he was obviously worried about the domestic impact of his policies, Eisenhower was also concerned about the influence of the civil rights issue on U.S. foreign policy. In an address to the American people he lamented:

> At a time when we face grave situations abroad because of the hatred that Communism bears toward a system of government based on human rights, it would be difficult to exaggerate the harm that is being done to the prestige and influence, and indeed to the safety, of our nation and the world.
>
> Our enemies are gloating over this incident and using it everywhere to misrepresent our whole nation. We are portrayed as a violator of those standards of conduct which the peoples of the world united to proclaim in the Charter of the United Nations.[31]

Another Pearl Harbor

Within weeks after the federal government's intervention in Little Rock, the Soviet Union shocked the world by launching *Sputnik*. The potential implications of the Soviet rocket capability had a profound impact on the Gaither committee and on how its findings would be received by Eisenhower, Congress, and the country at large. *Sputnik* raised questions about Eisenhower's ability to lead the nation, the U.S. military position vis-à-vis the Soviet Union, and the status of the United States among the world's scientific and technical elite.[32] David Beckler, a Gaither committee member, argued, "Although the satellite is not a military weapon, it tends to be identified in the minds of the world with the impressive military and technological strength of the USSR. In a military sense it underscores Soviet long-range missile claims. In a technological sense it shows the Soviets to have impressive technological sophistication and resources."[33]

Americans, who had become convinced of their scientific superiority, were amazed that the Russians could beat the world's most technologically advanced country to outer space. The implications of the launch of *Sputnik* were frightening. If the Soviet Union could send a satellite into space, why could it not launch a nuclear-tipped missile across the oceans? *Newsweek* concluded that *Sputnik* represented a "defeat in three fields: In pure science, in practical know-how, and in psychological Cold War."[34] *Life* argued, "Let us not pretend that *Sputnik* is anything but a defeat."[35] Public opinion polls revealed that 49 percent of the American people believed that the Soviet Union was "ahead of the United States in the development of missiles and long distance rockets."[36]

Senators and House members reached similar conclusions. Comparisons to the attack on Pearl Harbor were widespread. In special hearings to address the adequacy of U.S. missile programs, Senator Lyndon Johnson claimed, "We meet today in the atmosphere of another Pearl Harbor."[37] Charles Donnelly, a legislative assistant, explained that "there were few in January [1957] who foresaw that, before the end of the year, the United States would suffer a Pearl Harbor in the Cold War and be striving to repair its damaged prestige just as desperately as, in 1942, it was trying to reconstitute its battered naval strength."[38]

While the media, public, and Congress were stunned by *Sputnik,* Eisenhower exhibited little concern.[39] The president's initial reaction was to determine how and why the Soviet Union was able to achieve this capability first and what the possible implications were. The consensus of his advisers was that the Soviet Union had deliberately linked its missile and space programs to launch a satellite as quickly as possible. Deputy Secretary of Defense Donald Quarles told Eisenhower, "There is considerable intelligence to indicate that the Russian satellite work has been closely integrated with and has drawn heavily on their ballistic missile developments."[40] In contrast, the United States had followed a policy of developing a satellite capability separate from its military's missile programs.

Eisenhower decided that three facts should guide his administration's explanations to the American public concerning the Soviet achievement:

a. The U.S. determined to make the Satellite a scientific project and to keep it free from military weaponry to the greatest extent possible.
b. No pressure or priority was exerted by the U.S. on timing, so long as the satellite would be orbited during the IGY [International Geophysical Year] 1957–1958.
c. The U.S. Satellite program was intended to meet scientific requirements with a view toward permitting all scientists to share in information which the U.S. might eventually acquire.[41]

Eisenhower emphasized that *Sputnik* posed no significant military threat to the United States. He recognized that launching a satellite into space was much less difficult than hitting a target thousands of miles away with an ICBM. By stressing these principles he hoped to address the concerns raised by his advisers about the implications of *Sputnik*. Quarles believed that "two main Cold War points are involved: (1) the impact on public imagination of the first successful invasion and conquest of outer space, and (2) the inferences, if any, that can be drawn about the status of their [the Soviet Union's] development of military rocketry."[42] Eisenhower calculated that his military prestige and popularity would reassure the nation and hoped he would not have to initiate new and expensive military projects. He could not have been more wrong.

Before his first press conference after the Soviet launch, Eisenhower explained that his goal was "to allay histeria [*sic*] and alarm," while not belittling the Russian accomplishment.[43] In a two-page statement released on October 9, he described the development of the U.S. satellite program and defended its progress. He mentioned the Soviet achievement only once, congratulating the "Soviet scientists upon putting a satellite into orbit."[44] In answering questions at the press conference, Eisenhower asserted that the United States was not in a race with the Soviet Union. He emphasized that the U.S. satellite program would still be directed toward scientific, not military, goals and would continue on its current pace toward a launch in

December. He tried to reassure the country that *Sputnik* did not pose a security risk.[45]

Over the next few months, Eisenhower continued his attempts to calm fears. He argued that the planned launch of a satellite using the Vanguard missile in December was an opportunity to prove that the United States possessed capabilities similar to the Soviet Union's. But on December 6 Vanguard exploded on takeoff "as if the gates of Hell had opened up."[46] The implications seemed clear. The United States was far behind the Soviet Union in missile capabilities.[47]

The president failed in his attempts to persuade Americans that *Sputnik* did not represent a significant threat. Even he began to question his response. He told a group of legislators that he "had been trying to play down the situation, but perhaps had been guilty of understatement in regard to the strength of the Nation's defenses despite *Sputnik*."[48] In a recent study of the impact of *Sputnik* on the United States, Robert Divine reaches the same conclusion: "Eisenhower, for all his prudence and restraint, failed to meet one of the crucial tests of presidential leadership: convincing the American people that all was well in the world. His inability to understand the profound uneasiness and sense of impending doom was a political failure of the first order."[49]

Challenges to the New Look

The launch of *Sputnik* brought to the forefront possible deficiencies in Eisenhower's New Look military strategy. Since 1953, critics had questioned whether the strategy could effectively meet U.S. commitments and objectives: Did the New Look strategy guarantee that nuclear weapons would be used in any future conflict? Did it rely too heavily on nuclear weapons at the expense of conventional forces? Was it based on an accurate analysis of the targets to be attacked in the Soviet Union and its satellites in the event of hostilities? Did the strategy place too much emphasis on offensive weapons while leaving the country vulnerable to attack? While these questions had circulated since 1953, they now became more relevant.

Although many criticisms were leveled at the New Look, no statement received more attention than Secretary of State John Foster Dulles's address to the Council on Foreign Relations on January 12, 1954. In this speech he introduced the doctrine of massive retaliation, which became synonymous with the New Look. Dulles argued, "Local defenses must be reinforced by the further deterrent of massive retaliatory power. A potential aggressor must know that he cannot always prescribe battle conditions that suit him."[50] He then emphasized that "the way to deter aggression is for the free community to be willing and able to respond vigorously at places and with means of its own choosing."[51]

Dulles's speech raised considerable controversy both inside and outside the government. For those who were already skeptical about the New Look, Dulles's emphasis on "massive retaliatory power" seemed to indicate that any future conflict, big or small, would be resolved through the use of nuclear weapons. This belief raised at least two major concerns. First, the reliance on nuclear weapons would produce extraordinary casualties in any future conflicts. Second, by emphasizing the importance of nuclear weapons, the administration seemed to be subordinating the role of conventional forces. While Dulles may have overstated the importance of nuclear weapons to the New Look, Eisenhower had no intention of sacrificing the nation's ability to wage a variety of different types of conflicts.[52] "We had never proposed to strip ourselves naked of all military capabilities except the nuclear weapon," he remonstrated during a National Security Council discussion in June 1954. "It was ridiculous to imagine anything of this sort."[53] But, despite the president's insistence that the New Look did not mean exclusive reliance on nuclear weapons, critics remained unconvinced.

By the time of *Sputnik,* debate raged over the adequacy of Eisenhower's New Look strategy. Some critics believed that by relying so heavily on nuclear weapons, the United States was restricting its options in future conflicts. Others argued that the emphasis on nuclear weapons was correct, but that the administration had cut the budget too much to maintain a viable nuclear deterrent force. Still others claimed that the New Look strategy was too ambiguous and did not provide adequate guidance for military planning. The debates over these strategic questions were heightened by military service rivalries and the bureaucratic conflicts that plagued the implementation of the president's policies.

Eisenhower constantly reminded his military advisers that they represented the nation, not a particular military branch. From his own experiences as the Army's chief of staff and as an adviser to the JCS, he was well aware of the potential for conflicting interests. In fact, he called himself "a fanatic" on the need for cooperation among the military services.[54] During his presidency, Eisenhower reiterated on several occasions "the need for each Chief to subordinate his position as a champion of a particular Service to his position as one of the overall national military advisers." [55] In one particularly frustrating moment, Eisenhower exclaimed, "Everyone in the Defense establishment should nail his flag to the staff of the United States of America, and think in terms of the whole." [56]

Eisenhower was concerned that comments from military officials were producing the impression that the administration was not united behind its national security policies. [57] At least one subcommittee of the Senate Armed Services Committee reached this very conclusion. Senator Stuart Symington (D-MO), a former secretary of the Air Force who chaired the Air Power Subcommittee, delivered a scathing indictment of Eisenhower's policies at the beginning of 1957. The subcommittee concluded, "Financial considerations have often been placed ahead of defense requirements, to the serious damage of our air-power strength relative to that of Russia; and hence to our national security." [58] Although Eisenhower obviously disagreed with these conclusions, what bothered him most was that they were reached because of the advocacy by many military officials of greater spending for their particular military branch.

Critics also raised questions about the selection of Soviet targets to strike in the event of a war. [59] In his seminal essay on the influence of targeting on nuclear strategy, David Rosenberg criticizes Eisenhower for failing to limit the growth of the United States nuclear arsenal. Rosenberg argues that the president's inability to resolve the disputes between the military branches over strategy and targeting led to the growth of a nuclear arsenal well beyond what the United States needed. [60] He concludes, "Eisenhower never took action to cut back the production of weapons designated for the strategic air offensive, despite his growing conviction that the nation already had more than adequate striking power." [61]

One of the main debates that Rosenberg analyzes concerned the types of targets that the United States should attempt to destroy if war occurred with the Soviet Union. In 1950 the JCS adopted targeting guidelines that provided the foundation for U.S. nuclear war planning for the entire decade. The chiefs of staff assigned first priority to destroying the Soviet Union's capability to deliver atomic bombs, second priority to retarding Soviet military advances, and third priority to destroying Soviet war-making capacity. Code-named BRAVO, ROMEO, and DELTA, respectively, these plans led to a continually increasing target list and, in conjunction, an expanding nuclear weapons stockpile. [62]

Targeting debates revolved around how the New Look strategy should be implemented. There were clear divisions between the positions of the Army and Navy and that of the Air Force.[63] The Air Force recommended attacking BRAVO or counterforce targets—the Soviet air-missile nuclear forces—first. After destroying these, it would then focus on other targets. The Army and the Navy, on the other hand, stressed that it would be virtually impossible to destroy the enemy's entire offensive nuclear capability even under the best conditions; therefore, they argued, priorities should be established to recognize the limited number of targets that could and/ or needed to be hit. Army and Navy representatives recommended giving equal emphasis to counterforce and countercity (DELTA) targets.[64] By developing a more limited yet more defined target list, they hoped to create a nuclear strategy that was not dependent on the availability of the entire U.S. nuclear striking force.[65]

The debates also revolved around the timing of military strikes. Although it is clear that Eisenhower considered and rejected plans to launch a preventive war against the Soviet Union in 1953 and 1954, the possibility of preemption remained part of U.S. policy throughout the 1950s.[66] Preemption meant that if the United States discovered preparations for a Soviet attack, it would launch a military strike to prevent or preempt it. The Air Force's emphasis on counterforce strategy reflected this belief.[67]

The preemptive strategy can clearly be seen in the thinking of Air Force General Curtis LeMay, commander of the Strategic Air Command (SAC) from 1948 to 1957. In December 1949, he told Air Force Chief of Staff Hoyt Vandenberg:

> It would appear economical and logical to adopt the objective of completely avoiding [an] enemy attack against our strategic force by destroying his atomic force before it can attack ours. Assuming that as a democracy we are not prepared to wage a preventive war, this course of action poses two most difficult requirements:
>
> (1) An intelligence system which can locate the vulnerable elements of the Soviet striking force and forewarn us when [an] attack by that force is imminent, and
>
> (2) Agreement at [the] top governmental level that when such information is received the Strategic Air Command will be directed to attack.[68]

He reiterated this strategy in a lecture at the National War College in 1954. He argued, "We [SAC] think the best chance of preventing attacks on this country is to get those airplanes on the ground before they take off, rather than depending on the Air Defense Command to shoot them down after they got [*sic*] here." [69]

LeMay's views are important because they shed light on a debate that was raging among Air Force commanders and because he was an influential witness before the Gaither committee. At their annual conference in 1957, Air Force commanders discussed a recently completed report emphasizing that the basis of a successful strategy in a future war was "to select and destroy a target system, the destruction of which is possible in the event of initiation of war by the U.S. or after Soviet surprise attack." [70] As indicated, one strategic option envisioned the United States initiating a war with the Soviet Union. On at least two other occasions, the commanders discussed preventive and preemptive wars. While they did not recommend either strategy, it is clear from their discussions that as late as 1957 they had not ruled out such actions. [71]

As important as the debates were about targeting and preemption, they paled in comparison to questions concerning the capability of the United States to wage limited military operations. [72] In 1957 two of the decade's most influential books on nuclear strategy were published—Robert Osgood's *Limited War* and Henry Kissinger's *Nuclear Weapons and Foreign Policy.* Numerous articles appeared at the same time emphasizing the need to abandon or reduce the Eisenhower administration's reliance on strategic nuclear weapons. [73] Eisenhower generally did not follow the debates of civilian strategists closely, and he reportedly questioned, "What the hell do they know about it [nuclear strategy]?" [74] Nevertheless, he was aware of their arguments and even passed a brief of Kissinger's book to Secretary of State Dulles. [75]

The various limited war strategies owe much to the writings of British Rear Admiral Sir Anthony Buzzard, the former director of British Naval Intelligence. [76] In January 1956 Buzzard argued that "all our fighting should be limited (in weapons, targets, area, and time) to the minimum force necessary to deter and repel aggression, prevent any unnecessary extension of the conflict, and permit a return to negotiation at the earliest opportunity—without seeking total victory or unconditional surrender." [77] He explained that this strategy, "by providing an intermediate deterrent, guards against these dangers [limited wars], and gives more latitude for our diplomacy, without reducing our deterrent against all-out attack." [78]

In 1957 Buzzard elaborated on these ideas in an unpublished paper that circulated among members of the Gaither committee. He argued that "the key to achieving this essential balance of power is to establish a firm distinction between local tactical atomic war and total global war." [79] He explained, "If only we would firmly and publicly establish that tactical atomic war was a strictly limited affair and need not spread to total war, it would of course, take a large step towards counterbalancing the inherently superior Communist conventional strength, and thus restoring the *tactical* balance of power" (6; emphasis in original). He further expounded on why a limited war capability added to U.S. deterrent power. He stressed, "It is sometimes forgotten that a deterrent has two elements—*severity* and *certainty* of application, and—particularly, with the Russians—it is more important for our deterrent to be reasonably severe and certain of being applied than for it to be disastrous in its consequences and quite uncertain of being applied" (6; emphasis in original). He concluded that for a limited war strategy to be successful, the belligerents must have agreed before the outbreak of a conflict to limit war aims, the boundaries of the conflict, the types of weapons to be used, and the number of legitimate targets (8–9).

Kissinger adopted many of Buzzard's arguments in his study of nuclear weapons. [80] He explained, "In a limited war the problem is to apply graduated amounts of destruction for limited objectives and also to permit the necessary breathing spaces for political contacts." [81] He stressed, "The purpose of limited war is to inflict losses or to pose risks for the enemy out of proportion to the objectives under dispute. The more moderate the objective, the less violent the war is likely to be." [82] He further added that "the result of a limited war cannot depend on military considerations alone; it reflects an ability to harmonize political and military objectives." [83] By laying out a clear explanation of U.S. intentions and providing an alternative to all-out war, Kissinger and Buzzard believed that they were outlining a strategy that allowed greater flexibility.

Osgood reached similar conclusions. He argued, "Only by carefully limiting the dimensions of warfare can nations minimize the risk of war becoming an intolerable disaster." [84] He then explained that for a limited war strategy to succeed, there had to be agreed-upon limits in political objectives, geographical areas of conflict, weapons, and targets (237–59). Of particular importance were his arguments concerning the establishment of political objectives and the use of tactical nuclear weapons. Osgood contended that it was necessary that "the government establish concrete, feasible objectives, sufficiently well defined yet flexible enough to provide a rational guide for the conduct of military operations, and that it communicate the general import of these objectives . . . to the enemy" (239). He also explained that by limiting weapons that might be used in a conflict, a country was not forsaking the use of tactical nuclear armaments. Osgood concluded that "if the American government were to adapt tactical nuclear weapons to a well-conceived strategy of limited-war, based upon a policy of graduated deterrence, then it should not be difficult to erase this stigma [that tactical nuclear bombs were substantially different from conventional explosives] by publicizing the facts in a sober and candid fashion" (257).

The ideas of Buzzard, Kissinger, and Osgood triggered an intense debate by other limited war strategists concerning nuclear strategy in 1957. Officials within the Eisenhower administration pondered the need for acquiring more diversified military capabilities in order to achieve greater policy flexibility. Robert Cutler told Eisenhower that the question of limited war was receiving widespread attention in the NSC's planning board meetings. He advised the president "that continuing attention should also be given to the U.S. capabilities to deal with hostilities short of general war." [85] He finally suggested that "some way be found to *elevate* in the highest councils the need for such continuing attention, without calling for increased financial expenditures" (emphasis in original).[86]

Within the State Department, the Policy Planning Staff also discussed a paper that called for the development of an alternative policy to massive retaliation. It concluded, "Unless there is a national doctrine for limited war and a definition of means by which limited war will not expand into global holocaust, the United States stands in danger of starting a chain of events which might lead to national disaster." [87] It rationalized that with the development of increasingly more powerful nuclear weapons, the possibility of victory in a general war becomes unlikely. The paper recommended limiting objectives and the types of weapons, and relying on indigenous forces to wage wars.[88] In a not-so-veiled critique of the administration's policies, the paper concluded, "A philosophy for limited war implies cool-headed policy and self-restraint in the choice of objectives and the tactics to achieve those limited ends." [89]

Even John Foster Dulles, the author of the phrase "massive retaliation," left room for modifying his own strategy. In an October 1957 article in *Foreign Affairs,* he explained that it may "be feasible to place less reliance upon deterrence of vast retaliatory power. It may be possible to defend countries by nuclear weapons so mobile, or so placed, as to make military invasion with conventional forces a hazardous attempt."[90] If such a policy were adopted, "would-be aggressors will be unable to count on a successful conventional aggression, but must themselves weigh the consequences of invoking nuclear war."[91] While these comments do not indicate the abandonment of the massive retaliation doctrine, they do indicate that key officials in the Eisenhower administration were beginning to question whether the United States possessed adequate military capabilities to wage limited military operations.

The discussions concerning limited war capabilities were most relevant to the military branches. Of the three, the Army was the most persistent advocate of a limited war strategy. In defending their positions, Army leaders stressed that most wars throughout history had been fought for limited objectives and that the advent of multimegaton nuclear weapons would increase the incentive to keep them that way. Both Generals Matthew Ridgeway and Maxwell Taylor resigned from the JCS in 1955 and 1959, respectively, because of what they saw as the administration's lack of commitment to the Army's needs.[92] They did not necessarily advocate the abandonment of massive retaliation, but they sought a better balance among the military branches so that the Army could meet its commitments in all types of military conflicts.

While the Army was the most consistent advocate of a limited war strategy, both the Air Force and the Navy seriously considered it as well. In December 1957 the Air Force Science Advisory Board held a conference on limited war.[93] Although it was not designed to reach specific conclusions, the conference did provide an opportunity for open discussions of both the advantages and disadvantages of a variety of limited war strategies. In January 1958 the Navy completed a report that concluded, "Military *superiority* in unlimited war no longer connotes an ability to 'win'—nobody wins a suicide pact. Thus all-out war is obsolete as an instrument of national policy" (emphasis in original).[94] While both the Air Force and the Navy had their own reasons for embracing a strategy that provided greater flexibility, their efforts to incorporate limited military operations into their plans reflected the influence of limited war arguments.

Conclusions

The dramatic events and debates of 1957 transformed the setting in which the Gaither committee's findings were going to be assessed. The crises over the budget, the debacle in Little Rock, and the start of an economic recession damaged Eisenhower's reputation and hamstrung his attempts to govern the nation. Furthermore, *Sputnik* raised concerns about the Soviet Union's ability to attack the United States and expanded debates about Eisenhower's national security policies. After all of these crises, Eisenhower could no longer rely on his own reputation to reassure the nation.

By the time the Gaither committee delivered its report in November 1957, conditions had markedly changed from its inception the previous May. When the committee was created, Eisenhower still hoped that his budget would be passed with few modifications; he saw a victory on the horizon in the passage of the first civil rights legislation since Reconstruction; and he viewed U.S. military strength with pride. He could not know that the future would not be nearly so bright. When the Gaither committee presented its conclusions and recommendations, the nation was prepared to believe its dire outlook. Six months earlier that would not have happened, but in this case, timing meant everything.

4 | The Activities and Conclusions of the Gaither Committee

When Eisenhower ordered the establishment of the Gaither committee in May 1957, he conceived of a group that would analyze two important, yet limited, national security issues: active and passive defense. He believed that by making improvements in these areas the United States might be able to strengthen its deterrent power against the Soviet Union. This strategy of deterrence formed the basis of Eisenhower's national security policies.[1] He assumed that if the United States maintained sufficient military power to strike the Soviet Union under even the worst circumstances, the Kremlin would be unwilling to initiate war and risk annihilation. The president's press secretary, James Hagerty, summarized the administration's position in 1955. The strategy of deterrence, he said, was based on "blunting the threat of attack by establishing an adequate continental defense and building up our guided missiles here at home, and secondly, to emphasize the retaliatory concept of warfare by putting more money into the air and developing a better early warning system."[2] Two key parts of this strategy, continental defense and early warning, fell into the areas of active and passive defense that Eisenhower asked the Gaither committee to study.

After listening to countless briefings, studying numerous reports, and examining the most secret intelligence estimates, the committee reached some troubling conclusions. It found the United States facing an adversary that was expanding its military power at an alarming rate and that sought world domination. It argued that the United States had to make significant changes and additions to its active and passive defenses. It also recommended that the United States expand its offensive retaliatory capabilities in order to present a greater deterrent to the Soviet Union. The programs that the committee proposed would cost $44 billion over five years. The final Gaither report challenged the effectiveness of the Eisenhower administration's national security policies and forced its advisers to confront some very complicated issues.

Parameters and Organizational Structure of the Gaither Committee

As the summer of 1957 began, Gaither had the unenviable task of organizing the study that he had been appointed to lead. He had to work with Eisenhower's assistant for national security affairs, Robert Cutler, and the director of the ODM, Gordon Gray, to determine exactly what the committee would study. He also had to identify and recruit potential committee members. Finally, he had to carefully organize the new advisers so that the committee could present a final report to the president by the beginning of November.

Some government officials who knew about the proposed study were concerned that the Gaither committee's analysis would expand beyond what the NSC initially requested. Gaither met with Deputy Secretary of Defense Donald Quarles on June 19 to discuss the parameters of the proposed study.[3] Quarles worried that if the Gaither committee made recommendations like those of the Killian panel, the Defense Department would have difficulty implementing them. In the early summer of 1957, the Defense Department was just beginning to deal with the adverse effects of congressional cuts on "the operational readiness dates of the early warning system, the Continental Air Defense System, and the dispersal of the Strategic Air Forces."[4] Requests for additional programs would only have exacerbated this dilemma.

Eisenhower gave Cutler and Gray the responsibility for formulating the guidelines of the Gaither committee study. After Quarles expressed his concerns, Cutler reassured him that the president's intention was not to obtain a thorough reevaluation of U.S. national security programs. Rather, Eisenhower wanted broad advice "derived from wide experience" and careful study.[5] Cutler told Quarles, "The broad-brush study which is sought from the [Gaither] Committee relates to whether it is advisable for the U.S. Government in future years to embark on a greatly enhanced program of passive defense (shelters) or whether monies that would be devoted to that purpose had better be used instead for active defense, accepting whatever risk may be entailed." Cutler then added, "The last thing the President wants to come out of this study is a series of detailed recommendations for changing our defense programs."[6]

Gordon Gray. Eisenhower swears in Gray as director of the Office of Defense Mobilization in March 1957. Gray helped establish the guidelines for the Gaither committee. (National Park Service/Dwight D. Eisenhower Library)

Robert Cutler. Eisenhower swears in Cutler as U.S. director of the Inter-American Bank in 1960. Cutler served as Eisenhower's assistant for national security affairs in 1957 and helped establish the guidelines for the Gaither committee. (National Park Service/ Dwight D. Eisenhower Library)

At a meeting on June 27, 1957, Cutler presented instructions to Gaither and a few other committee members that emphasized the importance of performing a broad overview of U.S. active and passive defense measures, but one that did not offer specific guidelines for the president to follow.[7] Cutler elaborated:

> In arriving at its broad opinion with respect to protection of the civil population against nuclear attack, the Panel should take into account (a) the degree of protection afforded by *passive* defense programs now in being and programmed for the future, (b) the degree to which such protection would be afforded by existing and programmed *active* defenses, and (c) the benefits and risks to our military and non-military defenses which would be entailed, and the economic and political considerations which would be involved, in any decision to undertake a significant shift of emphasis with regard to either active or passive defenses. The end result of the study should be to suggest which of the various active and passive defense measures are likely to be most

effective, in relation to their costs, in protecting the civil population (emphasis in original).[8]

In late July or early August, Gaither and William Foster approached Cutler to expand the parameters of the study.[9] Cutler readily consented because he believed that a larger view of U.S. national security programs would facilitate the development of the most accurate opinions. In his memoirs, he recalled this exchange. "Its leaders, Rowan Gaither and William Foster," Cutler wrote, "asked permission to extend its [the Gaither committee's] inquiries into the overall U.S. defense programs, as having an obvious relation to what the national economy might be called upon to bear. The request seeming reasonable, I gave my assent without foreseeing the result."[10]

The request to expand the scope of the study may have stemmed from a meeting between members of the committee and Eisenhower on July 16. The president reportedly asked the panel, "If you make the assumption that there is going to be a nuclear war, what should I do?"[11] By offering credibility to a Soviet action that he did not expect, Eisenhower may have inadvertently given the committee the wrong premise from which to work. Instead of developing opinions based on the belief that the Soviet Union might attack but probably would not, it assumed that there would be a nuclear war. Foster, in fact, believed that Eisenhower "thought it was time for a fresh assessment of the balance of this country in relation to Russia in science, education, foreign trade, domestic economy, national morale, military strength and world friends."[12]

As the committee and the president's assistants attempted to sort out the study's parameters, Gaither, with the help of the ODM, continued to select advisers.[13] By the end of July, he had created a steering committee and an advisory panel as well as obtained the services of the Institute for Defense Analyses.[14] He organized four subcommittees: Evaluation Quantitative Assessments, Active Defense, Social-Economic-Political, and Passive Defense. These subcommittees were co-chaired by Robert Prim and Stan Lawwill, Jerome Wiesner and Hector Skifter, John Corson and Robert Calkins, and William Webster and James Perkins, respectively.[15] Each subcommittee examined specific issues and developed conclusions that the steering committee and advisory panel used in making their final analysis.

While the specific activities of the subcommittees remain unclear, their main concerns can be ascertained. The Active Defense subcommittee focused on the effectiveness of various defense programs against aircraft and missiles, as well as the relationship between defensive programs and offensive retaliatory capabilities.[16] The Passive Defense subcommittee examined the feasibility of constructing fallout shelters, the importance of strategic warning, and the necessity of stockpiling essential materials.[17] The Social-Economic-Political subcommittee studied the cost of current and proposed defense programs and the economic threat posed by the Soviet Union.[18] The final group, the Evaluation Quantitative Assessments subcommittee, provided quantitative assistance to the other three subcommittees by evaluating major war-gaming studies and analyzing the cost effectiveness of specific active and passive defenses.[19]

The exact number of meetings that the Gaither committee and its advisory groups held is unknown. However, from the available record it is clear that the committee and its subcommittees met frequently.[20] Early in its study, the committee discussed some of the major national security issues facing the country and addressed some specific questions. Economically, the committee members wanted to know the costs of current and proposed programs for active and passive defense and their impact on the economy. Socially, they planned to examine how the country could be made more aware of the dangers posed by a nuclear attack and how the government could continue to operate after a war. In the area of foreign policy, they were concerned with the reaction of U.S. allies and potential enemies to any changes in its defense programs.[21]

In its discussion of military issues, the committee had more pointed questions. Was the policy of massive retaliation still plausible in the wake of technological changes? Was a disarming attack plausible only as part of a preventive war? Were current limited war plans still adequate? What were Soviet intentions in relation to missile development? Would continuing current policies lead to the United States becoming a second-rate power within a decade?[22]

The committee evidently reached some tentative answers to these questions fairly quickly. It concluded that if a war occurred, the United States needed to focus on the destruction of military and civilian targets rather than on disarming the Soviet military. A new limited war strategy was necessary to replace the current reliance on general nuclear war. The government needed to initiate a ballistic missile defense system, possibly using a "Manhattan-type" program. U.S. missile programs should be dispersed as much as possible. U.S. security programs should be developed based on

Soviet actions and programs rather than on fixed budget ceilings. The development of new weapon systems should be constantly monitored to avoid overlap. Finally, the United States must be better prepared to meet "the racing change of the times."[23]

Briefings Received by the Gaither Committee

Despite entering the study with some preconceived beliefs, the Gaither committee still vigorously pursued its assigned task of evaluating U.S. active and passive defenses. While performing its examinations, it had access to voluminous sources that detailed U.S. offensive and defensive capabilities. The committee received briefings from the Defense Department, the Net Evaluation Subcommittee of the NSC, the CIA, the AEC, the FCDA, the ODM, and the NSC representative on internal security.[24] In addition to these briefings, the committee had access to both CIA and Air Force intelligence estimates, to special studies performed by the agencies mentioned above, and to studies by private organizations like the RAND Corporation and the National Academy of Sciences.[25] The committee members also questioned the nation's top military leaders and inspected its key defense installations.[26]

The Gaither committee's subcommittees and their various staff groups met frequently to discuss the key issues concerning U.S. capabilities for resisting a Soviet attack. The content of these meetings remains a mystery. With only a few exceptions, the notes are either classified, lost, or incomplete.[27] However, an analysis of the briefings that have become available, along with the known views of some of the participants, provides a revealing picture of the advice that the Gaither committee received.

The Gaither committee met some initial resistance from within the military establishment in its attempts to acquire information, but ultimately received the assistance it requested.[28] The JCS denied the committee's request for eight briefings but agreed to provide three. The first covered all aspects of the Soviet threat, the second identified U.S. continental defense capabilities, and the third reviewed U.S. retaliatory capabilities.[29]

The Air Force initially provided the committee "the 50-cent tour for visiting firemen" of SAC headquarters.[30] Later, however, General Thomas Power, the new SAC commander after General LeMay was promoted to vice chief of staff of the Air Force, presented a much more detailed briefing. The committee received presentations on SAC intelligence activities, reconnaissance operations, alert procedures, and tactics for penetrating enemy territory.[31] During a three-and-a-half-hour question-and-answer period at the conclusion of the day, General Power described SAC's most secret intelligence estimates of Soviet capabilities and answered "questions with great precision and competence and, as requested, philosophized with clear forethought and understanding about deterrence, Soviet future capabilities and intentions, and so on."[32]

On another occasion, General LeMay "was completely candid in answering questions, and regained for the Air Force the respect of the panel leaders."[33] While notes and memoranda from this briefing are unavailable, an examination of LeMay's statements around the same time provides an idea of what advice he gave the committee.[34] In 1956 he argued that the Soviet Union was "bent upon dominating the world by imposing upon nations and peoples everywhere a way of life radically and irreconcilably opposed to all of the things we believe in."[35] He then explained that the outcome of the next war would be determined in the first few days of the conflict. He stressed that the only way to prevent a Soviet attack was to make its leaders realize that they would face a devastating counterstrike.[36]

In remarks before the Air Force Science Advisory Board in May 1957, LeMay discussed several issues relevant to the Gaither committee. He enunciated that a strategy of deterrence would be successful only if the enemy was positive that it could not successfully attack the United States. He emphasized that "unless our forces are clearly capable of *winning* under operational handicaps of bad weather and no more than tactical warning, and despite any action the enemy may take against them, our forces are not a genuine deterrent. By '*winning*' is meant achieving a condition wherein the enemy cannot impose his will on us, but we can impose our will on him" (emphasis in original).[37] He then described how "the most important contribution of air defense systems is provision of warning to enable the air offensive forces to get underway before they are destroyed at base."[38] He stressed that while the United States currently maintained the capability to strike the Soviet Union, he feared that if SAC did not improve its ability to penetrate Soviet defenses by 1962, then he "could not be confident of winning the Air Power Battle."[39]

Fred Kaplan argues that in LeMay's briefings to the Gaither committee, the Air Force vice chief of staff was even more explicit in his plans for defeating the Soviet Union. On one of the committee's visits to SAC headquarters, it witnessed a surprise alert drill. When SAC bombers were unable to take off in less time than six hours, Robert Sprague questioned why LeMay was not upset. The general responded that the United States flew intelligence missions over the Soviet Union every day and would know about any attack well in advance, and his bombers would have more than six hours to get off the ground. He then argued that if attack plans were discovered, the United States would not hesitate to launch a preemptive strike.[40]

On September 17 Air Force Chief of Staff General Thomas White briefed the Gaither committee. He made three key arguments. He explained that the United States was facing an evolving and growing military threat from Soviet bomber and missile capabilities. He argued that the country's military had to be designed primarily to counter this growing threat from the air. Finally, he explained, "Today, more than ever before, defense is in large part, even primarily, a product of offensive capability. The two are tightly joined and each defies decision in isolation from the other. This stems from both military and economic considerations."[41] He concluded by arguing that while the Air Force could operate effectively on a $20 billion budget in 1958, there would have to be significant increases in the future.[42]

Each of the other military branches also briefed the committee. However, the only briefing of which there is a complete record is the one given by Commandant of the Marine Corps Lt. General Randolph Pate in late September 1957. In his presentation, he focused on two issues that were significant to the committee: the role of tactical nuclear weapons in warfare and the growing relevance of limited war capabilities. He stressed that the Marines "must possess these characteristics: READINESS, VERSATILITY, FLEXIBILITY, [and] OFFENSIVE POWER" (emphasis in original).[43] He lamented that the Marine Corps' ability to accomplish its tasks had "already been appreciably lowered by personnel losses" (10).

In his explanation of why the Marines remained essential to U.S. military efforts, Pate differentiated between general and limited war. He argued that after the initial atomic exchange in a general war, the Marines and other mobile forces would "most likely be the ultimately decisive element in insuring defeat of the enemy" (8). He also explained that he had "become increasingly convinced that the deterrent forces of each side are such that the mutual holocaust of an all-out, unlimited nuclear war suddenly starting is unlikely. This being the case, I believe that wars of limited forces and scope are much more likely" (11). Accordingly, the United

States had to be prepared to wage limited military operations. He then stressed that the military's only amphibious force, the Marines, could use tactical nuclear weapons to help achieve their objectives. "We found," he claimed, "that atomic weapons are not just to be feared. By the exploitation of these weapons, the amphibious force can compress days of preliminary bombardment into a few minutes of time" (4).

According to Paul Nitze and George Lincoln, the Gaither committee's various meetings raised two categories of questions about limited wars. The first category dealt with the political questions surrounding such wars: Where were these wars most likely to occur? What level of support would the United States receive from the people and the governments in the areas of the conflict? And what should U.S. objectives be in view of its overall world strategy? The second category involved the military implications of limited wars: What forces, both U.S. and indigenous, were available? What types of weapons should be used? And what targets should be attacked? [44]

From the briefings, Nitze and Lincoln concluded that the Air Force believed that U.S. capabilities to wage limited wars were restricted by the forces and weapons available to the enemy. If the adversary possessed comparable capabilities, it would be difficult to keep the conflict limited and still achieve a successful resolution of the conflict. But if SAC maintained its superiority, the Air Force argued, it would deter limited as well as general wars because it did not think an adversary would risk annihilation (2). The Navy, on the other hand, questioned the efficacy of nuclear weapons in limited wars, fearing that they would lead to the escalation of a conflict into a general war (5). The Army insisted that the key to a successful limited war strategy was maintaining flexibility to respond in a variety of ways. This flexibility would include the use of tactical nuclear weapons "if their use is to our military advantage" (5).

The Army's views on limited war can be elaborated further by examining presentations delivered by Army Vice Chief of Staff General Lyman Lemnitzer in 1957. He made similar presentations to the Army Policy Council in September and to the Air Force Science Advisory Board Conference on Limited War in December.[45] Lemnitzer criticized the doctrine of massive retaliation. He contended, "Those who talk of a war for survival or who insist that we must first fight and win the air battle, or who assert that the capacity to retaliate massively is the vital element in any war strategy are being tyrannized by their own doctrine. . . . This doctrine implies that every modern war must inevitably be a total war."[46] Lemnitzer elaborated:

The decisive limitation in limited war is that the war must be fought for a limited objective. . . . The only rational course is to act on the assumption that wars can be limited and develop a strategy which will at the same time enable us to deal with limited wars and to minimize the risk of an all-out war.

If we proceed on the assumption that total war is not inevitable, and if we develop a doctrine for limited war, then we should be able to employ armed forces as required to support national security policies, and still avert an all-out conflict.[47]

The Army and Air Force also argued that the nation's missile defenses needed to be improved. The Soviet announcement in August 1957 that it had successfully tested an ICBM raised considerable concern about the vulnerability of the United States. Representing the Air Force position, General E. E. Partridge, the commander of the Continental Air Defense Command, argued, "It is apparent that, in the ballistic missile field, the Soviets are developing a serious threat to our survival. To counter this threat, the United States must take positive and immediate action with the state-of-the-art to attain a defensive capability."[48] Army Chief of Staff General Maxwell Taylor also emphasized that "development of the anti-ICBM system should be accelerated to the extent of a national priority equal to the national priority accorded the development of the ICBM."[49]

One of the last military questions examined by the Gaither committee was the Navy's role in U.S. military strategy. In the areas under study by the committee, the most important ones involving the Navy were the Polaris submarine–launched missile system and antisubmarine capabilities. At an all-day meeting in August, the Navy briefed the committee on the threat posed by Soviet submarines and potential defense measures against them. Furthermore, it explained to the committee how Navy offensive capabilities, in particular the Polaris system, could add to the country's retaliatory striking power.[50]

The briefings received by the Gaither committee were not limited to presentations by the military. On at least two occasions the State Department's Policy Planning Staff met with the committee to discuss U.S. national security policies. As with the military briefings, one of the most important topics was limited war capabilities. Possibly influenced by Secretary of State Dulles's apparent shift away from the massive retaliation doctrine, a PPS study argued that "unless there is a national doctrine for limited war and a definition of means by which limited war will not expand into global holocaust, the United States stands in danger of starting a chain of events which might lead to national disaster."[51] The report concluded,

"A philosophy for limited war implies cool-headed policy and self-restraint in the choice of objectives and the tactics to achieve those limited ends."[52]

Studies and Reports Examined by the Gaither Committee

When Cutler discussed the parameters of the study with Gaither in June, he told the committee chairman that the panel would have access to any information pertinent to its study, including Air Force, SAC, and CIA estimates of the Soviet Union's military capabilities.[53] In addition, it could examine the reports produced by the NSC's Net Evaluation Subcommittee (NES), which had been charged to consolidate the various intelligence estimates of the Soviet Union's capability to damage the United States. Finally, it would have the authority to acquire any other government or nongovernment study that would assist in its examination.

While no complete record exists that details the specific sources of intelligence that the Gaither committee used in making their evaluations, the evidence indicates that the committee eventually gained access to every report or study it requested.[54] A review of the declassified national intelligence estimates between 1955 and 1957 reveals certain common conclusions. The Soviet Union was unlikely to initiate a nuclear war in the near future.[55] While it was not likely to start a war, the Soviet Union's strategic capabilities were increasing at an alarming rate and represented a significant potential threat if used against the United States.[56] Although the institution of a nationwide fallout shelter program would initially cause some confusion and alarm throughout the world, it would eventually be seen as an understandable defensive program.[57] These three broad trends can be seen in the Gaither report. While a Soviet attack was not expected, it could not be ruled out; therefore, the United States needed to prepare for all possible Soviet actions.

The National Intelligence Estimates (NIEs) suggested that the Kremlin sought world domination but would not jeopardize the security of the communist regime itself in pursuit of this goal.[58] NIE 11-4-54 reported, "The Soviet leaders almost certainly believe that during the period of this estimate [to mid-1959] the non-Communist world will possess such strength in major components of military power that general war would involve not only the certainty of widespread destruction within the USSR but the possibility of the destruction of the Soviet system itself."[59] An estimate in 1956 reached a similar conclusion: "The Soviet leaders probably recognize that the US nuclear-air capability remains superior to that of the

USSR, and have probably concluded that at present the USSR, even if it launched a surprise attack, would receive unacceptable damage in a nuclear exchange with the US."[60] Another NIE predicted that the Soviet Union would avoid actions that would "gravely risk general war," but would "probably regard itself as progressively achieving greater freedom of maneuver in local situations."[61] These estimates were consistent in predicting that the Soviets would not attack, but they never questioned the assumption that the Soviet Union sought world domination. If a general war was to occur, it would most likely result from miscalculation, not deliberate actions.

In their attempts to predict whether the United States would be able to detect a Soviet attack, the NIEs presented somewhat contradictory estimates. Special National Intelligence Estimate (SNIE) 11-8-54 examined the probable warning that the United States would receive in the event of Soviet aggression. It argued that such an offensive would be preceded by heightened political tensions that should provide fifteen to thirty days of warning.[62] But NIE 11-6-55 concluded that if the Soviet Union could keep political tensions low, it might strike the United States with "a high degree of surprise."[63]

The NIEs consistently predicted military capabilities based on estimates of maximum Soviet production levels. NIE 11-4-57 concluded that while the Soviet Union was not producing as many bombers as earlier predicted, it still maintained a long-range bomber force of 1,500 airplanes.[64] Another estimate asserted that the Soviet Union would have 10 ICBMs in 1958, 100 in 1959, and 500 in 1960. By comparison, it reported that the United States planned to have only 10 ICBMs in 1959, 30 in 1960, and 50 in 1961. Even if IRBMs were included, the picture was not much brighter. By 1961 the United States planned to have only 120 IRBMs and 3 nuclear submarines carrying 16 Polaris missiles each.[65]

The last NIE of significance to the Gaither committee, SNIE 100-5-57, examined the possible world reaction to a U.S. fallout shelter program. It concluded that among allied countries, such a program would initially produce doubts about U.S. commitments and strategies, but that most countries "would probably come to recognize that the shelter program, taken by itself, was a defensive measure and did not necessarily indicate any basic change in US foreign policy or substantially affect the likelihood of general war."[66] It stressed that the Soviet Union would attempt to exploit the program by arguing that it was one more piece of evidence that the United States was preparing for war. However, it emphasized that the Soviets would probably not believe that the program represented any significant shift in U.S. strategies.[67]

In addition to the NIEs, the Gaither committee relied on SAC and Air Force intelligence estimates. The Air Force and SAC consistently developed estimates of Soviet bomber and missile strengths that were higher than those of the CIA and the other military branches. Sherman Kent, the director of the Office of National Estimates, recalled that in determining the Soviet Union's emphasis on long-range bomber production, the Air Force argued "that the Soviets would continue to give a high priority to the Bison [long-range bomber] Force and enlarge it very considerably."[68] At Senate hearings in 1956, General LeMay asserted that between 1958 and 1960 the Soviet Union "will have a greater striking power [in long-range bombers] than we will have . . . under our present plans and programs."[69] The Gaither committee had to decide whether the Soviet Union was producing bombers at maximum levels, as SAC argued, or at the more moderate levels estimated by NIE 11-4-57.

The Gaither committee also relied heavily on the intelligence assessments developed by the NES. Under the guidelines contained in NSC 5511, the NES was established to develop "integrated evaluations of the net capabilities of the USSR, in the event of general war, to inflict direct injury upon the continental U.S. and key U.S. installations overseas, and to provide a continual watch for changes which would significantly alter those net capabilities."[70] Composed of the chairmen of the JCS, the AEC (starting in 1956), the Interdepartmental Intelligence Conference, and the Interdepartmental Committee on Internal Security, and the directors of the ODM, FCDA, and CIA, the NES integrated the intelligence estimates of the various military and government agencies to produce annual reports for the president.[71]

By the time the Gaither committee completed its final report, the NES had already presented assessments to the NSC in 1955 and 1956. The 1955 analysis focused on the consequences of a Soviet attack on the United States. It war-gamed two potential attack scenarios. Plan A involved an attack in which the United States received no warning prior to the launch. Plan C assumed that the United States would obtain sufficient strategic warning of an impending attack to place its military and civil defenses on full alert.[72] In analyzing both plans, the NES had access to the best estimates of Soviet military capabilities through 1958.[73] Under both scenarios, the NES concluded that approximately 65 percent of the American population would need some form of medical attention after the attack, and that for at least six months the economy would be practically inoperable.[74] The only significant difference between the two plans was that Plan C would allow the United States the initiative to launch a preemptive strike if it discovered Soviet preparations for an attack. In either a preemptive or retaliatory strike, the subcommittee concluded that the United States would inflict even worse damage on the Soviet Union.[75]

The NES performed its 1956 evaluation using the same two scenarios as in its first study. In this report, the NES concluded that if the United States did not maintain an adequate alert status for its nuclear retaliatory forces, a Soviet nuclear attack in 1959 would kill or injure more than 50 percent of the civil population and lead to the Soviet Union's emergence as the world's greatest power. It stressed that regardless of U.S. nuclear capabilities, a Soviet nuclear attack would, in the age of the ballistic missile, cause massive damage if adequate civil defense plans were not introduced.[76]

Although the Gaither committee had access to NIEs, the NES evaluations, and top-secret briefings, it does not appear that it examined intelligence gathered by the U-2. At least three members of the committee—James Killian, Herbert York, and Paul Nitze—claim that they did not see any of the U-2 intelligence at the time of the study.[77] York, who analyzed Soviet military capabilities for the committee and later had access to the U-2 data, explained, "At that time I knew much of the intelligence we had concerning the status of Soviet developments and deployments, but I knew little about how we got it."[78] While it appears that the committee did not have access to the U-2 intelligence, at least some of its individual members did know about the overflights. Richard Bissell, a consultant to the committee, ran the U-2 program for the CIA, and Killian had participated in the establishment of the U-2 program in 1954.[79]

A significant issue raised by the Gaither committee's apparent inability to examine the U-2 photographs is whether that information would have altered its ultimate conclusions. While it is impossible to know with certainty, the answer is probably no. This conclusion can be reached for two reasons. First, when the committee met, the U-2 program was only a year old. While it produced excellent intelligence, there were limits to what the few overflights that had already occurred could reveal. Second, while the CIA used the U-2 to prove what military capabilities the Soviet Union actually possessed, it was also attempting to show what the Soviets did not have. When no ICBMs were photographed, it seemed to show that they did not exist. However, with the relatively limited coverage provided by the U-2, it could also be argued that the Soviet missiles simply had not been seen. Between January 1959 and June 1960, only 13.6 percent of Soviet territory considered suitable for maintaining ICBM forces had been photographed by the U-2.[80]

Government Reports Examined by the Gaither Committee

Even without the U-2 photographs, the Gaither committee still had access to a full range of information. Beyond the briefings, intelligence estimates, and the NES evaluations, the committee was able to examine reports produced by government agencies. In August 1956 the Air Force presented its own views on SAC vulnerability to the NSC. In a briefing, General R. C. Lindsay identified four major weaknesses in SAC's capabilities. There were an insufficient number of air bases to provide effective dispersal of SAC's long-range and medium-range bombers. There were gaps in radar coverage, especially at high and low altitudes, that could be exploited by the Soviet Union in a surprise attack. Since at best only 11 percent of SAC forces could take off given fifteen minutes' warning, this was a significant vulnerability.[81] SAC's communications and control systems remained underdeveloped and relatively unprotected from a nuclear blast. U.S. nuclear weapons were stockpiled at only forty-five locations, and more than 50 percent of the weapons were at thirteen sites.[82]

The Air Force made several recommendations to remedy these problems. It argued that the government should construct additional air bases to facilitate a wider dispersal of SAC forces and should study the possibility of using civilian airfields in wartime. It also recommended allotting additional funding to fill the gaps in coverage at high and low altitudes by building additional radar sites. It requested money to accelerate its implementation of an alert force program. It asked for additional funding to construct more efficient and secure communication lines. Finally, it advocated further study of how to reduce the vulnerability of the nuclear weapons stockpiles.[83]

The JCS followed this Air Force study with the creation of an ad hoc committee to study U.S. air defenses.[84] The impetus for this study originated from both SAC and CIA estimates that indicated the Soviet Union might possess the capability to launch ballistic missiles from submarines.[85] In November 1956 the JCS appointed Albert Hill, a future member of the

Gaither committee, to chair a panel, which included General Carl Spaatz, General Thomas Handy, and Admiral John Ballentine, to study U.S. air defense needs.[86] This committee, which completed its report in June 1957, argued, "The goal for the defense of North America against air attack should be the achievement and maintenance of a level of air defense effectiveness sufficient to give a reasonable chance of defending approximately 80 percent of the vital target areas of the nation."[87] Although the report remains classified, analyses of Soviet strategies from the time period indicate that if the Soviet Union launched an attack, its military forces would concentrate first on U.S. retaliatory capabilities and then political, industrial, and economic centers.[88] The committee concluded that most target areas were very vulnerable.

The other study that the Gaither committee explicitly requested was the Continental Air Defense Objectives Plan, 1956–1966. Its assumptions about the Soviet Union's ultimate goal and objectives in a general war are illuminating. "It is accepted," the report stressed, "that the ultimate national aim of the Soviet Union is world domination."[89] It then argued that if a general war developed between the two superpowers, the Soviet objectives would be:

a) to secure the Soviet Union against a retaliatory attack, by both offensive and defensive operations against any force capable of significantly threatening its security.

b) To gain control of Eurasia, and to gain control of or neutralize the United Kingdom and the island chains of the Far East.

c) To neutralize North America's war-making capacity to the extent necessary to success in a. and b.

d) If possible, without prejudice to a., b., or c., to reduce North America's economic and social structure to the point where North America could not, for many years, constitute a threat to the expanded Soviet Empire.[90]

According to the report, the most important U.S. requirement was developing the necessary defenses to prevent a successful Soviet attack.

The Gaither committee also had access to government studies from nonmilitary agencies. Most important, numerous NSC studies provided invaluable information related to the committee's tasks. Of obvious importance was the final report of the Killian committee. Not only did this group address some of the same issues as the Gaither committee, but it also was composed of some of the same people. Six additional studies undertaken

either by the NSC itself or by groups under its direction were very significant: NSC 5606, an FCDA study, Part 5 of NSC 5720, a report by a special
committee on shelters, and economic analyses of shelter programs performed by both the CEA and the Treasury Department.

In 1956 the NSC issued its first full report on continental defense in
nearly two years—NSC 5606. Heavily influenced by Robert Sprague, the
report concluded, "The strength of the United States which must be maintained is an integrated complex of offensive and defensive elements. Each
of these elements has its proper role in deterring an attack [by the Soviet
Union] and in the defense of the United States should an attack occur."[91]
Additionally, the report contended, "The deterrent effect of U.S. power
will be dangerously lessened if Soviet production of multimegaton weapons and an adequate delivery capability is achieved before the United States
develops an adequate warning and defense system and significantly reduces
the vulnerability of its retaliatory nuclear power."[92] It therefore recommended achieving maximum tactical warning, defending against both air
vehicles and ballistic missiles, expanding the passive defenses of the country's retaliatory capability, and implementing new civil defense programs.
NSC 5606 proposed a gradual increase in spending on these measures
from $3.8 billion in 1956 to $11.5 billion in 1960.[93]

Later in 1956, the findings of an FCDA panel added weight to the recommendations of NSC 5606.[94] After studying the effects of a nuclear attack on the United States, the panel delivered a set of alarming conclusions
to the president and the NSC. The panel analyzed the consequences of an
all-out Soviet attack that struck at least half of the metropolitan centers in
the United States. Such an attack, it predicted, would cause 50 million
American casualties, including between 30 and 35 million deaths.[95] It argued, "*In the event of a massive nuclear attack on the United States, of the
proportions assumed without drastically improved preparation of the people,
support of the National Government and of the war effort would be in jeop-
ardy, and national disintegration might well result*" (emphasis in original).[96] To avoid such devastation, the panel advocated stockpiling essential
food and medical supplies, developing plans for recovery after an attack,
rehearsing carefully developed evacuation plans, and building shelters for
those unable to leave a target area.[97]

Part 5 of NSC 5720, the NSC's assessment of the status of U.S. national
security programs in 1957, reached similar conclusions. Produced by the
FCDA, this report did not predict a Soviet attack but concluded that "the

USSR has the capability of attacking any target within the United States or its possessions."[98] Soviet intentions were not important to the FCDA unless the possibility of an attack could be eliminated. Since U.S. military plans were based on what the Soviet Union might do, the FCDA operated under similar assumptions. It concluded that if the Soviet Union attacked in 1957, current evacuation plans and shelter space would be inadequate. It stressed, "Most of the radiation casualties resulting from [a Soviet] attack (and these would have numbered in the millions) could be attributed to insufficient protection from fallout, plus inadequate radiological defense programs."[99]

Although the preceding studies were significant, the reports developed by three groups that were created simultaneously with the Gaither committee were even more important. As with many of the other studies discussed earlier in this chapter, the reports developed by the special committee on shelters, the CEA, and the Treasury Department remain restricted. However, recently declassified memoranda do contain important summaries of the assumptions used by these groups in reaching their conclusions. The special committee studied the effectiveness of different shelter systems in limiting the casualties from a Soviet attack. The CEA and Treasury Department then analyzed the economic implications of implementing these programs.

After developing possible Soviet targeting strategies, the special committee examined the effectiveness of eight different shelter programs, ranging from fallout shelters to protect a limited part of the population to combinations of blast and fallout shelters to shield the entire population.[100] The first three programs represented partial shelter plans costing from $5.1 to $16.5 billion, while the last five provided at least complete national protection from fallout and ranged in costs from $24.5 to $70.0 billion. Each program would be implemented over an eight-year period beginning in FY 1958 and concluding in FY 1965.[101] The committee calculated that if the United States did not build any new shelters, casualties resulting from a Soviet attack would range between 67 million and 116 million, depending on the strike pattern.[102] Each successive shelter program would reduce the number of casualties. However, the most significant improvements in survival rates would occur between the most expensive partial shelter plan ($16.5 billion) and the least expensive complete shelter program ($24.5 billion). After this point, the potential return on the shelter investment diminished.[103]

After the special committee finished its examination, the CEA and Treasury Department analyzed the economic implications of the shelter programs. The CEA examined four of the eight shelter plans—the $10.1, $24.5, $49.4, and $70.0 billion programs.[104] It calculated that if the U.S. Gross National Product (GNP) grew $16 billion annually, federal revenue increased $3 billion annually, and federal expenditures were held to a 1 percent increase, then the economy would produce a $30 billion surplus between FY 1959 and FY 1962. These assumptions, however, depended on the country avoiding a recession, maintaining current tax levels, and keeping spending in check. The CEA concluded that while the first three shelter plans could be accommodated by the federal economy, only the $10.1 billion program was really manageable. It argued that the programs costing beyond $10.1 billion would have an inflationary impact and would strain steel, cement, and labor supplies.[105]

Treasury Department officials examined ways to finance a shelter program. They studied the possibility of providing tax incentives to industry and civilians to encourage the construction of private shelters. They also calculated possible ways to raise federal revenues to pay for shelters. They concluded that tax incentives would primarily aid the wealthy while providing only limited additional shelter space, and that increasing federal expenditures would measurably increase tax liabilities.[106] Accordingly, the Treasury Department opposed the construction of any shelters because of the potential drain on federal revenues. More pointedly, it argued that even if the United States could finance a shelter program without raising the current level of expenditures, it would still oppose such a venture because the country "would have to forego tax reductions to release funds for the activity and investment necessary for sustained economic growth through private initiative."[107]

Reports by Nongovernment Organizations and Experts

The Gaither committee's study groups supplemented these government estimates, studies, and briefings with books and reports produced by civilian experts. The study groups turned to the works of leading experts to analyze the best possible national security programs. On issues concerning SAC vulnerability, active defense measures, and military preparedness, reports by the RAND Corporation, Stanford Research Institute, Rockefeller Foundation, and Johns Hopkins University significantly influenced the committee's conclusions. The studies examined by the committee concerning passive defense measures are too extensive to list, but a sampling of the organizations that produced them should be sufficiently revealing: the Stanford Research Institute, the Walter Reed Army Institute of Research, the National Academy of Sciences, and Johns Hopkins University.[108] Finally, the works of Henry Kissinger and Anthony Buzzard influenced the Gaither committee's assessment of U.S. military strategies.

The RAND Corporation played a particularly influential role in helping the Gaither committee develop its conclusions. The committee received briefings from several RAND experts, including Albert Wohlstetter, Spurgeon Keeny, and Herman Kahn.[109] In addition, the committee had access to several RAND studies of SAC vulnerability and weaknesses in U.S. air defenses. In particular, "Selection and Use of Strategic Air Bases" (R-266) and "Protecting U.S. Power to Strike Back in the 1950s and 1960s" (R-290) laid the bases for the Gaither committee's conclusions that U.S. strategic retaliatory forces were vulnerable to a Soviet nuclear attack.

In their monumental study of U.S. air bases, Wohlstetter and his colleagues at RAND examined four different alternatives for selecting SAC base locations and analyzed which of them provided the optimum balance between offering security from an enemy attack and maintaining the capability to reach enemy targets effectively. The first alternative represented the U.S. strategy in the early 1950s of placing SAC forces at overseas bases to allow the quickest access to enemy targets. The second alternative proposed maintaining SAC forces overseas but at bases further from the front lines. The third alternative was to locate SAC forces in the United States and depend on aerial refueling to reach enemy targets. The last alternative called for basing SAC forces in the United States while relying on overseas bases as ground-fueling staging areas.[110] It concluded that U.S. retaliatory forces were currently vulnerable to a Soviet nuclear attack because SAC overseas bases were located within range of Soviet aircraft and were poorly designed to withstand attacks.[111] It stressed that the best base system would be the fourth alternative because it reduced the vulnerability of SAC forces without adding the cost of aerial refueling.[112]

Another RAND study that examined measures to protect U.S. strategic power proved equally influential. It evaluated the vulnerability of the United States to a surprise Soviet attack and discovered that with relatively limited forces, the Soviet Union could cause mass destruction. It asserted that a surprise Soviet attack involving as few as 150 heavy bombers and

150 ICBMs could devastate the ability of SAC to launch a counterattack. To meet this potential threat, the report recommended dispersing existing forces, hardening SAC bases, constructing active defenses around SAC bases, and developing better early warning capabilities.[113]

Two other groups involving some Gaither committee members performed studies in 1957. The Army contracted with the Operations Research Office (ORO) at Johns Hopkins University to study U.S. air defenses. At the same time, the Rockefeller Foundation established several panels to examine U.S. domestic and foreign security. One panel, including Gaither committee members Colonel George Lincoln, James Fisk, and General James McCormack, studied the military aspect of international security. Both groups completed their reports by January 1958.

According to Ellis Johnson, the director of the Johns Hopkins study, the objective of the ORO study was to find weaknesses in U.S. air defenses and determine ways to eliminate them. The study concluded that "the U.S. is falling behind the Soviets in military power."[114] Furthermore, it stressed that the country "absolutely must face up to the fact that the price for moral leadership is that we must spend much more than the Soviet on thermonuclear attack and defense systems since we *will* be attacked if we are so weak as to invite attack, and the U.S. *will* be that weak unless we are sure of having enough SAC left, after the surprise Soviet attack, to clobber them in return" (emphasis in original).[115] To meet the Soviet threat, it recommended increasing annual defense spending by $15 billion for an indefinite period.[116]

The Rockefeller Foundation acquired the assistance of more than 150 experts, who worked on seven different panels, to study U.S. domestic and foreign security in the late 1950s.[117] Panel II, which examined the military aspects of international security, performed a study similar to the Gaither committee's. The panel concluded, "Mankind . . . is faced by two somber threats: the Communist thrust to seek world domination that seeks to exploit all dissatisfactions and to magnify all tensions; and the new weapons technology capable of obliterating civilization" (97). Furthermore, while it stated that the United States would be able to meet any Soviet attack during the next two years with "a crushing reply," it was concerned about the period beyond that time frame (108). It lamented, "In looking at the strategic equation for all-out war there is reason for serious concern. Our retaliatory power is imperiled by Soviet advances in the missile field and by the inadequate dispersal and protection of our Strategic Air Command.

Our active defense designed against manned planes will have to be redesigned for the missile age. Our civil defense program and that of our allies is completely inadequate" (111).

To remedy the deficiencies that it saw in U.S. military programs, it recommended spending an additional $3 billion annually on defense programs (152). It specifically recommended modernizing the Air Force with new aircraft; developing ICBM and IRBM capabilities; reducing SAC vulnerability by improving warning, reaction times, and base structures; expanding the military's capability to wage limited military operations; and constructing fallout shelters (150–51). In its argument for improving U.S. civil defenses, the report claimed that "it is long overdue. It does not make sense for the free world to engage in a major military effort without at the same time protecting its most important resource: its civilian population" (141).

The Gaither committee also examined some special reports created by its own advisers. In particular, Foster and Sprague reviewed budget studies that indicated that the United States could afford to spend more on defense programs. Two consultants, in a study that Sprague called "thoughtful" and Foster labeled "Good!," concluded that a larger defense budget was economically feasible without an increase in inflation or higher taxes.[118] The consultants examined four possible defense budgets for FY 1960 ranging from $44 to $75 billion.[119] They concluded that the United States could maintain a $54 billion annual defense budget without serious detriment to the economy. Furthermore, if the country was willing to accept tax rates at the same level as during the Korean War, it could afford to spend $64 billion annually for defense programs.[120]

Evidently influenced by this report and his own beliefs, Paul Nitze proposed that the Gaither committee view its report as a unique opportunity to offer an alternative national security strategy to the president's policies. "It seems to me," Nitze wrote, "that a group such as this . . . can take a different view. It can discuss whether the resources being provided are adequate, whether the allocations within those resources are as wise as possible, and whether one line of strategic development or another would appear to be most to the common interest."[121] Nitze argued that the United States should increase its defense spending from $38 to $48 billion by 1960. It should reduce its reliance on nuclear weapons by increasing conventional forces, dispersing SAC, improving continental defense warning and missile systems, and beginning a shelter program for the civil population. Finally, the president should encourage European powers to increase their own conventional forces and make nuclear weapons available to them.[122]

The last items that the Gaither committee examined were the writings of civilian strategists. Lincoln, who himself had been active in publishing his views on strategy, sent a memorandum to other committee members that contained excerpts from Henry Kissinger's *Nuclear Weapons and Foreign Policy*.[123] The passages that Lincoln cited reveal a fundamental critique of Eisenhower's national security strategy. Kissinger argued, "The purpose of our capability for all-out war will be to deter Soviet aggression against us by developing a retaliatory force of a size which can inflict an unacceptable amount of damage on the enemy, no matter what level of destruction he may accomplish by a surprise attack."[124] In addition, he emphasized that the United States needed to develop a capability to wage a limited war in Europe. Kissinger stressed that if the United States did not develop this capability, "In every crisis it will force us either to resort to a suicidal nuclear war which would not save Europe from being overrun or to violate our solemn pledge [to defend Europe]."[125] He concluded that while it was understandable that some government officials wanted to maintain defense spending at current levels, it was also foolish.[126]

Views of Gaither Committee Members in the Late 1950s

One last way that the reasons underlying the Gaither committee's conclusions can be explored is to examine the reports and testimony produced by some of its members in the late 1950s. Many of the committee members studied specific problems for the Defense Department and testified before congressional committees. Sprague and Jerome Wiesner publicly discussed the Soviet threat and capabilities. Doolittle and Mervin Kelly testified to weaknesses in U.S. air defenses. Nitze and Lincoln wrote a report emphasizing the need for increased conventional forces to wage limited war. Fisk and James Corson analyzed the weaknesses in U.S. military defense organizations. James Baxter, David Beckler, and Foster stressed the need for fallout shelters. Finally, Albert Hill criticized the Eisenhower administration's emphasis on a balanced budget at the risk of national security.

Wiesner told a national television audience in June 1958 that "the Soviets have managed to make a considerably more effective air defense system than we have; I think it is perfectly obvious to everyone that they are ahead of us in the missile field. I believe that their limited war capability both in quantity and quality is superior to ours, and their submarine fleet is certainly a much larger one than we have at the present time." [127] In the same broadcast, Sprague argued that "in the near future, we are vulnerable to a surprise air nuclear attack on our continental bases of our Strategic Air Command, and if such an attack were successful, this would neutralize our ability to massively retaliate, which, in turn, would destroy our national policy of deterrence, and in the long future—and I am thinking possibly from 1970 on—our people face the possible danger of total annihilation in a nuclear war." [128]

Doolittle and Kelly served together on the Air Force Science Advisory Board and maintained close ties to that military branch. Kelly told Senator Lyndon Johnson's preparedness subcommittee, "When we look at where we stand in the missile field in relation to our competition, it is shattering and very worrisome." [129] At the Air Force's annual conference, in November 1957, Doolittle told his fellow officers that the Air Force needed to request a defense budget in excess of $38 billion and emphasize air defense more. [130] He testified before the Johnson subcommittee that the goal of the Soviet Union "is world communization and world domination." [131] He stressed the importance of increasing the number of aircraft, developing and accelerating missile programs, dispersing SAC forces to hardened bases, and improving SAC alert status. [132] He did not believe that the Soviet Union was currently stronger than the United States, but argued that "Russia's Rate of Progress is more rapid than ours, and, unless we continue to forge ahead at full speed, she will soon overtake us." [133]

In December 1957 Nitze and Lincoln co-wrote a report on U.S. limited war capabilities. They stressed that the United States needed to give greater attention to waging limited wars. They argued, "It is conceivable that a general war can be avoided for the indefinite future. It is almost inconceivable that limited military operations can be deterred indefinitely in all the various areas where United States interests are presently committed." [134] They questioned whether the United States could fulfill its declaratory policy, that is, its various commitments around the world. "At some point," they declared, "there must be a connection between this psychological deterrent and the actual military situation." [135] Assessing the military capabilities that the United States needed to maintain, they emphasized that conventional military capabilities should be augmented because of the dangers of escalation produced by nuclear weapons. "If the enemy is presumed to have nuclear weapons," they wrote, "serious questions arise as to the military advantage if any which we would obtain through initiating their use."[136]

One area of particular concern to the Gaither committee was the slow and ponderous pace of the Defense Department in developing new strategies and incorporating new scientific and technological advances into military plans. Both Corson and Fisk argued that there were serious problems in the organization of the defense establishment. Corson stressed that the United States faced a critical danger within two years "from an aggressively posed and rapidly developing enemy."[137] He concluded, "To maintain superiority for conducting military operations, there is a vital need for creating organizational machinery that will expedite [*sic*] the translation of technological concepts into weapons systems that can be produced prior to conflicts."[138] Fisk argued, "The Russians appear to have matched the United States in many significant areas of science and military technology and are surprising the United States in others."[139] He concluded that the United States needed to emphasize research and development much more.[140]

Baxter, Beckler, and Foster complained that U.S. leaders failed to recognize the importance of protecting the civilian population in the case of nuclear war. Baxter argued that the construction of fallout shelters would enhance the credibility of the massive retaliation doctrine by making the use of nuclear weapons less threatening to the population.[141] Beckler stressed that "unless the shelter program is developed on a government-wide basis in the context of our over-all national policies and programs, it may not get the attention and support it merits as an essential protective measure for national survival during the uncertain days of nuclear parity in the years ahead."[142] Foster provided a different rationale for building shelters, arguing that it "is known that shelters would provide a tremendous extra burden *not on us,* but on Russian strategy. Shelters would mean that any Soviet missile or bomber attack would have to be almost doubled to paralyze the United States beyond recovery. Thus, a shelter program is not a many billion dollar gamble against the day that the Soviet Union might attack. Rather, it is as much a positive deterrent as are our missile and Strategic Air Command bombers" (emphasis in original).[143]

More than any other Gaither committee member, Albert Hill captured the committee's skeptical mood concerning Eisenhower's emphasis on maintaining a balanced budget. When the committee met in the fall, Hill sent Sprague a poem he had written describing his view of the president's policies. In the poem, entitled "Ode to Eternity," he wrote:

> I'd rather be bombed than be bankrupt,
> I'd rather be dead than be broke.
> Tis better by far to remain as we are.
> I'm a solvent if moribund bloke.[144]

The Reports of the Gaither Committee's Subcommittees

The Gaither committee's top-secret discussions intensified between August and November.[145] One committee member recalled, "It was like looking into the abyss and seeing Hell at the bottom."[146] Foster recalled the sensitivity of the committee's work: "Documents taken from our office at night had to be carried by security officers. And when sessions were held at my home, guards were stationed at the house for protection of the documents."[147] The committee had to process the information in these documents and then write a coherent and persuasive final report. Before this could occur, the committee had to analyze the reports of the four subcommittees that had been created to study specific problems. The final conclusions of these groups were compiled into three volumes: Active Defense and SAC Vulnerability; Passive Defense; and Economic, Social, and Political.[148]

The subcommittees examining U.S. active defenses and SAC vulnerability concluded that U.S. air defenses were inadequate to meet the Soviet threat. They argued, "At the present time the ability of either military or civilian activities to utilize warning is essentially zero."[149] They feared that the Soviet Union could possibly launch an attack without strategic warning. Even worse, with the deficiencies they found in both high- and low-altitude radar coverage, they believed the United States might not even have tactical warning of a Soviet attack.[150]

One of the major problems faced by the Gaither committee in assessing the capabilities and intentions of the Soviet Union was the lack of actual information from within the Communist bloc.[151] Herman York described how he and Jerome Wiesner calculated Soviet ICBM strength for the committee. He explained that they knew the Soviet Union had been working on missiles for a long time and had conducted successful tests. They also possessed information on the Soviet Union's manufacturing capabilities. York then stressed, "In the absence of any contrary indications, we assumed the worst. I recall Jerome Wiesner and I estimating that they could produce 1000's of ICBM's in the next few years and urging that the Gaither Committee base its conclusions and recommendations on that fact."[152] Using this type of information, the subcommittees had the Soviet Union launching 1,800 ICBMs against the United States in a hypothetical attack: 125 at SAC bases, 675 at U.S. ICBM bases, and 1,000 at civilian targets.[153] Nitze recalled, "We calculated that ninety percent of our bomber force could be knocked out on the ground by a surprise Soviet bomber attack, let alone an attack by Soviet ICBMs."[154]

The subcommittees lamented that "there is only meager intelligence directly concerning their [Soviet] ICBM and IRBM programs. The estimates of Soviet capabilities . . . are based almost entirely on the U.S. ICBM and IRBM capabilities, and on inferences from Soviet achievements in related fields."[155] Given the paucity of estimates based on concrete intelligence, analysts tended to credit the Soviet Union with capabilities based on the maximum that Soviet industry could produce. They admitted, "Since there is recent evidence that the Soviet technical and economic capabilities have been underestimated in the past, the threat described in this report may reflect an unconscious corrective bias tending toward overestimation."[156] They argued that the United States needed to harden SAC air bases against the pressures produced by a nuclear blast and to construct active defenses against both bombers and missiles.[157] They emphasized that "[a]n all-out crash program must begin immediately in order that these defense capabilities can be achieved."[158]

The Passive Defense subcommittee created three subgroups to study the effectiveness of passive defenses in protecting industry, ensuring the safety of civilians, and reducing SAC vulnerability.[159] The subcommittee examined current FCDA plans for evacuation and for shelters designed to protect the civilian population and military equipment in the event of an attack. It argued that "evacuation is no longer an acceptable alternative for shelter to protect the civil population."[160] The committee members concluded that shelters would "forcibly augment our deterrent power in two ways: first, by discouraging the enemy from attempting an attack on what might otherwise seem to be a temporarily unprepared target; second, by reinforcing his belief in our readiness to use, if necessary, our strategic retaliatory power."[161]

After examining different types of shelters, the subcommittee concluded that a nationwide fallout shelter program costing $25 billion over six years should be initiated, while the effectiveness of blast shelters should be studied further.[162] It recommended that shelters be constructed no more than a mile apart or in locations that the average person could reach in ten minutes.[163] However, it emphasized that there is "a common aspect of all [shelter] programs: none offers absolute protection, and even with a prohibitively expensive program we must anticipate heavy casualties if we are attacked."[164]

The final volume of reports contained background information on the Soviet Union's economic potential, on the ability of the United States to pay for the proposed programs, and on how the recommendations should be implemented.[165] The subcommittees found that while the Soviet GNP amounted to only 40 percent of the U.S. GNP, the Kremlin devoted nearly the same funding to the military. More important, the committee members stated that while U.S. defense spending was expected to remain constant at approximately $38 billion annually in the future, the Soviet Union was expected to increase its expenditures. Based on these calculations, they concluded:

> If the Soviet threat is measured in terms of annual expenditures for defense and investment purpose, relative to our own, it is formidable indeed. Soviet economic strength has already been sufficient to build an impressive military capability. It is reinforced by a political structure that permits (or forces) single-minded concentration of economic resources on military objectives and promises to be sufficient to build a military capability substantially greater than our own before 1970, in the absence of increased effort on our part. In addition, increasing Soviet economic strength makes possible a continuing politico-economic offensive to extend Soviet influence throughout the world.[166]

Writing and Presentation of the Gaither Report

Using the findings of the four subcommittees and the other evidence discussed earlier in this chapter, the steering committee spent most of late October devising its own conclusions and writing a final report. Most of its members were requested to write brief summaries of the specific issues that they had been involved with during the study.[167] The committee then assigned Sprague and Baxter the unenviable task of drafting this report. Almost immediately, Sprague deferred much of the writing to Baxter, who had won a Pulitzer Prize in history for his 1946 study, *Science against Time.*

Realizing the gravity of the task of distilling hundreds of pages of research into a short report, Baxter asked Lincoln and Nitze to assist him.[168] Nitze and Lincoln quickly assumed primary responsibility for writing the final report. Nitze later recalled that "Abe [Col. Lincoln] and I were mentioned as 'project members' at the back of the report, which masked the fact that we shared importantly in shaping the substance of the final version."[169]

As Nitze and Lincoln composed the final report, the advisory panel presented a summary of its conclusions and recommendations to Eisenhower. Gaither spoke for the committee and identified six major conclusions. The currently planned active defense system was inadequate. The programmed passive defenses did not provide sufficient protection for the civilian population. SAC was vulnerable to a Soviet surprise attack. By 1959 U.S. vulnerability would increase with the advent of ICBMs. The risks to the country would continue to grow until there was a workable arms control agreement. Finally, Gaither stressed, "The long-run peril to the U.S. civil population demands prompt and effective measures for increasing our basic and inherent strengths and for melding the will and resources of the free world."[170]

After identifying these conclusions, Gaither discussed the rationale for the committee's findings:

> The employment of this Russian military power must be deterred and contained by the United States and its allies until an enforceable worldwide arms limitation plan is achieved. In this interim of unpredictable duration our security must rest primarily upon the full effectiveness of deterrents and, if deterrents fail, upon our capability to survive as a nation and to retaliate with swift decisiveness. Any weakness in deterrents and any important gap in our defenses if deterrents fail, imperil the U.S. civil population and national survival. A sober appraisal of the threat and of U.S. and allied strengths has, as we have indicated, brought us to the conclusion that today and in the decade ahead our deterrents are inadequate and that the U.S. civil population might be exposed to casualties of fifty percent or more of our total population—a catastrophe which defies imagination and which almost certainly would bring national disintegration. (4–5)

Gaither proposed that the United States protect and augment its strategic offensive striking power, reorganize the defense establishment, coordinate the free world's procurement and use of vital resources, educate the public to the dangers of a Soviet attack, and strengthen passive defenses (5–8). On this last point, Gaither explained, "A 'fall-out shelter program' may in our final deliberations be recommended as the only feasible protection for millions of people who will be increasingly exposed to the hazards of radiation. We frankly confess surprise that a fallout shelter program may be recommended. Our initial skepticism is yielding to the analysis of the megatonnage which will elude the best defensive systems now predictable" (7).

On November 7, the Gaither committee presented its complete report to the NSC. Five committee members participated in describing specific parts of the report. Sprague introduced the committee's task and discussed the timetable on which the committee based its conclusions. Wiesner addressed the need for expanding active defenses. William Webster made a presentation on shelters. Robert Calkins gave a briefing on the costs and feasibility of the committee's recommendations. Finally, Foster summarized the proposed changes in defense organization and offered some concluding remarks.[171]

The committee members wasted little time defining the Soviet threat in the final report. Instead, the committee accepted the basic American Cold War attitude that the Soviet Union sought world domination. It stated, "We have found no evidence in Russian foreign and military policy since 1945 to refute the conclusion that the USSR intentions are expansionist, and that her great efforts to build military power go beyond any concepts of Soviet defense." [172] The threat as the committee members envisioned it encompassed both economic and military factors.

Although it recognized the current economic superiority of the United States, the committee viewed this advantage as fleeting. It argued that while the United States was economically much superior to the Soviet Union, this difference was shrinking at a rapid rate. When coupled with the Soviet Union's emphasis on military spending rather than on producing consumer goods, the decline of U.S. economic strength in comparison to the Soviet Union seemed even more stark. The Gaither report emphasized that while the two adversaries presently spent almost equal amounts on defense, current trends in spending indicated that the Soviet Union would surpass the United States in defense spending by the 1960s. It concluded: "This extraordinary concentration of the Soviet economy on military power and heavy industry makes . . . available economic resources sufficient to finance both the rapid expansion of their impressive military capability and their politico-economic offensive by which, through diplomacy, propaganda and subversion, they seek to extend the Soviet orbit" (4).

The committee found the Soviet military threat closely paralleling the economic one. After examining recent military and technological developments, the committee presented a picture of an ever-strengthening Communist menace. It stressed that the Soviet development of atomic weapons, long-range aircraft, both ICBMs and IRBMs, a huge submarine force, an extensive air defense system, and an army composed of 175 divisions posed a serious threat to the United States and its allies. Together with the economic threat, the Soviet Union's growing military strength challenged the supremacy of U.S. world power (4–5).

The committee issued three "broad-brush" opinions. First, the active defense systems currently in place and those planned for the future offered little defense against a determined Soviet attack. Second, the passive defense measures designed to protect the civilian population provided little or no protection from the effects of a nuclear blast and/or radioactive fallout. Finally, because of the low levels of both active and passive defenses, the security of the United States rested primarily on SAC. The committee warned, "The current vulnerability of SAC to surprise attack during a period of lessened world tension (i.e. a time when SAC is not on a SAC 'alert' status), and the threat posed to SAC by the prospects of an early Russian ICBM capability, call for prompt remedial action" (5).

The committee made several recommendations to help strengthen U.S. continental and civilian defenses. The highest priority was to reduce SAC vulnerability and to increase the strategic retaliatory capability of U.S. nuclear forces. SAC forces, the committee argued, should be able to react with a warning of between seven and twenty-two minutes. Additional air bases needed to be constructed to augment the dispersal of strategic forces. Active defenses surrounding SAC bases should be strengthened through the use of Nike-Hercules or Talos surface-to-air missiles. Additionally, the committee emphasized the need to accelerate and expand the introduction of both ICBMs and IRBMs into U.S. strategic retaliatory forces. It recommended expanding the number of planned IRBMs and ICBMs from 60 to 240 and from 80 to 600, respectively. Finally, it stressed that the United States needed to improve the ability of its military forces to wage limited operations that fell short of general war (6–7).

In addition, the committee advocated programs of slightly less priority. The committee made its recommendations based on the belief that "protection of the civil population is a national problem requiring a national remedy" (10). It estimated that if the Soviet Union launched a nuclear attack, the American civil population would suffer between 70 and 150

Nike-Hercules Missile. The Gaither committee recommended install-
ing Nike-Hercules surface-to-air missiles for defense around Strategic
Air Command bases. (Dwight D. Eisenhower Library)

million casualties (between 35 and 75 percent of the estimated 1965 population) (18–20). It questioned the capability of the United States to acquire sufficient warning of a Soviet attack to initiate civil defense plans and
to notify the population if an attack was indeed underway (7–8). It concluded that the implementation of a $25 billion program of fallout shelters
and civil defense planning "would symbolize *our will to survive,* and our

Talos guided missile. The Gaither committee viewed the deployment of the Talos surface-to-air missile around U.S. military bases as essential for protecting the country's retaliatory capabilities. (National Archives)

understanding of our responsibilities in the nuclear age" (22; emphasis in original).

The committee also made recommendations in other areas. It stressed the need to improve the organization of the Defense Department so that it could effectively incorporate scientific and technological advances into its programs. It emphasized the importance of obtaining a greater understanding of Soviet intentions through hard intelligence. Finally, it argued that any changes in U.S. policies to reduce its vulnerability needed to be integrated with a broader foreign policy that would insure that allied countries would not see it as "a retreat to 'Fortress America'" (11).

The committee calculated that these recommendations would cost approximately $44 billion spread over five years (FY 1959–FY 1963). The active defense measures, including the reduction of SAC vulnerability, the construction of missile defense systems, and the expansion of U.S. military capabilities, would cost $19 billion, while the measures to protect the civilian population with improved radar and fallout shelters would cost $25 billion (22). The committee concluded that the United States could afford these programs although they "would necessitate . . . an increase in taxes, a somewhat larger federal debt, substantial economies in other government expenditures, and curbs on inflation" (12).

The committee stressed the importance of implementing these recommendations immediately or risk losing the military advantage to the Soviet Union. It argued that during the next two years, 1958 and 1959, the United States would be in a position to launch a decisive attack on the Soviet Union if necessary, while at the same time, it would remain able to negotiate from a position of strength. Beyond this period, the committee expressed grave concerns about the future of the United States. "The next two years," the committee emphasized, "seem to be critical. If we fail to act at once, the risk in our opinion will be unacceptable" (14).[173]

After the presentation to the NSC, Sprague and Foster were granted one more opportunity to express the committee's concerns to the president. At this invitation-only meeting, Sprague presented information that he believed was even too sensitive for the NSC.[174] He wanted to warn the president about the vulnerability of SAC.[175] He believed that one of the best ways to minimize the vulnerability was to obtain better intelligence of Soviet intentions and capabilities. He argued that the acquisition of strategic warning and hard intelligence of a planned Soviet attack "would be extraordinarily important to the United States and permit it to take an aggressive reaction, rather than just a retaliatory reaction."[176] While it is unclear what Sprague exactly meant by "aggressive reaction," at least three members of the Gaither committee thought that the United States should launch a preventive war.[177]

Conclusions

Why did the Gaither committee reach the conclusions that it did? The evidence points to two primary reasons. First, when Eisenhower established the committee, he was asking for assistance from people who had already developed opinions about Soviet intentions and U.S. and Soviet military capabilities. As noted in earlier chapters, many of the committee members had previously examined topics such as active and passive defense and SAC vulnerability. In addition, most of them had been associated with organizations or specific policies that influenced their thinking. When taking into consideration Sprague's recommendations for more spending on continental defense, Killian and Hill's advocacy for improved early warning radar, Doolittle and Kelly's support for reducing SAC's vulnerability, and

Berkner and Nelson's arguments concerning civil defense, the conclusions the committee reached should not have been a surprise. The committee members entered this study with backgrounds that were bound to influence the way they interpreted the available evidence.

A second reason for their conclusions is that the evidence they collected and used to evaluate the effectiveness of U.S. active and passive defenses seemed to confirm their preconceived beliefs. Some of the most important information that the committee used were the intelligence estimates produced by the CIA and military services. The NIEs revealed a growing apprehension of the Soviet threat and an emphasis on increasing Soviet capabilities. While they did not predict a Soviet attack, they did not rule out that possibility. Furthermore, as the two superpowers approached nuclear parity, the NIEs predicted that the Soviets would probably become more assertive on the periphery, increasing the risk of a war arising from miscalculation.

One of the fundamental problems that helped skew U.S. intelligence estimates was the lack of careful analysis of Soviet intentions. U.S. officials and analysts assumed that the Soviet Union sought world domination and would use military force, if necessary, to achieve it. As shown earlier, Doolittle echoed this theme when he testified that the Soviet goal was "world communization and world domination." The Gaither committee never carefully considered why the Soviet Union would want to dominate the world or assume the risks it would have to take to do so.[178] In his analysis of the influence of perception on policymakers, Robert Jervis provides an apt comparison to the mindset of the Gaither committee. He argues that "all too often statesmen assume that their opposite numbers see the world as they see it, fail to devote sufficient resources to determining whether this is actually true, and have much more confidence in their beliefs about the other's perceptions than the evidence warrants."[179]

By assuming Soviet hostile intentions, policymakers and intelligence analysts heightened the importance and the difficulty of analyzing Soviet capabilities and U.S. vulnerabilities. As the Gaither committee members attempted to estimate Soviet strategic capabilities, they were hampered by Soviet leaders' exaggerations of their country's military capabilities and by the lack of concrete intelligence. Two leading scholars of Soviet propaganda in the late 1950s and early 1960s claim, "For four years [1957–1961], Khrushchev and other Soviet leaders gave every indication in their public statements that they were indeed in a hurry to capitalize on their initial advantage and that they were bent on acquiring a large force of first-generation ICBM's." [180] During its deliberations, the Gaither committee also had to contemplate threatening statements from within the Soviet Union. One week after the launch of *Sputnik,* Khrushchev claimed, "We now have all the rockets we need: long-range rockets, intermediate-range rockets and short-range rockets." [181] Commander in Chief of the Soviet Air Force Air Marshall K. A. Vershinin was even more threatening:

> The calculation that America's remoteness will safeguard it from military blows in case of another world war is no longer tenable. Great distances will no longer play a decisive role in the age of reactor technology and atomic energy. What was inaccessible before has now become quite accessible. The modern means of air attack which have tremendous speeds and can operate over vast distances, are capable of striking at any point of the globe. The means of conveyance for hydrogen bombs, the most formidable weapons, make it possible to bring them instantly to the remotest areas of any continent of the world by intercontinental ballistic missiles. . . .
>
> It stands to reason that should the adversary make use of these weapons, the Soviet Union would suffer losses. But these losses would be smaller than those of the countries with a greater density of population and greater concentration of industries.
>
> This applies, above all, to the west European countries and to the United States of America. . . . Many of the major cities of the United States and some Western countries may, in the event of war, be attacked by rockets and bombers as well as by submarines. [182]

Compounding the difficulties created by Soviet bombast, intelligence analysts who estimated Soviet capabilities had to rely on the few photographs provided by the U-2 or other spy planes, electronic intercepts from along Soviet borders, interviews with political refugees, Soviet announcements and published statements, observations of Soviet military parades, and extrapolations of manufacturing capabilities. Needless to say, their conclusions were speculative. As Herbert York recalled, in calculating estimates of the number of ICBMs the Soviet Union would build, he assumed it would produce the greatest number of missiles possible. Having accepted Soviet hostile intentions, the Gaither committee believed that the Russians would increase their military capabilities to maximum levels.

Once the committee determined that the Soviet Union posed a threat and concluded that it was producing weapons at maximum levels, it had to decide where the United States was vulnerable and how the country should respond. Based on the committee's assumptions and the information it examined, several of its recommendations were obvious. Many of its members had already concluded that if SAC was made less vulnerable through dispersal and by reducing reaction times, it would pose a much greater deterrent to the Soviet Union. Others had realized that shelters could reduce the vulnerability of the civilian population. These conclusions were confirmed in their analyses of other studies. Whether produced by some government agency, by the RAND Corporation, or by some other organization, the reports examined by the Gaither committee presented a consistent conclusion—the vulnerability of the United States could be reduced by a combination of active and passive defenses.

A final factor that must be considered in explaining why the Gaither committee reached the conclusions that it did are the debates concerning various military strategies. The committee advocated increasing U.S. nuclear striking power, building active and passive defenses, constructing a nationwide shelter system, and expanding the military's capabilities for limited military operations. This last recommendation was of particular importance to the strategic debates of 1957. Many strategists, including Nitze and Lincoln, had published their views on limited war. Kissinger's study of nuclear weapons and U.S. foreign policy was particularly influential. The Gaither committee's recommendation to augment U.S. limited war capabilities reveals the influence of these arguments.

The Influence of the Gaither Report on the Eisenhower Administration in 1958

Four decades after the meeting of the Gaither committee, mystery still surrounds how Eisenhower and his advisers actually reacted to the November report. Did the president simply reject the report as a product of war-mongering extremists? Did he have access to intelligence information that undermined the basis of the committee's conclusions? Was he so blinded by his devotion to a balanced budget and controlling inflation that he failed to see an actual Soviet threat? Was his willingness to accept only some of the committee's conclusions and recommendations a product of an astute understanding of U.S. economic, military, and political power, or was it simple fortune?

The Gaither committee's findings raised some significant issues. Its assessment of Soviet military capabilities posed serious questions for U.S. security. If the committee's conclusions were accurate, the president faced a real dilemma. He based his approach to government on carefully balancing the nation's many needs and responsibilities. He once told a friend that "the critical problem of our time is to find and stay on the path that marks the way of logic between conflicting arguments advanced by extremists on both sides of almost every economic, political and international problem that arises."[1] Now, however, the Gaither committee was making recommendations that would fundamentally alter the balance on which Eisenhower's policies were based. To accept such consequences, the president had to be convinced that the United States was really at risk.

One of Eisenhower's most pressing concerns in contemplating how to handle the committee's findings was to determine what impact the proposals would have on the economy. He feared that increasing defense spending to the levels proposed by the committee would create budget deficits and inflation. If either of these economic problems developed, Eisenhower believed, the federal government would have to regiment the economy through such policies as higher taxes, price controls, and rationing. At all costs, he wanted to avoid these infringements on individual rights.

Eisenhower turned to the NSC and other government agencies to address the many issues raised by the Gaither report. Paul Nitze identified some of them when he recalled four questions that perplexed the committee and remained to be answered by the president himself and his closest aides:

1. "What is it we [the United States] should be attempting to deter by our nuclear offensive and defensive armament under conditions which seem likely to arise in the foreseeable future?"[2]
2. "In the years ahead is it to our interest that there be more or less emphasis upon nuclear weapons and nuclear strategy?"[3]
3. "Should we prepare primarily for a strategy of disarming the U.S.S.R. in a strike which precedes the receipt of an attack by the U.S.S.R., or should we prepare primarily for a strategy of deterrence through having a capability to do unacceptable damage to the Russians through a retaliatory blow—even though we had been struck first?"[4]
4. "How much emphasis should be given to quick reaction capabilities and how much to delayed reaction capabilities?"[5]

Eisenhower and his advisers spent most of the first half of 1958 attempting to answer these questions. Between January and July, the committee's recommendations remained at the forefront of the Eisenhower administration's deliberations concerning national security issues. The first three NSC meetings of 1958 dealt primarily with the Gaither committee and the comments made by the various government agencies concerning specific recommendations. Beyond these meetings, the NSC over the next six months periodically examined issues raised by the committee. In particular, the administration evaluated ways to limit SAC vulnerability; accelerate ballistic missile capabilities, including ICBMs, IRBMs, and the Polaris system; improve limited military operations capabilities; reorganize the defense establishment; improve continental defenses; and implement various shelter strategies. It can be argued that the Gaither committee did not present any revolutionary new ideas or programs, but "it certainly helped, and pushed and prodded" many of them.[6]

The National Mood and Initial Reactions to the Gaither Report

By the time the NSC received the Gaither report on November 7, 1957, Eisenhower was already under intense pressure to modify his national security programs. The launch of *Sputnik* and the Soviet announcement of a successful ICBM test had raised considerable public concern about U.S. military strength.[7] Previously, Eisenhower had been able to quell criticisms of his defense policies by reminding the American people of his widespread experience and knowledge in these fields. After October 1957, things were different. Eisenhower's status as a war hero and popular president was no longer sufficient to allay the people's doubts about weaknesses in U.S. security. In late October, *Aviation Week* argued that Eisenhower and his advisers "have been and still are embarked on a fiscal policy that is shaking the military, scientific and industrial foundations of our national defense system so badly that only emergency action with the utmost speed will prevent a major deterioration of our atomic airpower strength in relation to the Soviets in the immediate future."[8] The following week the publication claimed, "In the face of this overwhelming mass of evidence on the growth of Soviet military strength from new technological weapons, our own national leadership has been executing a policy aimed at reducing our own atomic-airpower strength in being, artificially retarding the pace of our military technological development and thoroughly discouraging the best efforts of both military and scientific leaders concerned with this vital program."[9]

Similar concerns were shown by the general population. A public opinion poll in late November 1957 found only 26 percent of Americans satisfied with U.S. defense policies and 53 percent advocating that they be reexamined.[10] After the embarrassing failure of the Vanguard rocket in December, the national mood grew more somber. *U.S. News & World Report* claimed that the "U.S., today, is far behind Soviet Russia in the big race for superrockets."[11] A week later, it reported a growing awareness and fear of nuclear war. "These new fears about war," it stated, "seemed more immediate and personal than war fears in the past. When past wars threatened, people worried about whether their sons might be called into service. . . . Now, all at once, war became a personal thing for everyone— something that could hit you, yourself, right in your home."[12]

Nevil Shute captured the mood of disillusionment and despair in 1957 in his best-selling novel *On the Beach,* which vividly portrays the consequences of nuclear proliferation and radioactive fallout. Shute traces how survivors of a nuclear war that has destroyed the Northern Hemisphere cope with the knowledge that the radiation released in the conflict will kill them within six months. As the characters attempt to deal with their impending deaths, they struggle to understand how the world could come to an end this way. Shute moralizes through the character of Peter Holmes, "Some kinds of silliness just can't be stopped. . . . I mean, if a couple of hundred million people all decide that their national honour requires them to drop cobalt bombs upon their neighbor, well, there's not much that you or I can do about it."[13]

The Soviet Union did nothing to discourage such fears. During Eisenhower's second term, he faced a Soviet disinformation campaign designed to raise Soviet military and technological prestige while undermining U.S. strength.[14] In November 1957, Khrushchev gave two seemingly threatening interviews. He argued, "If war is not averted, the Americans will experience the most devastating war ever known to mankind. It will rage not only in Europe and Asia, but, with not less fury, in the United States."[15] A little over a week later, he bragged, "The fact that the Soviet Union was the first to launch an artificial earth satellite, which within a month was followed by another, says a lot. If necessary, tomorrow we can launch 10, 20 satellites. All that is required for this is to replace the warhead of an intercontinental ballistic rocket with the necessary instruments. There is a satellite for you."[16]

In December, *Newsweek* interviewed senators and members of the House from both parties about the feelings of their constituents and found, "The American people have been severely shaken by the sputnik era and are losing confidence in their leadership." The interviews indicated these common feelings: "a crisis in national confidence produced by the conviction that the Soviet Union was now the world leader in science and technology"; "an aching need for bold leadership—and a shaken faith in the soldier-statesman whom they had twice elected as the man best qualified to deal with national security"; and "a readiness to make the sacrifices necessary to 'catch up.'"[17] In an analysis of public opinion in the aftermath of *Sputnik,* one scholar concludes:

> In general, American opinion in the post-Sputnik era may be characterized (a) as being aware of foreign and defense problems and attributing substantial importance to them; (b) as being aware of American vulnerability in the present military situation; (c) as having been shocked, in the short run, by the Soviet demonstration of scientific and technological prowess, and as having lost confidence in the conduct of American foreign policy in the immediate post-Sputnik period; and (d) as having substantially recovered from this loss of confidence and accepted the Administration interpretation of the relative positions of the United States and the U.S.S.R.[18]

Eisenhower was quite dismayed by such fears. He did not understand why Americans could not recognize the continued superiority of U.S. military strength. Although he was quite concerned about Soviet technological achievements and increasing Soviet military strength, he disagreed with those who criticized his policies. He believed that current and planned U.S. defense programs would continue to deter the Soviet Union and provide adequate military forces to handle any limited war situations. After Gaither's presentation on November 4, Eisenhower explained that "he thought our strategic forces are stronger than the group may have indicated." He then stressed, "With regard to the ICBM, here is one case in which a central position is not an advantage to the Soviets. The free world holds the periphery and can pose a threat from a multiple of points." [19]

On the same day the Gaither committee presented its report to the NSC, Eisenhower began a campaign to reassure the American people of the country's continued military strength and technological excellence. In a series of public appearances, he attempted to address Americans' concerns and discuss what the United States was going to do to improve its strategic position. Many of his comments reflected his initial assessments of the Gaither committee's conclusions. He told a national television audience that advances in science and technology would enhance, rather than undermine, national security. In particular, he explained that technological advancements would improve U.S. defenses. [20]

On November 13, Eisenhower delivered a widely publicized speech in Oklahoma City. He identified four tasks for U.S. military forces: possessing sufficient retaliatory strength to deter the Soviet Union, insuring flexibility in military capabilities in order to meet any form of aggression with an effective response, maintaining continental defenses in a high state of readiness, and retaining reserve strength to handle any emergency situations. [21] To fulfill these tasks, he said that a high level of citizen participation would be necessary, as well as a willingness to bear any additional financial burdens. He concluded by detailing U.S. plans:

> To continue, over the years just ahead, to maintain the Strategic Air Command in a state of maximum safety, strength, and alert, as new kinds of threats develop, will entail additional costs. This means accelerating the dispersal of Strategic Air Command to additional bases. . . . We have been providing facilities for response to emergency alarm. This, too, should be speeded up. . . . To achieve maximum possible warning of any future attack, we must carry on additional improvements throughout our warning line that are

now scientifically feasible. . . . Another need is to develop an active defense missile system against missiles. . . . To increase retaliatory power, we shall be adding long-range missiles.[22]

While the president attempted to encourage the American people, the NSC asked various government agencies to make initial comments about the Gaither committee's findings. It requested that the Defense Department evaluate the feasibility of the committee's recommendations related to the military. It asked the State Department to examine how the implementation of the committee's conclusions would affect U.S. allies. It ordered the Bureau of Budget, the Council of Economic Advisors (CEA), and the Treasury Department to assess the impact of the committee's recommendations on the nation's economy. It asked the CIA to examine ways to improve intelligence and to acquire strategic warning of a Soviet attack. Finally, it requested that the FCDA, in collaboration with other agencies, study the committee's shelter recommendations.[23]

Secretary of Defense Neil McElroy assigned the JCS responsibility for developing the military's response to the Gaither committee's findings. The JCS completed its report in early December and reached several significant conclusions. It opposed the extension of the DEW line south of Midway because there was little likelihood that the Soviet Union would attack from that direction.[24] It directed that the protection of SAC bases be augmented.[25] It recommended dispersing SAC's forces to a greater number of airfields.[26] It stressed that "an anti-ICBM is an urgent requirement."[27] Finally, it argued that "a reasonably effective air defense system against all types of aircraft and missiles, including ballistic missiles, can be achieved."[28]

The JCS made three other recommendations. First, it agreed with the Gaither committee that the country's limited military operations capabilities needed to be reevaluated in relation to all U.S. military objectives and in terms of the Soviet threat and the resources available during the period under consideration.[29] In addition, the JCS accepted that a fallout shelter program was "the only feasible means of providing shelter protection that can be undertaken on a nation-wide scale at the present time."[30] Finally, it supported the construction of hardened ICBM launch sites as soon as feasible.[31]

Defense Secretary McElroy presented similar recommendations to the NSC in December. He addressed four issues: improving SAC reaction times, protecting SAC bases, accelerating the development of IRBMs and ICBMs, and strengthening the country's capabilities to wage limited military operations. He explained that during 1958 and 1959, defense officials were primarily concerned with the threat from enemy bombers. In the years that followed, they saw the main threat emanating from missiles. He recommended that by January 1958 SAC should be able to launch 157 bombers with 30 to 120 minutes' warning. By July 1959, he expected SAC to get 515 planes off the ground with the same warning.[32] After the introduction of ICBMs, with the expected reduction of warning time to fewer than 15 minutes, McElroy requested that SAC be able to launch 240 bombers in July 1960 and 465 by July 1961 with 15 minutes' notice.[33] As far as reducing SAC's vulnerability, the defense secretary ordered the construction of Nike-Hercules surface-to-air missile sites around SAC bases. He advised protecting 4 of 31 SAC bases by January 1958, 16 of 44 bases by July 1959, and 29 of 52 bases by July 1960.[34] While recommending these air defenses, he viewed the construction of shelters for SAC bombers as impractical.[35]

While the Gaither committee had recommended augmenting the number of U.S. IRBMs from 60 to 240 and ICBMs from 80 to 600 by 1963, the Defense Department requested increases on a smaller scale. Defense officials believed that the first IRBMs and ICBMs would quickly become obsolete, and more money should be spent on developing second-generation missiles; therefore, the Defense Department initially recommended the construction of only 120 IRBMs (60 Thor and 60 Jupiter missiles) and 130 ICBMs (90 Atlas and 40 Titan missiles).[36] The committee also advised increasing U.S. capabilities to wage limited military operations. McElroy agreed that "action should be taken to augment the capabilities and increase the readiness of U.S. and allied forces which are organized and equipped to combat local aggression and to increase the mobility and flexibility of these forces." [37]

The NSC asked the State Department to analyze the possible impact of the implementation of the committee's recommendations on U.S. allies. There was concern that if the United States constructed fallout shelters, U.S. allies might perceive such an action as a move toward isolationism. The State Department argued that if the Eisenhower administration decided to build shelters, it needed to offer assurances to its allies that it would remain committed to them. The State Department stressed, "If not carefully integrated into our foreign policies, any substantial new programs to reduce the vulnerability of the United States might be widely misinterpreted as a fundamental change in U.S. policy which could have most serious effects on U.S. relations with our allies and the uncommitted nations." [38]

The three agencies dealing with the economic implications of the Gaither committee's recommendations—the Bureau of Budget, the CEA, and the Treasury Department—expressed serious doubts about some of the committee's economic assumptions. The Budget Bureau asserted that the Gaither committee had made two key mistakes in calculating the economic implications of its programs, namely, overestimating the future growth of the federal budget and underestimating nondefense expenses. [39] The CEA emphasized that the committee had exaggerated federal revenues and underrated the inflationary impact of its recommendations. [40] The Treasury Department concluded that the committee had failed to recognize the economic costs and consequences of its recommendations. Treasury officials were particularly concerned that the implementation of the Gaither committee's programs would result in an overly regulated economy and would lead to demands from the American people for the immediate construction of shelters. [41]

The last two agencies to present their evaluations of the Gaither committee's conclusions were the CIA and the FCDA. The CIA agreed with the committee that the United States needed to strengthen its intelligence-gathering capabilities. [42] The FCDA supported the committee's recommendations for assigning the shelter program the highest priority. [43]

As the various government agencies examined the Gaither committee's recommendations, Eisenhower was completing his proposed FY 1959 budget. Before *Sputnik,* the administration was trying to limit defense spending so that it could meet the budget guidelines produced by Congress earlier in the summer. [44] After October 4, priorities changed. Amid the uproar and shock created by the Russian achievement, people questioned how the Soviet Union could have made such a technological advancement before the United States and wondered what the president would do about it. [45] Administration officials now deemed that the current proposals for the FY 1959 budget were inadequate.

At a meeting between Eisenhower and his military advisers on November 11, the president explained that the country had to raise the pay of its military personnel and accelerate the alert and dispersal of SAC. Furthermore, he added, "We must keep up our 15 carriers, and we must build submarines." [46] Considering his earlier views, his pronouncement about defense spending was surprising. He "stressed that there is nothing sacrosanct about the $38 billion figure [for defense spending]. . . . He felt we could do what needs to be done for approximately $39 billion or $39.5 billion." [47]

At two other meetings during the next few weeks, Eisenhower articulated why the additional appropriations were needed and how the decisions about them should be made. He explained that he wanted to approach proposals for increased expenditures for national security programs "not on the basis of 'can we do it in response to the public outcry,' but 'should we do it.'" [48] To obtain the right balance in his proposals, Eisenhower understood the importance of both meeting military requirements and building the confidence of the people. He described in December how he was "really giving a lot of thought to what is the [defense budget] figure that will create confidence. He thought that a feeling of greater confidence in the security sphere might go over into economic confidence as well, and thus help the economic picture." Eisenhower added that "he thought two-thirds of the supplementary funds are more to stabilize public opinion than to meet a real need for acceleration." [49]

Eisenhower did not rush to judgment or try to make immediate decisions in response to either *Sputnik* or the Gaither report. He wanted his advisers to analyze carefully what changes and additions needed to be made in his administration's national security policies. By the third week in November, Eisenhower received preliminary figures for additions of $2.14 billion to the planned $37.66 billion defense budget for FY 1959. The increases would cover pay raises for military personnel, improvements in SAC alert and dispersal, enhanced ICBM detection, accelerated IRBM and ICBM programs, increased research and development, new satellite and outer space programs, improvements in antisubmarine warfare, and the reorganization of the Army's divisions along Pentomic lines. [50]

Discussions involving the president came to a temporary halt when he suffered a mild stroke on November 25. After convalescing in Denver, Colorado, however, Eisenhower was able to resume most of his activities by early December. When he returned to the White House, he had to decide what additional increases needed to be made to the FY 1958 defense budget, since the additional appropriations in the FY 1959 budget would not go into place until July 1958. McElroy proposed and Eisenhower agreed to seek an additional $1.26 billion for the FY 1958 defense budget to accelerate and/or augment the Polaris missile system, SAC dispersal, missile detection, and the development of IRBMs and ICBMs.[51] While reactions to *Sputnik* could have accounted for some of these increases, the specific recommendations indicate the influence of the Gaither committee's conclusions. Robert Cutler, Eisenhower's assistant for national security affairs, explained, "Many of the measures assigned the highest relative value by the [Gaither] panel have been included in the Defense Department program for FY 1959 and the augmentations for FY 1958."[52]

Leak of the Gaither Report

On November 23, the White House released a statement that identified the members of the Gaither committee's steering and advisory panels and announced that the committee had performed a secret study for the administration.[53] The statement did not describe the activities of the committee or the contents of its report. Not surprisingly, information about the committee began to filter out after the announcement, and requests for access to the report bombarded the White House.[54] Noted *New York Times* columnist Arthur Krock hypothesized about the contents of the report after hearing a speech that committee member William Foster delivered in early December at West Point. "We," Foster proclaimed, "must get away from the strange dichotomy with which we have traditionally viewed force, refusing to consider it except as a last resort, then approaching it in a crusading manner with a 'punish-the-bandit' view which has been prevalent in our recent conflicts."[55] In his analysis, Krock wrote, "This [speech] strongly implies that the [Gaither] report to the N.S.C. gave the most powerful support thus far in the United States to the military policy of striking an enemy before an assault he obviously is about to make on this country."[56]

In addition to its specific recommendations, the Gaither committee advised the president and the NSC that the administration needed to raise public awareness about the steps the nation had to take to meet the Soviet challenge. In late November, Foster met with Eisenhower about this proposal, and the president "seemed anxious to mobilize public opinion."[57] They decided that Foster should arrange "an off the record unpartisan discussion of national security matters."[58] From this discussion, the White House hoped to gain support for both its mutual security and defense reorganization programs.[59]

Sparked by Eisenhower's apparent interest, Foster invited more than twenty national leaders to his home to discuss the challenges facing the nation.[60] Along with Foster, the other Gaither committee members present included Paul Nitze, Colonel George Lincoln, and Frank Stanton. Other guests at dinner were Roswell Gilpatric, Laurence Rockefeller, Elmo Roper, John Cowles, Thomas Dewey, Frank Lindsay, Eric Johnson, Hugh Calkins, Bradley Gaylord, Harold Boeschenstein, George McGhee, and Vice President Richard Nixon.[61] The group's actual discussions were not recorded. However, one reporter described the meeting as an attempt by Eisenhower to organize "a group of leading Americans who feel that the country requires a special, abrupt and continuous alarm bell on the danger from the Soviet Union."[62]

On December 20, any remaining secrecy concerning the Gaither committee's conclusions disintegrated in a front-page story in the *Washington Post*. The headlines read: "NATO VOTES MISSILE BASES, PEACE TRY; SECRET REPORT SEES U.S. IN GRAVE PERIL." In the ensuing article, reporter Chalmer Roberts disclosed the committee's most important findings. He wrote:

> The still top-secret Gaither Report portrays a United States in the gravest danger in its history.
>
> It pictures the nation moving in frightening course to the status of a second-class power.
>
> It shows an America exposed to an almost immediate threat from the missile-bristling Soviet Union.
>
> It finds America's long-term prospect one of cataclysmic peril in the face of rocketing Soviet military might and of a powerful, growing Soviet economy and technology which will bring new political propaganda and psychological assaults on freedom all around the globe.[63]

Roberts's article intensified requests that the report be released. George Reedy, a key legal assistant of Senator Lyndon Johnson on the Senate preparedness subcommittee, recalled that "one of the big struggles was to get hold of a copy of the Gaither Report."[64] During the subcommittee's hearings between November 1957 and January 1958, Johnson stated he had held between ten and fifteen conversations with administration officials about releasing the report.[65] Senator Stuart Symington, an outspoken critic of Eisenhower's policies, claimed that he had also taken part in about fifteen conversations with administration officials on the same issue.[66]

There remains much confusion as to the origin of the leaks of information from the Gaither report. At least eighty-five copies of the report were distributed, and most of those involved with the committee had access to it.[67] Several committee members lobbied for the release of the report or at least a sanitized description of its contents.[68] *Newsweek* reported that Roberts's article was based on more than twenty interviews.[69] Killian recalled that Roberts had received a general draft of the report that Jerome Wiesner developed in fuller detail.[70]

Public knowledge of the report made the administration's evaluations more difficult. Eisenhower and his advisers had great freedom in assessing the report's worth as an internal document. However, to the public, which was still reeling from the shock of *Sputnik,* the report took on another significance: it seemed to symbolize U.S. weaknesses. Eisenhower had no assurances that the release of a sanitized version of the report would alleviate fears, but by refusing to do so, he was creating the impression that he had something to hide.[71]

Through most of January 1958, the administration remained split over whether to release some version of the report. The debate within the administration focused on whether the release of the report would quell national fears or whether it would multiply demands for more information about other presidential advisory panels. Secretary of State Dulles, Vice President Nixon, and, at times, Eisenhower himself favored the release of a sanitized version.[72] Dulles reported that Nixon's "feelings are becoming strong that in order to kill it [the Gaither report] we should put something out."[73] This position, however, was balanced by Robert Cutler's adamant disapproval. Cutler explained, "There is no way in which to release to the American people information vital to the national security without it becoming available to those dedicated to destroying the American people."[74]

Eisenhower's final decision to withhold the report may have stemmed from the opposition to its release expressed by key Gaither committee members. In early January, Killian asked Gaither whether he would "be willing to prepare and release the substance of the recommendations contained in your Panel's report, without revealing information that I might consider must remain secret for the protection of the nation?"[75] Gaither responded that after discussing the request with Robert Sprague and James Perkins, he was opposed to the release of either the final report itself or a sanitized version. He argued that the former "would be a dangerous precedent for the invasion of executive privilege for receiving private advice," while the latter "would be ineffective and dangerously mislead-

Eisenhower and John Foster Dulles. Eisenhower and Secretary of State Dulles meet in January 1958 as the administration evaluates the Gaither report. (National Park Service/Dwight D. Eisenhower Library)

ing."[76] Echoing some of the same concerns, Eisenhower decided to deny all requests for the report. He told Senator Lyndon Johnson:

> Throughout history the President has withheld information whenever he found that what was sought was confidential or that its disclosure would jeopardize the nation's safety or the proper functioning of our Government.
>
> I mention this consideration because of my conviction, which I am sure you share, that in such a matter as this we must be careful to maintain the proper separation of powers between the Executive and Legislative Branches of the Government. . . .
>
> Only by preserving the confidential nature of such advice is it possible to assemble such groups or for the President to avail himself of such advice.[77]

Handling of the Gaither Committee Recommendations in 1958

At the same time that the president and his advisers wrestled with whether to release the Gaither report, Eisenhower presented his annual message to the Congress. He vividly described the threat posed by the Soviet Union:

The threat to our safety, and to the hope of the peaceful world, can be simply stated. It is communist imperialism. This threat is not something imagined by critics of the Soviets. Soviet spokesmen, from the beginning, have publicly and frequently declared their aim to expand their power, one way or another, throughout the world.

The threat has become increasingly serious as this expansionist aim has been reinforced by an advancing industrial, military, and scientific establishment.

But what makes the Soviet threat unique in history is its all-inclusiveness. Every human activity is pressed into service as a weapon of expansion. Trade, economic development, military power, arts, science, education, the whole world of ideas—all are harnessed to this same chariot of expansion.

The Soviets are, in short, waging total cold war.[78]

Eisenhower then identified eight specific areas that needed immediate attention. The U.S. military establishment required reorganization to facilitate more effective decision making and operations. The United States had to improve its military capabilities, especially in acquiring warning of a Soviet attack and in protecting and increasing retaliatory forces. The United States needed to continue its mutual aid programs. The United States had to expand trade. Congress needed to pass legislation to allow the freer exchange of scientific and technical information between the United States and its allies. The country needed to increase spending for education and research. The people had to be willing to accept additional burdens and sacrifices. Finally, the United States had to seek the peaceful exchange of information throughout the world.[79]

Less than a week later, the president presented to Congress his proposed FY 1959 budget and a request for supplementary funding for FY 1958. Eisenhower asked for an increase of approximately $1.3 billion in the current FY 1958 defense budget and an additional increase of $2.5 billion in the FY 1959 defense budget.[80] He explained that the increases did not reflect any substantial weaknesses in current U.S. military strength but would help the United States meet the challenges created by new scientific and technological advances. He argued, "Our defenses are strong today, both as a deterrent to war and for use as a crushing response to any attack. Now our concern is for the future."[81]

Congress acted quickly. On January 23, the House of Representatives voted unanimously to supplement the current FY 1958 budget by $1.26 billion. Congress allotted $218.6 million for SAC alert and dispersal plans,

$329 million for a ballistic missile detection system, $333.4 million for the acceleration of both IRBM and ICBM programs, $350 million for augmenting and accelerating the Polaris missile system, and $29 million for the SAGE air defense system.[82] The House stated that its purpose was "to accelerate and expand certain high priority programs in the interest of shortening the time by which our military capabilities will have been advanced so as to more arrestingly deter war and more swiftly and devastatingly respond to any attack. In short, it is to buy time."[83]

As the president and Congress implemented initial changes in U.S. national security programs in January, the NSC began to deliberate the Gaither committee's conclusions more fully. At the first NSC meeting of the new year, Deputy Defense Secretary Quarles presented his department's recommendations concerning the Gaither committee's proposals to expand U.S. ballistic missile capabilities. He presented a startling comparison of estimated U.S. and Soviet missile strength. He asserted that based on the best available intelligence estimates, the Soviet Union would have 10 ICBMs in 1958, 100 in 1959, and 500 by 1960. By comparison, he said the United States planned to have 10 ICBMs in 1959, 30 in 1960, and 50 in 1961. Even the addition of IRBMs did not make the picture much brighter. By 1961 the United States planned to have 120 IRBMs located in Europe and 3 nuclear submarines carrying 16 Polaris missiles each.[84]

Quarles reported that the Defense Department currently planned to have 130 ICBMs operational by the end of FY 1963 as opposed to the 600 recommended by the Gaither committee. He explained that the United States could potentially build 600, but the Defense Department questioned the practicality of committing so much money to first-generation missiles. "The problem," Quarles revealed, "was not the construction of the missiles, but building bases for them."[85] He argued that the selection, construction, and hardening of the bases would be very time-consuming and expensive. The Defense Department, moreover, was hesitant to make such a large commitment to first-generation missiles, which would soon be obsolete.[86]

In February, the Air Force began recommending an increase in the number of ICBMs to levels resembling those advocated by the Gaither committee. It recommended the construction of a 600-ICBM force by FY 1964.[87] The Navy also made requests concerning the Polaris missile submarines that were similar to those made in the Gaither report. It recommended accelerating the number of Polaris submarines to 3 in 1961, 13 in 1962, 25 in 1963, and 37 in 1964. By late February, it advised expediting the number of submarines from 1 in 1960 to 39 in 1964.[88]

In March 1958, the JCS asked for additional funding for other programs. It requested $400 million for the Polaris missile system, $100 million for developing solid-propellant IRBMs and ICBMs, and $100 million for the Titan ICBM.[89] Later, in the same month, the JCS recommended increasing the number of IRBM squadrons to 16 (240 missiles), just as the Gaither committee had requested.[90] The JCS based its decisions in part on a Weapons Systems Evaluation Group (WSEG) study of U.S. offensive and defensive capabilities that proposed hardening Atlas bases, acquiring more Titan missiles, and augmenting the number of Polaris submarines.[91]

In April, the NSC discussed the question of expanding the number of IRBMs. Secretary of Defense McElroy decided to request 12 squadrons (180 missiles). Eisenhower questioned why the country needed to expand its IRBM force beyond 120 missiles. He feared that they would become obsolete quickly and have to be scrapped.[92] Deputy Secretary Quarles told the president that the proposal for 12 squadrons had been selected as a compromise between the Gaither committee's recommendation of 16 squadrons (240 missiles) and the original Defense Department proposal of 8 squadrons (120 missiles). Quarles insisted that 180 missiles were the minimum needed to meet the proposed NATO deployment of IRBMs.[93] Although the recommendation did not meet his desire to limit spending, Eisenhower reluctantly agreed to the request.[94]

At the same time that administration officials were examining ballistic missile capabilities, they were also discussing how to reduce SAC vulnerability. The Gaither committee recommended five specific ways to reduce the vulnerability of U.S. retaliatory forces: increasing alert capabilities, dispersing SAC forces, obtaining greater warning, hardening SAC bases, and building anti-aircraft and antimissile defenses. In his memoirs, Eisenhower explained that of all the committee's recommendations, he "was personally interested most in the measures to put more SAC bombers on an alert status and to disperse our SAC bases."[95] With the exception of hardening SAC bases, the Eisenhower administration adopted these recommendations, at least in part.[96]

SAC worked under two scenarios in developing plans to reduce its reaction times. Under the first, the presumed Soviet attack would involve bombers that would be detected at least 30 minutes prior to reaching their targets. Until 1960, SAC expected any Soviet attack to provide this amount of warning. After 1960, SAC planned for the second scenario, in which the Soviet first strike would involve ballistic missiles. Under such an attack, SAC forces would receive less than 15 minutes' warning. One scholar aptly concludes, "It would be difficult to overstate the impact that this time reduction [after the introduction of the ICBM] had on the analysis of national security and on U.S. society."[97] At the end of January, SAC proposed the achievement of the following reaction times: by mid-1959, 515 bombers should be on 30-minute alert; by mid-1960, 321 should be on 15-minute alert; and by mid-1961, 465 should be on 15-minute alert.[98] In March, SAC again accelerated the implementation of 15-minute alert status. It proposed having 158 aircraft on 15-minute alert by mid-1958, 355 by mid-1959, 425 by mid-1960, and 480 by mid-1961.[99] Of these aircraft, SAC expected to have 85 B-52 bombers on 15-minute alert in 1959, 140 in 1960, and 165 in 1961.[100] SAC made substantial progress in achieving its goals. In October 1958, SAC commander Thomas Power announced, "Since initiating our alert force operations in October 1957, SAC has steadily progressed towards so posturing the force that one-third of the bombers can be launched within 15 minutes."[101] By May 1960, he could disclose the fulfillment of this goal.[102]

Tied closely to the reduction of reaction times was the Gaither committee's recommendation to disperse SAC forces to a larger number of airfields. The committee was concerned that U.S. nuclear retaliatory capabilities would be concentrated at a limited number of vulnerable airfields. It recommended the construction of additional SAC bases and possibly using non-SAC and/or commercial airfields as alternatives. In February 1958, Defense Secretary McElroy announced that the supplementary appropriations for FY 1958 and the funding contained in the FY 1959 budget would "provide for completion of the dispersal of the heavy bomber wings and of a substantial number of the medium bomber wings."[103] He told Senator Johnson's subcommittee that by 1960 all 33 B-52 squadrons would be located at their own bases.[104] As far as using non-SAC or commercial bases, both SAC and the JCS opposed the idea as unnecessary.[105]

While reducing the reaction time of SAC forces and dispersing SAC squadrons to more airfields won widespread support within the administration and in military circles, hardening SAC bases did not. The Gaither committee recommended building blast shelters to protect SAC aircraft, equipment, and personnel. The JCS and Defense Department concluded,

"Any program to harden other than the SAC numbered Air Force command control centers does not appear to be warranted at this time."[106] They explained that while hardening might protect personnel and planes, it would not prevent the destruction of the runways or reduce the dangers posed by radiation.[107]

In addition to the issues of alert, dispersal, and hardening, the Gaither committee made two other recommendations designed to reduce the vulnerability of SAC and to protect the continental United States. It advocated acquiring early warning of an attack and constructing active defenses against both aircraft and missiles. In October 1957, the JCS had identified major areas of weakness in U.S. defenses. It found that the United States would receive little warning of an attack carried out above 50,000 feet or below 2,000 feet, or launched by submarines.[108] It concluded that up to twenty-two SAC installations would receive no warning of a Soviet attack launched from submarines. Furthermore, even if the attack occurred at between 2,000 and 50,000 feet, some SAC bases would still receive little or no warning.[109]

In February 1958, the NSC issued NSC 5802, which described U.S. objectives and programs for continental defense. While it emphasized the need for an effective nuclear retaliatory capability, it also stressed, "The United States should continue to improve, and to maintain at a high state of readiness, an effective, integrated system of air surveillance, weapons, and control elements, providing defense in depth capable of detecting, identifying, engaging, and destroying enemy aircraft or missiles approaching over the North American Continent before they reach vital targets."[110] To achieve these objectives, the United States had to be able to detect a Soviet attack and possess the defensive capabilities to thwart the enemy's ability to reach its targets.

There were two types of detection that the United States could hope to achieve, the first being strategic warning that the Soviet Union was planning an attack. This type of warning was difficult to obtain since it depended on determining specific Soviet intentions prior to an attack. If strategic warning could not be achieved, the next best alternative was tactical warning: detecting the attack as soon as possible after it was initiated. The Gaither committee recommended improving U.S. capabilities in both areas, but it emphasized acquiring tactical warning since obtaining strategic warning was much more difficult.

The Soviet Union possessed, or would in the near future, the capability to launch an attack against the United States using airplanes, ICBMs, and submarine-launched missiles. Deputy Defense Secretary Quarles argued in January 1958 that while obtaining tactical warning was a desirable goal, it would be very expensive and could never provide 100 percent protection.[111] Nevertheless, Secretary McElroy approved spending $427 million to expand radar coverage of likely Soviet attack routes; the JCS recommended spending over $1 billion to acquire more anti-ICBM capabilities; and the Air Force began awarding contracts to companies that would study and implement an early warning system.[112]

After evaluating the Gaither committee's proposals for air defense weapons systems, the JCS decided to "provide for NIKE and/or HAWK protection at 55 SAC (41 bomber, 9 refueling and 5 missile) bases, with incidental protection afforded 15 (8 bomber, 6 refueling and 2 missile) additional SAC bases for a total of 70 projected bases, by end FY 1961."[113] Furthermore, it recommended "vigorous research" on the development of defenses against ICBMs.[114] It also emphasized that the "operational availability of BMEWS [Ballistic Missile Early Warning System] for ICBM should be actively pursued."[115]

Like the Gaither committee, the JCS and Defense Department were very concerned with advances in submarines capable of launching missiles. One joint committee of the Senate and the House of Representatives captured this fear when it argued, "The day is rapidly nearing when the Soviet Union can possess, first a few, and then a large fleet of intermediate-range ballistic missile-launching nuclear-propelled submarines. . . . Our existing and presently planned defensive system could not stop such a missile attack. Therein lies the peril."[116] Secretary McElroy echoed this view when he testified before the Johnson subcommittee that "the Navy did not request a [aircraft] carrier in the Fiscal '59 budget, electing instead to put the bulk of these funds against additional modern antisubmarine warfare readiness."[117]

The concern over the submarine threat led to an increase in the FY 1959 budget of $262 million more than had been requested prior to the Gaither committee report.[118] An even more telling indication of the fear generated by submarines was a JCS plan for dealing with them. The JCS argued that "the most practical solution [to the submarine threat] lies in establishing control over the launching submarine prior to the launching of its missiles. In peacetime, this control includes detection, tracking, identification, hold-down tactics, and in certain situations constituting an immediate and vital threat to the security of the United States, destruction of the submarine."[119]

One of the last Gaither committee recommendations concerned augmentation of U.S. limited military operations capabilities. The committee was very worried that the administration's reliance on nuclear weapons as the main deterrent against the Soviet Union reduced U.S. military options in the event of a crisis and made a nuclear war more likely. This concern was echoed by CIA analyst Raymond Garthoff, who argued that "the *employment* of nuclear and thermonuclear weapons is *necessary* in the United States concept [of war], but not in the Soviet one. The Soviets thus retain a greater freedom of choice. If a genuine stalemate in intercontinental capabilities is achieved in a prehostilities period, the United States might be endangered by the neutralization of its entire strategy, and hence of its ability to act, whereas the Soviet strategy would be served by this development" (emphasis in original).[120]

The debate over limited war capabilities coincided with General Nathan Twining's tenure as the JCS chairman. He later claimed that in the late 1950s, the JCS "never could . . . agree on a definition of limited war."[121] Civilian strategists had been debating various aspects of limited war strategies since at least 1954, with the discussions reaching a peak after the publication of Henry Kissinger's work in 1957. The Gaither committee did not recommend specific increases in limited war capabilities but did call for a study of whether the United States was prepared for such conflicts. The problem was that there was simply no consensus concerning an appropriate limited war strategy. Disputes centered on such issues as whether to use nuclear weapons, how to restrict the geographic areas of conflict, how to limit political objectives in a conflict, and exactly what forces were necessary to wage limited war.

Initially, the Defense Department opposed the creation of an interdepartmental committee to study U.S. limited military operations capabilities, as the Gaither committee recommended. It preferred to make its own study, independent of other government agencies. Its proposal ran into sharp opposition from the State Department. In fact, the State Department's Policy Planning Staff recommended that the NSC accelerate the creation of an interdepartmental panel to study limited military operations capabilities.[122] When the Defense Department, at a January NSC meeting, recommended a delay in the study, Secretary of State Dulles raised serious questions about a postponement.[123] He stressed the importance of a study of limited military operations by an interdepartmental committee, which could examine the varied implications of increasing U.S. capabilities.[124]

On March 5, the NSC ordered the creation of a study group to examine current and future limited war capabilities. For purposes of the study, the NSC stated that "*Limited Military Operations* include any armed conflict short of an overt engagement of U.S. and USSR armed forces which has been directed by or concurred in by competent political authority. There exists the possibility of isolated incidents involving small units of the U.S. and USSR forces which would not lead to war. The degree of participation in limited military operations by the United States may vary from furnishing of military supplies to the engagement of a portion of the U.S. armed forces."[125] The study group was charged with discovering the most likely areas for U.S. involvement in a limited war and with determining whether U.S. military forces possessed adequate strength to deal with such situations.[126]

While the study group performed its examination, the NSC discussed limited military operations capabilities in its review of U.S. basic national security policies in May 1958. Cutler introduced the subject by explaining how the planning board was trying to make changes in U.S. policies in light of the emerging nuclear parity between the two superpowers. He argued that the proposed changes were "designed to ensure that the United States would have a flexible capability so that it could determine the application of force best serving U.S. interests under the circumstances existing in each case of limited military aggression."[127] Cutler's recommendation received support from Army Chief of Staff General Maxwell Taylor, Chief of Naval Operations Admiral Arleigh Burke, and Secretary of State Dulles. Taylor explained that "the U.S. nuclear deterrent capability was essentially a shield, whereas our active military capabilities must be those designed for the conduct of limited war."[128] Dulles and Admiral Burke made similar arguments. Dulles said "new conditions are emerging which do not invalidate the massive retaliation concept, but put limitations on it and require it to be supplemented by other measures."[129] "Our need," Burke argued, "is not rigidity, but an ability to move effectively into big, intermediate or small operations."[130]

The Defense Department, the Air Force, and President Eisenhower questioned whether the United States did not already possess the necessary capabilities to wage limited military operations. Secretary McElroy expressed concern at the increased costs involved in augmenting U.S.

conventional forces.[131] Deputy Secretary Quarles said he doubted that any war with the Soviet Union could be fought without nuclear weapons, and he feared that if the United States announced that such a war could occur, it would encourage Soviet aggression with conventional weapons.[132] Both Air Force Chief of Staff Thomas White and JCS Chairman Twining "insisted that the United States already possessed strong capabilities for fighting limited war."[133] President Eisenhower acknowledged that he had concerns about augmenting U.S. forces for limited military operations. He said, "Each small war makes global [nuclear] war more likely."[134] He also raised the question of cost. He told his advisers:

> We really are faced with two possible courses of action. If we strengthen the mobile and tactical types of forces, either we do so by decreasing the strength of our nuclear deterrent force or else we will have to accept a massive increase in the resources to be devoted to our military defenses. If we accept the latter alternative, we have got to decide promptly by what methods we are going to maintain very much larger military forces than we have previously done. These methods would almost certainly involve what is euphemistically called a controlled economy, but which in effect would amount to a garrison state.[135]

While the NSC debated limited military operations capabilities, its interdepartmental study group completed a 250-page examination in June. Unfortunately, most of its report and the discussions related to it remain classified. However, the study group evidently reached several general conclusions. While the United States could use more limited war capabilities, its current forces were adequate. If a limited war did occur, the United States needed to notify the enemy of its intentions. The public needed to be educated about the role of nuclear weapons.[136] The NSC planning board expressed serious concern about informing the enemy of the country's intentions. It explained:

> The communication of limited objectives to potential aggressors is, as the Study states, an important means of minimizing the likelihood of miscalculation by the aggressor and the risk of general war. However, can communication of limited intentions be made in advance of every resort to limited hostilities without paying the unacceptable cost of encouraging the aggressor by reassuring him of the limited extent of the risk he is taking in initiating aggression? Should the communication of U.S. limited objectives be made

(a) generally, long before a limited military operation may be undertaken, (b) a short time before a limited operation may be undertaken, (c) just after a limited operation is undertaken? [137]

The interdepartmental group's final report did not lead to any substantial changes in Eisenhower's programs concerning limited military operations.

The last two Gaither committee recommendations dealt with the reorganization of the defense establishment and with constructing fallout shelters. Since the beginning of his administration, Eisenhower had attempted without much success to make the Defense Department operate more effectively. In making its recommendation concerning reorganization, the Gaither committee concluded that the defense establishment was not incorporating scientific and technological advances into its military programs in an efficient manner and was plagued by bureaucratic conflicts. Through its proposed changes, the committee sought to overcome these problems.

"The first need," Eisenhower argued in his 1958 State of the Union address, "is to assure ourselves that military organization facilitates rather than hinders the functioning of the military establishment in maintaining the security of the nation." [138] He found the defense establishment unable to meet the challenges posed by the modern world. He announced that he had established a special committee to study how the defense establishment should be organized. The committee members were William Foster and Robert Lovett from the Gaither committee, Charles Coolidge, General Alfred Gruenther, General Nathan Twining, Admiral Arthur Radford, and General Omar Bradley. [139] After receiving the committee's recommendations, the president submitted his proposal to Congress in April.

Eisenhower made six recommendations for changes in the organization of the defense establishment. Troops deployed overseas should be led by a "designated unified commander" rather than a commander from a particular service branch. The designated unified commander should answer directly to the secretary of defense, who answered to the president. The JCS should serve the secretary of defense directly rather than representing particular military branches. Each chief should concentrate on managing his respective branch, not on developing operational plans. A new position, director of defense research and engineering, needed to be created. Congress should appropriate funds to the secretary of defense rather than to the individual services. [140]

The president's proposals met some initial resistance in Congress. "The real problem," one scholar explains, "was how to apportion control of the modern military establishment, furnishing real security without compromising the traditional balance between executive and legislative power."[141] Some members of Congress, led by the venerable representative Carl Vinson (D-GA), believed that the proposals would weaken congressional influence over defense policies.[142] However, in August, Congress sent Eisenhower a bill that contained most of what he had requested. It increased the president's control over the defense establishment and strengthened the secretary of defense's authority over the service chiefs.[143]

The Eisenhower administration's response to the five-year $25 billion fallout shelter program was generally negative. Secretary of State Dulles found the Gaither committee's argument for shelters unconvincing. Sprague recalled that at the November 7 NSC meeting, Dulles asserted that the committee "had over-exaggerated our weaknesses and recommended a number of things that were militarily unnecessary and economically unfeasible. My general distress was that I thought Mr. Dulles had pretty well washed down the drain the six months work of, I thought, quite a competent group in carrying out an assignment they were asked to do."[144] Dulles explained to Eisenhower later that he was simply temperamentally opposed to shelters.[145] There may have been personal reasons as well for Dulles's rejection of the Gaither committee's recommendation concerning shelters. When he discovered that Paul Nitze had participated in writing the report, he was dismayed. He even questioned his brother, CIA Director Allen Dulles, how Nitze became an adviser to the committee.[146]

When the NSC examined the shelter recommendation in January, the FCDA was the only government agency to support the program without reservations. Leo Hoegh, the FCDA's director, argued that shelters would bolster the deterrent power of retaliatory forces, strengthen the position of U.S. negotiators, and reduce casualties in a war by 35 to 45 percent.[147] Opponents such as Secretary Dulles, Robert Cutler, and AEC chairman Admiral Lewis Strauss questioned the costs and effectiveness of shelters, thought they might make war more likely, and wondered about their impact on U.S. allies.[148]

Eisenhower and Vice President Nixon expressed serious reservations about the effectiveness of shelters in maintaining the viability of the country after a nuclear exchange. The president "noted that it had been said that fallout shelters might save 50 million people, a reduction of 35% in casualties. In talking about such figures, we were talking about the complete destruction of the United States."[149] Nixon was even more blunt. He "suggested that it be assumed that 40 million people would be killed in event of enemy attack if we had shelters, and 60 million would be killed if we did not have shelters. If 40 million were killed, the United States would be finished. He did not believe we could survive such a disaster. Our major objective must be to avoid the destruction of our society."[150] After these discussions, the NSC decided to reject the Gaither committee's shelter recommendation. But it did create an interdepartmental committee to study passive defenses, to institute a public education program, and to support research on different types of shelters.[151]

The Gaither committee's steering panel reconvened in February and met with Cutler to discuss how the administration was responding to its report.[152] Cutler wanted to assure the panel members that the administration was carefully considering their report. The steering panel members took the opportunity to question why administration officials seemed to be ignoring the recommendation for a nationwide shelter program. They argued, "The Gaither recommendations with respect to active and passive defenses should be regarded as an integrated combination. That is to say, a nation-wide fallout shelter program was to be taken in conjunction with recommendations for improving active defense and as a complementary thereto in protecting American lives."[153]

Over the next month and a half, Sprague corresponded with Killian and Cutler in an attempt to obtain their support for a shelter program. He explained that a one-megaton nuclear ground burst would kill 70 percent of the population within 13 square miles of the explosion because of either blast pressures or thermal heat. Unsheltered people within a radius of 600 miles would receive a lethal dose of radiation within seven hours.[154] "These figures," Sprague argued, "give very persuasive support to the urgent need of a fall-out shelter to protect military and civilian personnel, whether within urban or rural areas."[155] Although Sprague's arguments impressed Cutler, Killian was not convinced of the utility of shelters. He did not even want to educate the public about shelters lest it generate demands for a nationwide program.[156]

After the interdepartmental committee completed its report in March 1958, the NSC again addressed the question of shelters. Many of the same points made at the first meeting were heard again. After FCDA Director Hoegh spoke in favor of shelters, Treasury Secretary Robert Anderson argued, "The problem posed by a shelter program . . . was not only a grave financial problem. The main problem lay in the fact that we simply do not know enough at present to determine whether to go ahead with a large Federal program of shelter as a means which will really contribute to the survival of the United State in a terrible nuclear war." [157] Eisenhower later claimed that "this was one of the hardest problems in the world on which to make a wise decision." [158]

The NSC finally recommended spending $35 million in FY 1959 for certain minimal shelter studies.[159] It proposed the continuation of research and the development of prototypes of small fallout shelters. It advised surveying existing facilities nationwide to determine current available shelter space, and the construction of fallout shelters in new Federal buildings. Finally, it supported the expansion of public education programs addressing the consequences of nuclear war.[160]

Conclusions

Although surprised by some of its contents, Eisenhower did not dismiss the Gaither report, as some scholars have claimed. Stephen Ambrose argues that the president ultimately "rejected the Gaither Report. He refused to bend to the pressure, refused to initiate a fallout shelter program. It was one of his finest hours." [161] This is a rather shortsighted view of the influence of the Gaither report. The Gaither committee made recommendations in five main areas: increasing U.S. offensive striking power, reducing the vulnerability of SAC and the continent, improving U.S. limited military operations capabilities, constructing fallout shelters, and reorganizing the defense establishment. In every area except for fallout shelters and conventional forces, the administration either made major changes in its programs or initiated new studies in 1958. Eisenhower was more reluctant than some of his advisers to alter his programs, but he did accelerate U.S. missile development. He also emphasized the need for SAC alert and dispersal programs, ordered a study of U.S. limited military operations capabilities, and reorganized the defense establishment.

Eisenhower expressed reluctance at increasing the number of first-generation IRBMs and ICBMs that the United States should build. However, he did agree to deploy 130 ICBMs, 180 IRBMs, and additional Polaris missile-launching submarines.[162] While these force levels are far below the committee's recommendation of 600 ICBMs and 240 IRBMs, the distinction is not as clear as it appears. Eisenhower did not oppose increasing U.S. offensive striking power; he had doubts only about making first-generation missiles the basis of these forces. Because he had much more faith in the delivery capability of heavy bombers, he believed the United States should deploy a minimum number of first-generation missiles while concentrating on improving their accuracy. Eisenhower told the NSC in April 1958 "that he still had more faith in the delivery capabilities of the aircraft than he had in all these missiles at the present time." [163] Accordingly, while he supported enhanced alert and dispersal programs for SAC, he approved only a relatively limited number of first-generation missiles.

As for augmenting U.S. limited war capabilities, Eisenhower questioned the Gaither committee's contentions that small wars would remain limited. He did agree, however, to a new study of whether U.S. limited military operations capabilities were sufficient to address possible trouble spots in the world. The president ultimately based his decision not to expand conventional forces on his belief that future wars would be short and waged with nuclear weapons.[164] He explained his views in 1956: "I have spent my life in the study of military strength as a deterrent to war, and in the character of military armaments necessary to win a war. The study of the first of these questions is still profitable, but we are rapidly getting to the point that no war can be *won*. War implies a contest; when you get to the point that the contest is no longer involved and the outlook comes close to destruction of the enemy and suicide for ourselves—an outlook that neither side can ignore—then arguments as to the exact amount of available strength as compared to somebody else's are no longer the vital issues." [165]

Of all the Gaither committee recommendations, the most palatable to Eisenhower was the proposal to reorganize the defense establishment. The Gaither committee was only one of many groups recommending change. Eisenhower was already well aware of the problems, and he made reorganization one of his legislative priorities in 1958. He successfully persuaded Congress to make substantial changes in the defense establishment.[166]

While many of the Gaither committee's recommendations received widespread support within the administration, its call for a nationwide system of shelters met stiff resistance. There was some support from the FCDA, the Office of Defense Mobilization, and the State Department's Policy Planning Staff. However, most of Eisenhower's advisers opposed the recommendation because of the costs of shelters, the knowledge that in a nuclear exchange millions would die regardless of preventive measures, or the implications of a shelter program for U.S. allies. Cutler later recalled the administration's reasons for rejecting the recommendation. He explained, "All of this about the need for shelter from fall-out overlooks the many factors which have puzzled the NSC and are still being researched. It is too one-sided. It overlooks foreign repercussion, effect on economy, human practicality, whether it shouldn't be done at local level, effect on national morale, etc. It argues all on one side." [167]

The Gaither committee asked for an incredibly comprehensive security system. It requested military capabilities that would have allowed the United States to launch a preventive war or an overwhelming retaliatory strike, and to wage limited wars with or without nuclear weapons. Although Eisenhower wondered whether he could "carry out all of these plans and still maintain a free economy in the United States," he still carefully considered the committee's conclusions.[168] While he did not accept all of them, he did find many of the recommendations necessary and incorporated them into his national security programs with a careful eye on limiting their impact on the economy.

6 | The Legacy of the Gaither Committee

$\mathbf{B}$y July 1958, the Eisenhower administration had thoroughly evaluated the Gaither committee's conclusions and recommendations. In contrast to some interpretations, the committee's findings significantly influenced Eisenhower's national security policies.[1] While the Gaither report itself faded from NSC discussions after 1958, the issues and questions it raised continued to dominate policy making. For the remainder of his presidency, Eisenhower struggled to guarantee U.S. capabilities to strike the Soviet Union and preserve the security of the United States, while at the same time not undermining the American way of life that he treasured.

The influence of specific members of the Gaither committee on the Eisenhower administration continued to the end of his presidency. James Killian acted as Eisenhower's national science adviser until 1959. Herbert York served as the director of the Defense Department's Office of Research and Development. William Foster headed a delegation to Geneva in late 1958 to discuss with Soviet representatives ways to reduce the possibility of a surprise attack.[2] Many other committee members also continued to serve in a variety of capacities, including as advisers to the President's Science Advisory Committee (PSAC) and the Defense Department.

Although Eisenhower did not believe that the communist leaders intended to launch an attack, the presence of these advisers, additional technological advances, Soviet bombast, and intelligence estimates indicating that the Soviet Union had a quantitative lead in nuclear missiles forced the president to reexamine his policies. While he never seriously questioned his strategy of deterrence, he did conclude that he needed to strengthen the U.S. military. By the time he left office, he had expanded his initial proposals for approximately 350 nuclear missiles to almost 1,400. Furthermore,

157

he continued to disperse SAC, improve alert status, construct antimissile defenses, and build early warning radar.

Despite significantly expanding U.S. military programs in the three years after *Sputnik* and the Gaither committee, Eisenhower still faced almost constant criticism that his defense policies failed to provide adequate guarantees for the nation's security. More specifically, his policies were challenged in two areas: missile strength and limited war capabilities. Senators Stuart Symington, Lyndon Johnson, and John F. Kennedy led a chorus of opposition to Eisenhower's military programs. Symington claimed in early 1958, "It is a tragic fact that, even after the warnings contained in the Sputnik launchings, and despite the previously known deficiencies in SAC, nothing has been done to rectify those deficiencies."[3] The leak of the Gaither report played an instrumental role in furthering the perception that U.S. missile capabilities were inferior to those of the Soviet Union. One recent scholar aptly concludes that while the Gaither report did not create the missile gap or fears of a national emergency, it "was essential to their circulation beyond the intelligence community and, ultimately, outside the administration."[4]

Symington's accusations and the Gaither committee's findings were lent credence by the Soviet Union's claims of its technological superiority and more assertive policies in 1958. Khrushchev wanted the world to believe that the Soviet Union had surpassed the United States technologically. The Soviet leader and his military commanders regularly bragged about Soviet military prowess, especially in the area of rocketry.[5] Their bellicose speeches and statements appeared to corroborate a more aggressive Soviet foreign policy. 1958 witnessed what the Eisenhower administration saw as communist aggression in the Middle East, the Chinese offshore islands of Quemoy and Matsu, and Berlin.[6] Khrushchev's ultimatum in November 1958 to settle the Berlin question only heightened concerns.[7] Although each of these incidents was resolved relatively peacefully, they added to the perception that the United States was in a deadly struggle and needed to be prepared for any possible Soviet actions.

The debates over Eisenhower's national security policies became pivotal in the 1960 presidential campaign.[8] Democratic candidate Kennedy and his running mate, Lyndon Johnson, argued that the Eisenhower administration failed to recognize the deficiencies in U.S. military capabilities because it was too concerned with balancing the budget and controlling inflation. While Kennedy and Johnson saw these policies as admirable goals, they believed that the danger posed by the Soviet Union was much greater than Eisenhower and, more important at this time, Republican candidate Richard Nixon realized. Capitalizing on perceptions of the missile gap and deficiencies in the massive retaliation strategy, the Democratic nominee challenged whether the United States could survive the continuation of Eisenhower's military policies with Nixon as president. Kennedy won the election in part because of his promises to strengthen U.S. war-fighting capabilities.

During the 1960 election campaign and then in his presidency, Kennedy sought the advice of numerous Gaither committee members.[9] He studied the committee's report early in his administration. Paul Nitze, in particular, served as Kennedy's primary adviser on defense and foreign policy issues and became the new president's assistant secretary of defense for international security affairs. Foster helped negotiate the 1963 ban on atmospheric nuclear tests. Killian continued to advise Kennedy on science and intelligence issues. Jerome Wiesner became Kennedy's national science adviser. At least another eight Gaither committee members served the Kennedy administration in a variety of capacities. After his inauguration, Kennedy immediately began to alter the national security policies he inherited from Eisenhower. The new president expanded U.S. strategic missile capabilities, augmented limited war forces, and improved SAC's alert status. He also focused renewed attention on the question of civil defense. While it is impossible to tie the Gaither report directly to the policies introduced by Kennedy, the similarities between the committee's recommendations and the new administration's flexible response strategy are readily apparent.

Eisenhower's National Security Policies, 1958–1961

For the last two and a half years of his presidency, Eisenhower attempted to formulate national security policies that would continue his emphasis on balancing the country's economic and military needs. While he was also worried about Soviet military and technological advances, he questioned the willingness of the Kremlin to risk their own destruction by attacking the United States. He argued that "until an enemy has enough operational capability to destroy most of our bases simultaneously and thus prevent retaliation by us, our deterrent remains effective. We would make a mistake to credit him with absolute capabilities."[10] Rather than seeking to outproduce the Soviet Union or embarking on expensive and unproven programs to protect U.S. civilians, he pursued policies that he believed would guarantee U.S. capabilities to retaliate even under the worst possible conditions and would not hurt the economy.[11]

During the first six months of 1958, Eisenhower instituted alert and dispersal programs, expanded early warning radar coverage, programmed anti-aircraft and antimissile defenses, and accelerated the development and deployment of several different missile systems. While the specific recommendations do not reflect complete agreement with those of the Gaither committee, they do show its considerable influence. After the summer of 1958, the Gaither report was rarely discussed within the Eisenhower administration or mentioned in public debates. However, the report's obscurity during this time does not signify its lack of importance in helping shape debates concerning U.S. national security programs. The changes in these programs during the first half of 1958 were only the first of many to occur before Eisenhower left office.

While he often approved increases reluctantly, Eisenhower eventually accepted recommendations from his advisers to create a missile force substantially larger than the one proposed by the Gaither committee. Several factors influenced Eisenhower's decision making. Until the introduction of satellite intelligence at the end of 1960, estimates of Soviet missile capabilities remained speculative and continued to emphasize the communists' quantitative superiority.[12] The continued Soviet bombast precipitated pressures on the administration to regain the technological and military advantages over the Kremlin.[13] Eisenhower also received recommendations from his military advisers for expanded missile programs that reflected their inability to overcome interservice rivalries. While Eisenhower did not have to accept their recommendations, he faced great opposition if he did not. The rapid development of more reliable second-generation missiles, moreover, made their deployment more acceptable and important.

In addition to expanding missile forces, Eisenhower also continued to disperse U.S. nuclear delivery systems, increase SAC alert capabilities, expand radar coverage, and construct active defenses. The president viewed these policies as essential to guarantee the capability of the United States to retaliate regardless of the circumstances. He agreed with Secretary of State Dulles, who asserted that "the United States should not attempt to be the greatest military in the world. . . . In the field of military capabilities enough was enough. If we didn't realize this fact, the time would come when all our national production would be centered on our military establishment."[14] By expanding U.S. missile capabilities and reducing their vulnerability, Eisenhower felt confident that the Soviet Union would avoid taking any risks that might result in its own destruction.

The Gaither committee proposed the expansion of five separate offensive missile systems: Thor and Jupiter IRBMs, Atlas and Titan ICBMs, and the Polaris SLBM. By the end of FY 1963, it recommended the deployment of 240 IRBMs, 600 ICBMs, and 6 Polaris submarines carrying 16 SLBMs. In total, these forces would have consisted of almost 940 nuclear missiles.[15] During his last three years in office, Eisenhower met and then surpassed these force levels. In August 1958, the Defense Department studied the possibility of expanding the programmed ICBM force to 200 missiles (110 Titan and 90 Atlas).[16] In November 1959, the Defense Department proposed and Eisenhower approved a force of 270 ICBMs (140 Titans and 130 Atlas).[17] By Kennedy's inauguration in January 1961, Eisenhower had programmed the deployment of 810 ICBMs (130 Atlas, 140 Titan, and 540 Minuteman).[18]

Eisenhower also supervised a similar expansion of the development of Polaris missile submarines. He saw the Polaris as a major hedge against the Soviet Union's launching of a surprise attack. By providing a virtually invulnerable second-strike capability, the Polaris would force Soviet leaders to consider even more seriously the consequences of attacking the United States. In 1958, Eisenhower approved plans to construct 9 Polaris submarines. A year later, he agreed to expand the force even further to 15.[19] By July 1960, the president approved the construction of 24 Polaris submarines.[20] These 24 submarines added 384 SLBMs to the already planned 810-ICBM force.

In addition to the ICBM and Polaris forces, the Eisenhower administration implemented its plans to deploy both Thor and Jupiter IRBMs overseas. In April 1958, Eisenhower had agreed to a Defense Department recommendation to deploy 12 IRBM squadrons (9 Thor and 3 Jupiter) containing 15 missiles each. Ultimately, 4 Thor and 3 Jupiter squadrons became operational in Great Britain, Turkey, and Italy between 1959 and 1962.[21] The Eisenhower administration limited the deployment of IRBMs to 7 squadrons when it realized that reliable ICBMs would be available, which would make the IRBMs unnecessary and obsolete. However, while the IRBMs were plagued with shortcomings, they "demonstrated America's resolve to defend its allies and represented the only display of strategic missiles in Europe."[22]

The ICBM and IRBM forces and the Polaris submarines represented

Jupiter C missile being launched at Cape Canaveral Missile Test Annex in August 1958. The Gaither committee recommended the deployment of IRBMs like this Jupiter missile in Europe. (National Archives)

only two legs of the U.S. nuclear arsenal. The third part of the nuclear triad remained the SAC bombers. The Gaither committee did not recommend substantial increases in bomber force levels, but it did emphasize the importance of reducing SAC vulnerability. It proposed the implementation of alert forces, the further dispersal of bomber squadrons, the improvement of early warning, and the construction of active defenses. Eisenhower and the NSC focused on each of these issues between 1958 and 1961. Additionally, Eisenhower adopted proposals to modernize the composition of the bomber and tanker forces. While he phased out the B-36 in

Polaris missile being tested at Cape Canaveral. The Polaris SLBM represented the third leg of the nuclear triad that the Gaither committee thought essential for maintaining U.S. security. (National Archives)

1958 and began to reduce the importance of the B-47 in 1959, he increased the deployment of B-52 bombers from 243 in 1957 to 567 in 1961. Furthermore, he modernized the tanker force by introducing the KC-135.[23]

Besides determining strategic force levels, the most pressing military question addressed by the Eisenhower administration between 1958 and 1961 was to determine the optimal force requirements for fighting either

Boeing B-52 bomber on a test flight over Florida. To ensure a strong nuclear striking force while the weaknesses in early generation missiles were eliminated, the Gaither committee recommended the modernization of the U.S. Air Force's bomber force through the introduction of the B-52. (National Archives)

general or limited wars. As shown in earlier chapters, the distinction between limited and general wars had been a controversial topic for military strategists. Civilians like Bernard Brodie, Henry Kissinger, Robert Osgood, Paul Nitze, and William Kaufman insisted that the United States should develop greater military capabilities to wage limited wars. However, there was no consensus as to how these types of wars should be fought. Should nuclear weapons be used or should conventional forces be relied upon? How should political objectives be determined and conveyed to an enemy? How could the geographical areas of conflict be limited? Without providing specifics, the Gaither committee recommended that the United States perform a study to determine the best composition and role for its limited war forces.

As a result of these recommendations, the NSC created a task force in the spring of 1958 composed of representatives of the State Department, Defense Department, JCS, and CIA to study U.S. capabilities to wage limited wars through July 1961. The task force concluded that "United States capabilities for limited military operations are adequate to undertake and carry out limited operations."[24] However, this opinion was not unanimous within the administration. Another study completed in September 1958 by the Defense Department's Defense Science Board found otherwise: "The limited-war capability of the United States is inadequate from the viewpoint both of military operations and of research and development."[25] Furthermore, the study argued that the "present capability [of the United States] is limited in strength and cannot be exercised quickly or effectively."[26] This type of criticism reappeared on several occasions during the remainder of the Eisenhower administration.

In 1960, two separate committees, a PSAC panel and an interagency study group, examined U.S. limited war capabilities. The panel found what it believed to be several serious deficiencies. It concluded, in particular, that the military branches focused so much attention on maintaining forces for general war that they neglected "the specialized weapons and systems for limited war."[27] To remedy these deficiencies, the panel recommended augmenting U.S. airlift capabilities, developing ground support aircraft for limited war, and placing more emphasis on the development of nonnuclear weapons.[28]

The interagency study group, composed of representatives from the CIA, State Department, and the Department of Defense, performed a study similar to the one instigated by the Gaither committee recommendations in 1958. The impetus for this examination was the belief among some members of the Eisenhower administration that the 1958 study failed to resolve the role of nuclear weapons in limited war.[29] The group's final report remains classified, but discussions concerning its conclusions provide a revealing look at the disagreements over limited military operations.[30] The study group examined five possible locations of limited war confrontations: Berlin, Iran, Laos, Korea, and the Chinese offshore islands of Quemoy and Matsu.[31] It concluded that the United States had "an adequate capability for any one of the situations studied but cannot handle two at once."[32] More specifically, it stressed:

> U.S. capabilities in conjunction with those of our Allies are generally adequate to conduct any one of the limited military operations studied but these capabilities are dependent on prompt action, as required in each case, to

a. Initiate partial mobilization.
b. Augment existing military [air]lift capabilities.
c. Expand the war production base.
d. Waive financial limitations.[33]

The State Department found that U.S. capabilities in these fields were insufficient. State Department representative Gerard Smith told Secretary of State Christian Herter, "Although the language of the present study's conclusions is carefully hedged, its import seems to me inescapable. The US does not have now an adequate limited war capability."[34] Undersecretary of State Livingston Merchant emphasized, "There is unanimity in the State Department about the need for a greater limited war capability" (5), explaining further that "the State Department . . . believes it is difficult to have an effective and successful foreign policy if the US lacks the capability of dealing with at least two limited war situations concurrently without an unacceptable degradation of our general war capability" (6).

U.S. military leaders also analyzed the interagency group's report. Their overriding conclusion was "that our limited war capability is basically dependent on our general war capability and our determination to risk general war."[35] One of the key questions they could not answer was whether nuclear weapons would be used in limited war situations. JCS Chairman Twining explained that "we must assume that when we get in a shooting war we will have to have a supplemental budget and step up our airlift. . . . On the use of atomic weapons we cannot prejudge" (2). Army Chief of Staff Lyman Lemnitzer concurred. He argued that it is not "possible to decide in advance whether to use nuclear weapons. . . . Therefore, it is necessary to have a proper balance between nuclear and conventional forces so we won't get musclebound" (4). Overall, the JCS stressed that "the United States does not have forces in being adequate to cope with all envisaged limited war situations."[36]

Navy Chief of Staff Admiral Arleigh Burke and Air Force Chief of Staff General Thomas White raised the issues of U.S. prestige and will. Burke argued, "The US will is important. The Soviets will push us at every opportunity and we need to have the will to resist." He then provided as an example the crisis in Berlin, explaining that "in the Berlin situation it is easy to consider letting Berlin go rather than fight a general war. However, we need to stand up to the enemy if we want to keep the free world on our side. We must keep Berlin or lose our prestige and respect. If general war is necessary, we might as well have it now and take the risk of losing our nation."[37] White expressed his complete agreement. "We need," he stressed, "national determination in a situation where general war must be risked. We should use whatever weapons are necessary" (4).

Questions concerning U.S. capabilities to wage limited wars were also raised by Nitze and General Maxwell Taylor, who retired as the Army's chief of staff in 1959. Taylor believed that Eisenhower's reliance on massive retaliation significantly limited U.S. capabilities to respond to military crises short of general war. He argued that "Massive Retaliation as a guiding strategic concept has reached a dead end and that there is an urgent need for a reappraisal of our strategic needs. In its heyday, massive retaliation could offer our leaders only two choices, the initiation of general nuclear war or compromise and retreat."[38] Taylor claimed that the United States needed to expand the capabilities of its conventional forces to wage limited wars in order to insure that it would not have to respond to every military crisis with nuclear weapons.[39]

Nitze was the most vocal proponent on the Gaither committee for expanding limited war capabilities. In June 1959, he argued that as programmed by the Eisenhower administration, U.S. military forces were inadequate to meet the range of threats posed by the U.S.S.R. He explained, "If one grades the various threats which Soviet-Communist initiative can present to the free world in order of the violence of the means involved, one finds a wide band starting with reasonably mild but disturbing words at one end of the spectrum and an all-out surprise nuclear attack on the United States at the other end of the spectrum."[40] He believed that the United States needed to be prepared for all contingencies. The United States should possess a secure retaliatory capability, expanded limited war capabilities, and strong security alliances.[41]

Eisenhower saw several basic flaws in the arguments of the critics of his limited war policies.[42] He believed that they underestimated the deterrent factor of U.S. strategic capabilities and the convertibility of these forces for limited war operations. He questioned whether any limited war between U.S. and Soviet forces would remain that way for very long since he believed that any engagements would quickly escalate into a general war. He further argued that any other limited conflicts could be controlled with existing forces in being at least until the United States had time to mobilize additional manpower and armaments.[43] Accordingly, during his last few years in office, he did not waver from his reliance on nuclear weapons and strategic delivery systems as the principal deterrent to the Soviet Union.[44]

The last major issue that the Gaither committee addressed and the Eisenhower administration had to discuss was the question of civil defense, and in particular, fallout shelters. The Gaither committee recommended that the United States should spend $25 billion over five years to construct fallout shelters for the civilian population. No one seriously questioned that a system of fallout shelters would reduce substantially the number of casualties from a Soviet nuclear attack. As the NSC studied the Gaither committee's recommendation for shelters, it ordered an examination of the consequences of a massive nuclear exchange (approximately 15 million kilotons). The study concluded that in an attack of this magnitude, only 94 million out of the estimated U.S. population of 192 million would survive even with a nationwide fallout shelter system.[45] While the study found that 67 million people would have lived because of the shelters, the question was whether the loss of almost 100 million people would allow the continued existence of the United States as a nation.

Eisenhower and his advisers continually struggled with this question. The cost of the shelters created a dilemma. When FCDA director Leo Hoegh recommended modifying existing federal buildings for use as shelters at a cost of $5 million in FY 1960, Eisenhower did not oppose the idea. He simply did not feel "he knew exactly what to do about it."[46] In December 1958, the NSC decided to authorize up to $35 million to continue research, construct a small number of shelters, survey potential existing structures for shelter spaces, initiate a public education program, and incorporate shelters in new federal buildings.[47]

By the end of his administration, Eisenhower's civil defense programs revealed little influence from the Gaither committee. Based on the 1958 program, the FCDA studied possible existing shelter facilities and built almost 150 prototype shelters. However, it did not incorporate shelters into new federal buildings as was earlier planned, because of inadequate funding. A lack of consensus concerning shelters hamstrung the FCDA and the new Office of Civil and Defense Mobilization (OCDM).[48] While certain groups, like the Gaither committee and the Rockefeller Panel, and individuals, like Congressman Chet Holifield, recommended the construction of shelters, neither the public nor Congress showed a strong willingness to support expanded expenditures for shelters. Although people supported the idea of a community shelter, only 39 percent supported spending $500 to build a private, family shelter in 1960.[49] Even more glaringly, Congress

Proposed fallout shelter outside Kansas City, Missouri. The Gaither committee proposed using existing industrial spaces like these limestone caves as fallout shelters in the event of a nuclear attack. (National Archives)

cut the OCDM budget 40 percent between 1959 and 1961.[50] Without a consensus on shelters, Eisenhower felt no concerted pressure to expand his civil defense policies.

The Missile Gap and the 1960 Presidential Election

As Eisenhower and his advisers attempted to devise plans for strengthening U.S. strategic forces, they faced some of the same problems experienced by the Gaither committee. They wanted to maintain sufficient military capabilities to deter the Soviet Union from launching a nuclear war. To do this, they needed to know approximately how large the Soviet bomber and missile forces were and what the Kremlin's intentions were. Intelligence analysts from the CIA, military branches, and other government agencies had to rely on limited information to derive their estimates of Soviet capabilities.[51] A leading scholar of the missile gap controversy persuasively argues that after *Sputnik* "the question of Soviet intent assumed an even greater

Storage survival supplies for a 258-person fallout shelter in Baltimore, Maryland. Part of the Gaither committee's plans for the survival of the United States was to stockpile supplies for use in the case of a nuclear war. (National Archives)

importance in any effort to determine the future course of Russian missile programs and the Soviet's willingness to use this power to pursue their foreign policy goals." [52]

Claims of a missile gap periodically resurfaced between 1958 and the 1960 presidential election.[53] Senator Symington wrote Eisenhower in the summer of 1958 that "we [Symington and his advisers] believe our national intelligence system is underestimating the enemy's current and future ballistic missile capability. . . . As a result we also believe that our national defense plans and programs are not being effectively related to sound estimates of Soviet capability." [54] Others criticized the administration for failing to recognize and overcome the emergence of the alleged Soviet quantitative lead in missile capabilities. If the Soviet Union did have such a lead, Eisenhower's critics argued that the communist leaders might be more willing to take policy risks in pursuit of its goal of world domination. Senator Lyndon Johnson's chief legal counsel captured the essence of the critics' concerns when he argued that "we [U.S. leaders] have been unwilling to face the disagreeable facts that we are actually in a state of war, that the enemy has prepared for war and that unless we work 365 days a year with an urgency, as though we were in a war, we are liable to be licked and become a second-class country." [55]

Although the critics were wrong, there were legitimate reasons for concluding that there was a missile gap. The national intelligence estimates during these years consistently predicted a prospective Soviet missile force much larger than the one possessed by the United States. While the projected gap was always in the future, the estimates pointed to a period in the early 1960s when the Soviet Union would have a substantial quantitative lead in ICBMs. A NIE in June 1958 estimated that the Soviet Union could have 100 ICBMs in 1959, 500 in 1960, and 1,000 in 1961. [56] A NIE later in the same year predicted that the Soviet Union would have 10 ICBMs in 1959, 100 in 1960, and 500 by 1962. [57] NIE 11-8-59, which was not released until February 1960, estimated that the Soviets would have 35 ICBMs by mid-1960 and between 140 and 200 by mid-1961. [58] Finally, NIE 11-8-60 estimated that the Soviet Union would have between 10 and 35 ICBMs in 1960 and between 50 and 200 in 1961. [59]

The problem for intelligence analysts was determining the intentions of an adversary who resided in a restricted society and whose assumed goal was world domination. As Herbert York and Alan Greb explain, "In such circumstances [where the enemy resides in a closed society], it often becomes necessary to plan to cope with what the other side *might* be doing rather than what it actually *is* doing. And what it *might* be doing is limited only by human imagination rather than by physical reality" [emphasis in original]. [60] When the Gaither committee made its estimates, it assumed that the Soviet Union would produce military hardware at maximum levels. Based on this assumption, it reached some frightening conclusions. The intelligence community had to deal with some of the same problems.

In 1959, Defense Secretary Neil McElroy attempted to explain to a congressional committee one of the difficulties in making accurate intelligence estimates. He testified, "We concede the capacity of the Soviets to do a good many things, if they make the determination to do so. . . . We do concede them capacity, but no one that I know can be inside of the Russian mind and decide what proportion of that capacity they are going to use." [61] Because of the difficulty in determining Soviet intentions, the intelligence analysts adopted "the position that they were not very much interested in intentions, they were only interested in capabilities." [62] JCS Chairman General Nathan Twining elaborated on the difficulties of estimating Soviet capabilities, telling the Senate Foreign Relations Committee, "I would like to establish a point which should be borne in mind at all times when considering the United States versus the Soviet weapons comparison: Our information on what we now have is exact, while that given for the Soviets is often estimated from assumptions and requirements. . . . In other words, because we can do things, we assume they can and they have requirements, therefore, they are developing these missiles." [63]

With little concrete evidence, intelligence analysts had difficulty developing conclusive estimates. Their efforts were made even more difficult by Soviet propaganda highlighting that country's missile strength. Soviet leaders bragged in May 1959 that they possessed the nuclear capabilities "to wipe from the face of the earth all of our probable opponents." [64] The result was an overestimation of Soviet capabilities and, accordingly, a potentially much greater threat to the United States. [65] George Reedy, a legislative assistant to Senator Johnson, explained how these exaggerated estimates led to the belief of a missile gap:

> We [the members of the Senate Preparedness Subcommittee] didn't realize a very simple thing, that what they [the intelligence analysts] were doing was extrapolating on the basis of Russian capabilities, but using actual figures for what the United States was doing. Now their assumption was that the Soviet Union was producing missiles to capacity, and so when they extrapolated on that from the standpoint of what they knew the Soviet Union produced at one point, they were able to get such a tremendous imbalance between the Soviet Union and the United States. [66]

The press also made substantial claims about the supposed missile gap. Joseph Alsop reported in July and August 1958 that the United States was falling dangerously behind the Soviets in missile capabilities. He argued that while the U.S.S.R. would have 100 ICBMs in 1959, 500 in 1960, and 1,000 in 1961, the United States would have 0 in 1959, 30 in 1960, and 70 in 1961.[67] Taken together, all of these calculations painted a frightening picture. Although they were only estimates, if they proved accurate the United States faced a potentially deadly threat. Robert Amory, a CIA analyst, remembered, "Taking our earliest estimate of when they [the Soviets] could have five hundred [ICBMs] and then comparing that with the known projection of American strengths, . . . you came up with a *potential* missile gap" (emphasis in original).[68]

The 1960 presidential election brought into focus many of the criticisms of Eisenhower's national security policies. Democratic candidate Kennedy and his running mate, Senator Johnson, were among the most vociferous critics of the Eisenhower administration. As the Senate majority leader and the chairman of the preparedness subcommittee, Johnson maintained constant pressure on the administration to improve U.S. military strength vis-à-vis the Soviet Union. He told Defense Secretary McElroy in July 1958 that he was disappointed in the progress made since the preparedness subcommittee reached its initial conclusions at the beginning of that year.[69]

Kennedy was an even more persistent critic. In August 1958, he delivered a scathing attack on Eisenhower's national security policies. He claimed the president and his advisers "tailored our strategy and military requirements to fit our budget—instead of fitting our budget to our military requirements and strategy."[70] He then accused the administration of losing the military advantage to the Soviet Union. "The fact of the matter," Kennedy argued, "is that during that period when emphasis was laid upon our economic strength instead of our military strength, we were losing the decisive years when we could have maintained a lead against the Soviet Union in our missile capability" (41).

After lambasting Eisenhower's national security policies, Kennedy described what the United States needed to do to overcome its military deficiencies. He advocated adding more tanker aircraft to SAC's forces; accelerating the development and deployment of ICBMs, IRBMs, and SLBMs; improving continental defenses; expanding airlift capabilities; and increasing manpower for limited military operations (42). He complained that if these measures were not implemented, the Soviet "missile power will be the shield from behind which they will slowly, but surely, advance— through Sputnik diplomacy, limited brush-fire wars, indirect non-overt aggression, intimidation, and subversion, internal revolution, increased prestige or influence, and the vicious blackmail of our allies. The periphery of the Free World will slowly be nibbled away. The balance of power will gradually shift against us." [71]

In a subsequent interview, Kennedy made similar claims:

> In military preparedness I think that the reasoning of the Eisenhower administration is comparable to the prediction of Britains [sic] Stanley Baldwin during the Thirties—the enemy's capabilities are grossly and constantly underestimated. There isn't any doubt that the Russians are able to build accurate intercontinental ballistic missiles. I believe that the dangers of an unbalanced budget are far less than the danger to which the administration is determined to subject us by keeping us behind the Soviet Union in the ultimate weapon. When some people still say we are equall [sic] with the Russians in military strength, I would ask how much of our strength will be left after we have sustained a surprise blow; How equal are we after the first attack had been made by them on us? [72]

As Kennedy sought the Democratic nomination, he turned to Paul Nitze and several other Gaither committee members for advice on national security issues. [73] Kennedy asked Nitze to chair a committee that included former Gaither committee member James Perkins, Roswell Gilpatric, and David Bruce to make recommendations concerning U.S. national security policies. During its deliberations, the group talked to many experts on defense issues, including Foster, Lincoln, and Robert Lovett from the Gaither committee. The group concluded that U.S. nuclear forces had to be expanded and improved to meet any possible Soviet challenge. [74]

These conclusions proved appealing to the new president. In his run for the presidency, he advocated increased defense spending and the acceleration of U.S. missile capabilities. Specifically, he proposed reducing SAC vulnerability by maintaining 25 percent of its planes in the air at all times, accelerating the production of Atlas missiles, increasing spending for the development of both the Polaris and Minuteman missiles, and augmenting conventional forces. [75] Kennedy recognized that these programs would require higher spending and possibly unbalanced budgets. He explained to his Senate colleagues the dilemma faced by U.S. decision makers and made a clear distinction between his position and that of the Eisenhower administration. He argued, "We cannot be certain that the Soviets will have, during the term of the next administration, the tremendous lead in missile striking power which they give every evidence of building—and we cannot be certain that they will use that lead to threaten or launch an attack upon the United States. Consequently those of us who call for a higher defense budget are taking a chance on spending money unnecessarily. But those who oppose these expenditures are taking a chance on our very survival as a nation." [76]

In a campaign speech in October 1960, Kennedy cited the Gaither report in his arguments that Eisenhower was not doing enough to meet the Soviet threat. He claimed that during the Eisenhower administration, "The Soviet Union decided to go all out in missile development. But here in the United States, we cut back in funds for missile development. We slashed our defense budget. We slowed up the modernization of our conventional forces—until, today, the Soviet Union is rapidly building up a missile striking force that endangers our power to retaliate—and thus our survival itself." [77]

Eisenhower reacted in dismay to such criticisms. He adamantly believed in the adequacy of U.S. military programs. He simply considered it foolish to expand U.S. military power further when there was little likelihood that it would ever be needed. Despite intense pressure, he successfully resisted demands for significant increases in military spending. He failed, however, to allay the nation's great concerns. [78] McGeorge Bundy succinctly explains this failure:

> Eisenhower did not adequately explain himself. His failure to give a full explanation of his disbelief in a prospective missile gap was reinforced in its unfortunate effects not only by his failure to spell out publicly his view of the deterrent strength of the forces on both sides, but also by his failure to press on his countrymen the understanding he had expressed so clearly back in 1954, that in matters of this magnitude Soviet leaders would predictably be most cautious. So while he did sensible things and resisted foolish ones, he allowed the ensuing public arguments to be led by men who did not understand matters as well as he did. [79]

The 1960 election proved a great disappointment to Eisenhower. Although he was not completely enamored of Nixon, he was adamantly opposed to Kennedy. When Nixon's chances looked dim in the month leading to the election, Eisenhower began to campaign vigorously for his vice president. His efforts proved to no avail. While still personally popular, Eisenhower could not rally the Republican party to victory. In one of the closest presidential races ever, Kennedy won by less than 120,000 votes of the 68 million that were cast.[80] Eisenhower viewed the results as a repudiation of his eight years in office.[81]

Kennedy's Defense Policies—An Overview

After winning the election, Kennedy resolved to alleviate any deficiencies in U.S. military strength and raise U.S. prestige abroad. Jean Smith concludes, "On military policy Kennedy's views remained fixed: the United States should maintain forces in being to deter and defeat aggression at any point on the spectrum of violence."[82] To carry out such a policy, Kennedy rejected the massive retaliation doctrine of the Eisenhower administration and adopted a strategic approach that emphasized the maintenance of a greater variety of military options to meet any possible challenge. While many factors influenced the development of these policies, the importance of the Gaither committee should not be overlooked. Over a dozen of the committee's members served as advisers to Kennedy, including Wiesner, Nitze, York, Foster, Killian, Robert Sprague, Spurgeon Keeny, Vincent McRae, Brockway McMillan, Richard Bissell, and John McCloy.[83] Furthermore, during his first weeks in office, Kennedy studied the Gaither report.[84]

Kennedy's strategy to expand U.S. military capabilities encompassed three requirements: augmenting U.S. nuclear forces, enlarging U.S. conventional forces for limited military operations, and strengthening civil defense.[85] Kennedy succeeded in expanding U.S. missile capabilities even beyond the levels prescribed by the Eisenhower administration. He placed a greater emphasis on limited war capabilities, and especially, the development of counter-insurgency forces. Finally, he announced a civil defense plan that, although not varying greatly from Eisenhower's approach, had a much greater impact because of the president's public pronouncements.

Despite his initial reluctance in 1957 and 1958, Eisenhower greatly expanded U.S. nuclear capabilities before he left office. Kennedy inherited the nuclear triad—SAC bombers, ICBMs, and SLBMs—that formed the foundation of the U.S. nuclear arsenal. Reflecting the advice of Nitze's advisory committee, Kennedy believed that the United States needed more. In his first message to the Congress in January 1961, the new president proposed the expansion of the entire missile program. By the time he was assassinated in November 1963, the United States had deployed 631 ICBMs and 160 SLBMs and had programmed the deployment of an additional 800 missiles.[86]

When Kennedy entered the White House, he had access to a new source of intelligence that had only become available in the last few months of the Eisenhower administration. In August 1960, Eisenhower received the first satellite photographs, which "in one mission provided more photographic coverage of the Soviet Union than all previous U-2 missions."[87] Although it is unclear whether Kennedy was informed of the new intelligence during the campaign, he did gain access to the intelligence information after the November election.[88] The satellite photographs dispelled any possibility of a missile gap in favor of the Soviet Union.[89] Despite this knowledge, Kennedy remained determined to expand U.S. missile capabilities. He immediately initiated plans to increase Eisenhower's proposed FY 1962 defense budget of $40.8 billion. During his first nine months in office, Kennedy added an additional $1.95 billion to the defense budget in March, $225 million in May, and $3.45 billion in July. By August 1961, Kennedy had expanded the defense budget by nearly $6 billion.[90]

The March 1961 appropriations were geared primarily to accelerate the expansion of U.S. strategic forces. In particular, Kennedy wanted to augment the Polaris submarine forces. While Eisenhower had planned to build 19 submarines carrying a total of 304 missiles by June 1965, Kennedy's program accelerated the deployment to 29 submarines carrying 464 missiles. In addition to expanding the Polaris forces, Kennedy also added 60 Minuteman ICBMs to Eisenhower's program of 540.[91] In the FY 1963 budget, Kennedy completed the deployment of the Atlas ICBMs (129 missiles) and Titan ICBMs (108 missiles) and funded 16 squadrons of Minuteman ICBMs totaling 800 missiles. Kennedy also again augmented the planned deployment of Polaris submarines to 41 carrying 656 missiles. Finally, he increased the B-52 bomber force to 600 aircraft.[92]

As part of the policy of flexible response, Kennedy advocated the growth of U.S. conventional military capabilities. As early as 1957, he had argued that the United States needed to adopt a military strategy that maintained large nuclear forces and sufficient conventional forces to meet any possible challenge.[93] The new president had been influenced by the thinking of General Maxwell Taylor, General James Gavin, and Nitze, who argued that the United States needed to expand its military options to meet the variety of military threats posed by the Soviet Union. In particular, Taylor and

Nitze saw the need for expanded conventional forces to wage limited wars. Herbert York, who served in both the Eisenhower and Kennedy administrations, remembered the change in emphasis in defense policies: "There was a definite change in attitude between the Eisenhower administration and the Kennedy administration. . . . I never got anywhere trying to sell much in the way of limited war ideas to Tom Gates [Eisenhower's last Secretary of Defense], or persuading him that it needed more, whereas [Kennedy's Secretary of Defense Robert] McNamara started off with the assumption, that more needs to be done in that area." [94]

Kennedy and his advisers believed that "a posture of flexible response was deemd [sic] to be more credible in support of American security interests and foreign policy objectives, because a clearer and closer correspondence could be struck between the military force that was to be applied by the President and the political stakes and the scope of the military conflict at issue between the United States and an enemy power." [95] In the March additions to the FY 1962 defense budget, $850 million was directed to improve U.S. limited war capabilities. Reflecting a general agreement with the limited war studies completed in 1960, most of the funding went to the expansion of air and sea lift forces and the procurement of conventional weapons. In May, Kennedy added $237 million to the defense budget to enhance U.S. limited war capabilities. The final $3.2 billion increase in July for FY 1962 facilitated increases in both conventional and nuclear capabilities. By the end of July 1961, Kennedy had proposed and Congress accepted the expansion of U.S. military personnel from the 2,493,000 requested by Eisenhower to 2,743,000. Over half the increase went to the army. [96]

Kennedy did not announce a position on civil defense during the presidential campaign. However, during his first year in office he gave more public attention to it than any other previous president. Kennedy stated in May 1961 that shelters should be viewed "as insurance for the civilian population in the event of such a miscalculation [a Soviet attack]. It is insurance we trust will never be needed—but insurance which we could never forgive ourselves for foregoing in the event of catastrophe." He then added that "there is no point in delaying the initiation of a nationwide long-range program of identifying present fallout shelter capacity and providing shelter in new and existing structures. Such a program would protect millions of people against the hazards of radioactive fallout in the event of a large-scale nuclear attack." [97]

In the midst of the renewed Berlin crisis two months later, Kennedy told a TV audience:

> In the event of an attack, the lives of those families which are not hit in a nuclear blast and fire can still be saved if they can be warned to take shelter and if that shelter is available. We owe that kind of insurance to our families, and to our country.
>
> In contrast to our friends in Europe, the need for this type of protection is new to our shores. But the time to start is now. In the coming months, I hope to let every citizen know what steps he can take without delay to protect his family in case of attack. I know you would not want to do less.[98]

Secretary of Defense McNamara presented Kennedy's civil defense plans to the Senate Appropriations Committee the next day. As the first phase of a plan to find shelter spaces for over 100 million people, McNamara requested $207.6 million to identify existing shelter spaces and to stock them with necessary emergency supplies. With the Berlin crisis acting as an impetus, Congress approved the entire amount.[99] When compared to the Eisenhower programs, there was not much difference. However, Kennedy's public announcements raised a national hysteria.[100]

Kennedy's proposals to build community shelters met much less success with Congress. Billed as the Shelter Incentive Program, Kennedy proposed giving $25 per shelter space to nonprofit facilities such as hospitals, libraries, and schools that built shelters. For FY 1963, the newly formed Office of Civil Defense (OCD) requested $695 million for this shelter program, but Congress only granted $113 million. For FY 1964, the OCD requested $346.9 million and received $11.6 million.[101] Congress' response to Kennedy's proposals reflected its general unwillingness to support major expenses for the construction of new shelters.[102]

Conclusions

Eisenhower reacted cautiously to the Gaither report and attempted to limit its influence on his national security policies. He approved those recommendations that he believed would strengthen the United States but resisted those proposals that he thought would undermine U.S. economic security. As a result of his caution, he constantly resisted calls for significant increases in defense spending; therefore, while he did expand U.S. nuclear capabilities and improve U.S. defenses, he refused to adopt a nationwide shelter program because he did not believe it would insure the continued viability of the United States after a nuclear war. In his mind, the cost of shelters simply would not reap many benefits. He also rejected demands to increase U.S. limited war capabilities because he believed that the United States already possessed the military forces to meet any likely conflicts of this type.

Eisenhower justified his military policies on two primary grounds. He continually argued that the Soviet Union would not risk a nuclear war in pursuit of its policy goals. Additionally, he stressed that there was little possibility of a limited war with the Soviet Union because such a conflict would quickly escalate into a nuclear war. He emphasized to the NSC in 1960 that "the only hostilities the U.S. was really concerned about was an all-out atomic attack." [103] Eisenhower did not mean to imply that limited wars might not occur, but he believed such conflicts would be waged between U.S. and non-Soviet forces. In these types of engagements Eisenhower was confident that U.S. forces in being were more than adequate. [104]

Although Eisenhower felt strongly that his policies would guarantee U.S. security, many people shared the Gaither committee's view that the United States needed to spend more on defense. Stimulated by *Sputnik,* the leak of the Gaither report, and Khrushchev's extraordinary claims, critics of the Republican administration claimed that Eisenhower was allowing the Soviet Union to obtain a lead over the United States in ballistic missile capabilities. These assertions of a missile gap dogged Eisenhower until he left office. In retrospect, it is clear that Eisenhower held a more nuanced view of the Cold War in the late 1950s than his critics. In actuality, there was little Eisenhower could have done to dispel his critics' claims. Almost all of the available evidence, both within the government and circulating in the public, pointed to a Soviet lead in missile development and deployments. The U-2 photographs, which helped confirm for Eisenhower the myth of the missile gap, would have provided little help in convincing a skeptical public, since they provided only limited coverage of the Soviet Union and could not refute the existence of extensive Soviet capabilities. What Eisenhower failed to do was to clearly articulate the deterrent value of existing U.S. military forces. [105] He realized what the public never understood. The United States possessed sufficient capabilities to absorb a Soviet attack and still launch a devastating counterstrike. Unfortunately for Eisenhower, he was never able to persuade the American public that the Soviet Union would have faced sure destruction if it had attacked the

United States. This failure allowed the Democrats to capitalize on the missile gap issue and regain the White House in 1960.

During his campaign and presidency, Kennedy asked many former members of the Gaither committee to serve in important advisory roles. The new president shared many of the committee's views and attempted to include them in his policies. In particular, he turned to Paul Nitze for advice on defense and foreign policy issues. After his election, Nitze continued to advise the president, along with Wiesner, Killian, Foster, and others from the Gaither committee. Not surprisingly then, by the end of 1963, most of the committee's recommendations, with the significant exception of fallout shelters, had become part of U.S. policy.

Unlike Eisenhower, Kennedy "believed that the economy could benefit from government spending, and he was therefore less concerned about allowing the military budget to rise during his presidency." [106] He expanded U.S. nuclear forces even more, increased U.S. capabilities to wage limited wars, and recommended an enlarged civil defense program. In implementing these changes, he increased expenditures for the military services from $41.3 billion in 1960 to $47.9 billion in 1963 and added approximately 225,000 military personnel to Eisenhower's recommendations.[107] At a news conference in 1963, Kennedy boasted, "The fact of the matter is, when we came into office we had 11 combat ready divisions; we now have 16. We increased the scheduling of Polaris, nearly double per year. We've increased the number of planes on 15 minute alert from 33 percent of our strategic air force to 50 percent. In a whole variety of ways . . . we've strengthened ourselves in defense and space." [108]

Conclusion

Beginning in 1957, Eisenhower faced tremendous pressures to reexamine U.S. national security policies. Through his first term, he had attempted to moderate the defense policies of the Truman administration and achieve a balanced budget. He was successful. However, with significant scientific and technological advances in nuclear weapons and delivery systems, the president's New Look policies came under increasing attack. One of the most important criticisms raised in 1956 and 1957 was whether the United States was doing enough to protect its civilian population. To answer this question, Eisenhower asked a panel of experts to examine U.S. active and passive defenses. The Gaither committee, as the panel became known, concluded that there were significant deficiencies in U.S. national security policies that could be rectified only by increased defense spending and expanded civil defense programs.

This study illuminates Eisenhower's decision-making process concerning national security issues. Until recently, records related to the Gaither committee remained hidden from the scholar's view. Although the Gaither report itself was declassified in the 1970s, most of the documents related to its development and dissemination continued to be restricted until the 1990s. The recent release of many of these records has allowed a clearer understanding of the significance of the committee's conclusions and, at the same time, provided another avenue to evaluate Eisenhower as a decision maker.

This study has drawn heavily from the depositories at the Eisenhower Library, the National Archives, the Library of Congress, the Massachusetts Institute of Technology, the George C. Marshall Foundation, and the United States Military Academy. By piecing together widely scattered documents, this study reveals that the Gaither committee was of vital importance in creating the impression of a missile gap and pressuring Eisenhower to change his national security policies. Furthermore, it underlines the difficulties Eisenhower experienced in trying to assess and implement the committee's recommendations. The president attempted to maintain a balance between the needs of national security and what the nation could afford.[1] Eisenhower feared that if he disrupted the economy through excessive spending on defense programs, the government would have to become more directly involved in everyday life. In his mind, such involvement would undermine the individual rights that he viewed as the basis of the American system of government and way of life.

When Eisenhower created the Gaither committee, he used an advisory system that had worked well previously. He entered the presidency believing that one of the central ingredients to decision making was to obtain advice that had been thoroughly discussed and analyzed by his key advisers. He viewed the NSC as the organization that could evaluate issues related to national security most effectively. During his first months in office, Eisenhower quickly approved the reorganization of the NSC to solidify its position in his decision-making system. For the remainder of his administration, the NSC served in this unprecedented role as one of the president's most important advisory organizations.[2]

In addition to revamping the NSC, Eisenhower turned to consultants outside the government for policy advice. The new president had realized during World War II that science and technology were evolving so quickly that no one person or group could understand all of the changes. The advances in nuclear weaponry and delivery systems in the late 1940s and 1950s made it even more difficult to comprehend the implications of the technological changes. While the members of the NSC were highly trained in certain fields, they lacked the expertise to understand fully the impact that scientific and technological advances would have. Eisenhower, therefore, sought the advice of specialists who had expertise in specific fields or a broad understanding of the technological changes that might impact U.S. national security.[3]

On three occasions during his two terms in office, Eisenhower asked the NSC to create advisory panels to evaluate national security issues. In 1953, the newly elected president initiated Project Solarium to study different strategies. Composed of three panels of consultants, Project Solarium provided advice that Eisenhower and the NSC used to develop the administration's New Look national security strategy. In 1954, Eisenhower again turned to a group of consultants, known as the Killian committee, to evaluate the threat of a surprise attack. After the committee submitted its report to the NSC in early 1955, Eisenhower accelerated U.S. missile programs and initiated the top secret U-2 intelligence program. Finally, in 1957, he created the Gaither committee to examine the effectiveness of U.S. active and passive defenses against an attack.

Since the completion of its examination in November 1957, the Gaither committee has been misunderstood by historians and other scholars. The committee has been described as of little importance.[4] This study does not corroborate this conclusion. The Gaither committee finished its report at a time of extremely high tension in the Cold War. The Soviet launch of *Sputnik I* in October and *Sputnik II* in November raised serious questions of the vulnerability of the United States. While it was much easier to launch a rocket into space than to hit a target with a nuclear weapon thousands of miles away, the Soviet satellites seemed to indicate that country's nuclear superiority over the United States. Khrushchev's claims that his country possessed this capability only heightened concerns. The American apprehension was shortsighted, especially when U.S. Strategic Air Command bombers were included in a comparison of U.S. and Soviet strengths. However, it was hard for most Americans to feel secure when *Sputnik* could pass over the United States with impunity.

The Gaither committee was not immune to the fears created by *Sputnik*. Its conclusions were pessimistic, and its recommendations reflected deeply held fears of the Soviet Union. But, with a few exceptions, the committee members did not want war, and in fact saw the strengthening of U.S. military forces as the only way to avoid it. The views held by the Gaither committee were not at the extremes of American society. There was a widespread fear of the Soviet Union and a belief that the United States needed to expand its military power. Consequently, the Gaither committee recommendations served as a catalyst for the reevaluation of Eisenhower's national security policies in late 1957 and early 1958.

Eisenhower ordered the creation of the Gaither committee after serious questions were raised about U.S. civil defenses and their ability to defend against a Soviet attack. The growing fears about radioactive fallout led the FCDA to recommend in early 1957 the construction of a nationwide system of fallout shelters. The advent of ballistic missiles brought into doubt U.S. capabilities to detect the launch of a Soviet attack, to defend the country if such an attack did occur, and to retaliate if necessary. These questions did not have easy answers; therefore, Eisenhower turned to consultants who either had expertise in specific technological fields or a broad understanding of the problems of active and passive defenses.

The committee met sporadically in the summer of 1957 and then much more intensely in the fall. It received briefings from the nation's ranking military leaders, examined numerous reports evaluating U.S. military policies, and studied intelligence estimates of Soviet military strength. By the time the committee presented its final report to the NSC in November 1957, it had examined U.S. military policies as thoroughly as time would allow. Its conclusions were frightening and its recommendations were unsettling, but based on the evidence it examined, perfectly understandable.

The committee concluded that within two years the United States would lose its nuclear superiority over the Soviet Union, therefore possibly finding itself vulnerable to a Soviet surprise attack. With these conclusions in mind, the committee recommended increasing nuclear forces to maintain U.S. superiority or, at a minimum, the ability to retaliate; expanding U.S. early warning radar capabilities; dispersing SAC forces; constructing antimissile defenses; building fallout shelters; reorganizing the Defense Department; and augmenting limited war capabilities. These programs would not be cheap. The committee estimated that they would cost $44.2 billion more than currently programmed in the defense budgets for FY 1959 through 1963.

The committee's recommendations created a dilemma for the Eisenhower administration. Spending, on average, an additional $9 billion a year would have meant increasing annual defense budgets by nearly 25 percent. If Eisenhower had accepted these increases, he would have had to accept higher taxes and deficits—both of which he abhorred. The president feared that higher taxes and deficit spending would force the government to regiment the economy and intrude on the rights of the individual. Nevertheless, Eisenhower was willing to accept higher spending if national security depended on it. In evaluating the Gaither report, Eisenhower sought to balance the consequences of higher defense spending with the preservation of national security.

Between November 1957 and July 1958, the Gaither report remained the centerpiece of NSC discussions. Various government agencies—including the Defense Department, the JCS, the State Department, the CIA, the Treasury Department, the Budget Bureau, and the FCDA—evaluated the Gaither report and presented their recommendations to the NSC. After numerous discussions, Eisenhower adopted changes to his national security policies that reflected the influence of the Gaither committee's recommendations. By July 1958, he increased force levels for IRBMs, ICBMs, and SLBMs; ordered the dispersal of SAC forces to more airfields and improvement in SAC's alert status; expanded early warning radar coverage; constructed additional antimissile defenses; reorganized the Defense Department; and initiated studies of U.S. limited war capabilities and fallout shelters. While he did not accept all of the Gaither committee's recommendations, their impact is nonetheless clear.

The influence of the Gaither committee did not end in the summer of 1958. For the remainder of his presidency, Eisenhower continually reevaluated the policies that the Gaither committee had brought into focus. During these years, the specific Gaither committee recommendations lost their relevance as new reports and intelligence estimates forced the administration to reevaluate U.S. strategic needs. However, the import of the committee's conclusions, specifically its calls for greater strategic capabilities, limited war forces, and fallout shelters, provided a continued impetus for discussions of U.S. national security needs.

Part of the lasting influence of the Gaither report rested in the political atmosphere it helped create. More than anything, *Sputnik* raised awareness that U.S. technological superiority was not guaranteed.[5] After the Gaither report was leaked to the press in December 1957, it furthered this fear by posing the possibility of a missile gap in favor of the Soviet Union. Without trivializing their real concerns about U.S. security, many Democrats saw the "missile gap" as an issue that they could use to criticize the Republican administration.[6] Eisenhower's refusal to release the report to congressional leaders fueled fears that the president was trying to hide the country's weaknesses. Until it was finally dispelled by new satellite intelligence in 1960 and 1961, the notion of a missile gap remained pivotal in debates about U.S. national security.

Senator John Kennedy was one of the most vocal proponents of the missile gap theory and harshest critics of the Eisenhower administration. He attacked U.S. military deficiencies on the Senate floor in 1958 and 1959, and campaigned against the Republican administration's policies in 1960. During his presidential run and administration, Kennedy on several occasions turned to former Gaither committee members for advice and even read the Gaither report. It would be too much to argue that the

Gaither report specifically influenced Kennedy's policies, but the ideas it espoused were surely important in the development of the new administration's flexible response strategy.

When Kennedy entered office in 1961, he saw two areas of U.S. military power that needed strengthening—nuclear missiles and conventional forces. Kennedy expanded the nuclear triad he inherited from the Eisenhower administration to insure U.S. superiority over the Soviet Union and augmented U.S. conventional forces to control conflicts short of general war. He further revisited the Gaither committee's call for a nationwide system of fallout shelters. During his three years in office, Kennedy successfully increased U.S. nuclear forces, augmented limited war capabilities, and located new shelter sites.

Along with showing the influence of the Gaither committee on the Eisenhower and Kennedy administrations, this study evaluates why the committee reached the conclusions it did. As they met in the summer and fall of 1957, committee members struggled to develop recommendations that reflected their understanding of the Soviet threat. While they were selected to advise Eisenhower, their opinions did not always coincide with the president's own views. They perceived a much greater Soviet threat than did Eisenhower. At later Senate hearings, both Robert Sprague and James Perkins questioned whether Eisenhower and his advisers really understood the threat posed by the Soviet Union. "I believe," Sprague testified, " . . . that the danger is more serious than the President has expressed himself to the American public."[7] Even more scathingly, Perkins argued that "the nature of the threat was not fully realized," and later concluded that "the Government did not have its eyes open in the summer and fall of 1957."[8]

Most of the committee members entered the study with deeply held opinions. With few exceptions, they had participated in other studies that addressed some of the issues found in the Gaither report. It is striking how closely the committee's conclusions resembled the findings of the MIT summer studies, Project East River, Project Solarium, and the Killian committee. Many members of these groups served on the Gaither committee. Furthermore, most of the members were influenced by their past or current affiliations. While it does not appear that the committee directly sought to benefit one group or another, its conclusions supported many of its members' affiliated groups. For instance, James Doolittle and Mervin Kelly were closely tied to the Air Force; James Fisk had been a consistent proponent for increased funding for research and development; and James

Killian, Albert Hill, and James McCormack maintained very close ties to MIT and were advocates for obtaining financing for improved early warning radar. The members' institutional ties and the knowledge they gained from earlier studies helped formulate the opinions they held when they began the Gaither study.

Once the committee began its examination, the members' preconceived opinions were reinforced by the evidence they analyzed. The military leaders consistently stressed deficiencies in their respective military branches and requested additional funding. Various reports created by government and civilian organizations concluded that the United States was deficient in strategic missile strength and vulnerable to a Soviet missile attack. Finally, the intelligence estimates predicted Soviet missile force levels that, if accurate, could have posed a significant threat to the United States. Taken together, this evidence provided committee members no reason to alter their earlier opinions.

In his memoirs, Eisenhower criticized the Gaither committee for failing "to see the totality of the national and international situation."[9] However, with their backgrounds and the available evidence, it is difficult to criticize the committee too much. It reached conclusions and made recommendations that were widely accepted.[10] Nevertheless, two significant criticisms can be directed at the committee. It made recommendations for significant increases in U.S. military force levels, yet it never articulated how or when they should be used. The implication of the committee's recommendations was that the United States should prepare for all possible contingencies without regard for their probability, their economic consequences, or their impact on foreign policy.[11]

Even more telling, the committee developed its conclusions based on an assumption about Soviet intentions rather than on a careful evaluation of why the Soviet Union might take particular actions.[12] At the beginning of its report, the committee stated that the Soviet Union's goal was world domination. At no point in the subsequent pages did the committee attempt to evaluate whether this really was the Soviet Union's goal or what risks its leaders would be willing to take to achieve it. The committee had available studies of the casualties that the United States could expect in a nuclear war, including several that predicted 100 million Americans would be killed. For the Soviet Union to risk a nuclear exchange with the United States, it would have had to consider the possible consequences for its own population. In making its recommendations, the committee failed to evaluate the likelihood of the risks the Soviet Union might take to achieve its goals; therefore, it proposed major increases in defense spending that did not reflect the improbability of a Soviet attack.

These criticisms are significant because without articulating a new strategy for how to utilize the expanded military forces and failing to analyze Soviet intentions, the committee placed a much greater emphasis on Soviet capabilities than it might have otherwise done. In doing so, it recommended the expansion of military forces to preserve the superiority of the United States without truly evaluating whether those forces and the costs associated with them were necessary.

As already explained, Eisenhower and his advisers carefully evaluated the Gaither report and, after much study, modified some of the administration's national security policies. Questions still remain as to the effectiveness of Eisenhower's decision-making system in dealing with the Gaither report. Was the establishment of the Gaither committee the best way to obtain the advice he wanted? Did his "hands-off" approach to management permit the committee to overstep the intended scope of its study? Did he articulate his administration's response to *Sputnik* and the Gaither report in a clear and reassuring manner? Did his national security policies after 1957 reflect a nuanced assessment of the Soviet threat and U.S. strategic needs? The answers to these questions provide a unique opportunity to reevaluate the effectiveness of Eisenhower as president.

During his administration, Eisenhower followed a strategy of deterrence in developing his national security programs. In pursuit of this strategy, he attempted to maintain a strong military while limiting defense spending. He believed his presidential responsibilities included protecting the nation's physical integrity as well as preserving a way of life. He recognized that a strong military could provide national security, but spending too much could undermine the economy and challenge freedoms guaranteed by the Constitution. He told a friend during the 1958 congressional election campaigns, "The brickbats that will be thrown at me I shall ignore, and I shall concentrate, as I have tried to do in the past, upon our national security, upon inching toward a just and durable peace for all the world, and upon sustaining the health of the American economy." [13] He therefore always carefully evaluated the economic impact of potential policies.

The changes Eisenhower made in his policies in 1958 and beyond represented his attempt to maintain a balance in his programs. He wanted to preserve national security, maintain an economy based on low inflation and balanced budgets, and protect individual rights. Although he was not convinced of the existence of a missile gap, he recognized that if the intelligence estimates were close to being accurate, he could not allow the Soviet Union to acquire a lead in missile capabilities. He thus reluctantly increased the country's offensive and defensive military capabilities.

Eisenhower established the Gaither committee to obtain advice that would allow him to find the proper balance in his policies. As he recalled, "With no vested interest in a particular department, and no federal jobs to protect, the panel was a means of obtaining independent judgments." [14] If he really believed that he could obtain such "independent" advice, he was mistaken. More important, this statement represents his failure to comprehend the views already held by the Gaither committee members. He had access to the reports of Project East River, Project Solarium, and the Killian committee, and had received briefings from Sprague, Doolittle, Killian, and Fisk concerning their perceptions of weaknesses in U.S. military or intelligence operations. Eisenhower knew their views and should have foreseen their conclusions. To have expected otherwise was remarkably shortsighted. There was simply no way the Gaither committee or any other group of experts could reach conclusions unaffected by preconceived beliefs or past affiliations.

Furthermore, Eisenhower's use of specialists and experts who were not elected and whose activities were generally unknown to the public brings into question his true understanding of the democratic principles that he readily espoused. He did face a dilemma. Because of the ever-expanding importance of specialized knowledge, Eisenhower needed to be able to acquire the best advice. However, by turning to experts who were neither elected, appointed by Congress, nor in any other way subject to the people's oversight, Eisenhower widened the gulf between democratic participation and decision making. By using this advisory system, Eisenhower severely hampered the citizenry's ability to oversee the activities of the government. Eisenhower belatedly recognized in his farewell address the dangers of becoming "the captive of a scientific-technological elite," but he failed to provide a possible solution to the individual's diminishing influence on decision making.

This assessment leads to a necessary reevaluation of Eisenhower's decision-making system. Fred Greenstein persuasively argues that Eisenhower followed a "hands-off" approach to decision making. [15] This approach is readily apparent in the president's supervision of the Gaither committee.

After ordering its creation, Eisenhower allowed his subordinates to oversee the selection of the committee members and their activities. Other than once in July, Eisenhower did not have direct contact with the group between May and the end of October. While it must be recognized that he had to allow the committee to do its work, his lack of oversight permitted the committee to expand its mandate well beyond an examination of active and passive defenses. The result was a report that evaluated the entire U.S. national security program and made extensive calls for revisions—an outcome the president did not want.[16]

After receiving the committee's report, Eisenhower and his advisers carefully evaluated its recommendations and conclusions. This stage of Eisenhower's decision-making system worked well. The NSC assigned the respective government departments relevant sections of the report to analyze. After receiving feedback, the NSC held discussions and made recommendations to the president. Through the entire process, Eisenhower participated actively in the NSC discussions and then made his decisions. By July 1958, the entire Gaither report had been thoroughly evaluated.

Where did Eisenhower's decision-making system fail him? In at least two places its shortcomings are readily apparent. By allowing the committee great autonomy, the president inadvertently permitted it to interpret its purpose broadly. The one time Eisenhower did meet with the committee members during their deliberations only strengthened their belief that they were supposed to review all U.S. national security programs. By remaining uninformed during the course of the committee's study, Eisenhower was unable to control the scope of its findings. Of equal importance, he never fully realized the importance of clearly articulating his views to the committee and, more important, to the population as a whole. He assumed his views were understood and accepted by most Americans. He was wrong. While Eisenhower was readily liked and respected, during his second term there were grave doubts about his policies. If he wanted the Gaither committee to limit the scope of its study and the people to trust his policies, he needed to articulate his views in a more effective manner. His failure to do so severely hampered his ability to govern during his second term.

Who was right? Did the Gaither committee illuminate a more potent threat than Eisenhower recognized, or was Eisenhower's caution a reflection of a more prudent analysis of the available evidence? In retrospect it seems clear that Eisenhower's more cautious approach was the most appropriate one. From the standpoint of the late 1950s, however, this view was hard to defend. The briefings, intelligence estimates, and the studies examined by the Gaither committee clearly indicate that many leading experts, both civilian and military, believed that the Soviet Union posed a significant threat to the United States. Although this assessment was inaccurate, it does not negate the fact that many people agreed with it.[17]

David Rosenberg has criticized Eisenhower for failing to regulate the expansion of the United States nuclear arsenal during the 1950s. He argues that Eisenhower recognized that the United States possessed sufficient nuclear weapons to destroy the Soviet Union but allowed the arsenal to continue to grow.[18] This conclusion has much validity, but it does overlook the control that Eisenhower maintained over delivery systems. The president faced tremendous pressure over his last few years in office to expand defense budgets and military programs even more. It is to his credit that he kept spending as low as he did. His shortcoming was his failure to convince the American people that his policies were the best for the country.

Eisenhower's handling of the Gaither report provides clear evidence of his struggle to limit defense spending. While defense spending increased after *Sputnik* and the Gaither report, these funds were used to address specific strategic needs. Even though Eisenhower did not think the Soviet Union would attack and believed that the intelligence estimates exaggerated Soviet capabilities, he recognized that he had to plan on the possibility that he might be wrong. He showed remarkable prudence in the implementation of his missile programs. He recognized the limitations of first-generation missiles and deliberately restricted their deployment. He only expanded ICBM force levels when the second-generation missiles, and especially the Minuteman, became available. Additionally, he foresaw the deterrent value of Polaris. Was it "overkill," as Rosenberg suggests? Yes, but it was predicated on the belief that the forces might be necessary to deter an enemy whose intentions remained unclear.

Final Thoughts

Heretofore, the history of the Gaither committee and its influence on the Eisenhower and Kennedy administrations was obscure. Changes in U.S. national security policies in the last few years of the Eisenhower presidency generally have been explained as the administration's reaction to *Sputnik*.

This study reveals that *Sputnik* offered only the most obvious incentive for change. The Gaither committee provided a blueprint for meeting any challenges posed by the Soviet Union. It recommended a U.S. military program that would have allowed the president to pursue any policy he chose. Eisenhower did not accept all of the committee's findings, but he was sufficiently persuaded by the panel of experts that he did modify some of his national security policies. Now, forty years later, it is clear that the Gaither committee played a pivotal role in the escalation of the Cold War in the late 1950s.

Much can be learned from this study of the Gaither committee. Eisenhower clearly made decisions based on well-defined principles and after receiving advice from a well-organized decision-making system. There is much to applaud in both areas. Eisenhower's basic values enabled him to develop policies that remained generally consistent throughout his administration. While it can be criticized, the president's New Look strategy was based on the belief that only by constraining defense spending could the United States maintain a political system based on democratic principles and an economic system based on capitalism. Eisenhower's decision-making system permitted thorough discussions of policy alternatives, allowing the president to receive the best possible advice. Eisenhower should be commended for his commitment to basic principles and effective organization.

On a more critical note, this study reveals several weaknesses in Eisenhower's presidency. His "hands-off" approach at times gave too much autonomy to advisory groups like the Gaither committee. As long as the president's objectives were clearly understood and accepted, the system worked well. The examples of Project Solarium and the Killian committee reveal the system at its best. However, when the president's views were not accepted, then problems could develop. This was clearly the case with the Gaither committee. Its members perceived a much greater Soviet threat than Eisenhower did and operated under assumptions that challenged some of the president's policies. Eisenhower's "hands-off" approach did not account for such differences of opinion.

Additionally, this study raises questions about how a president should define his policies. Throughout his administration, Eisenhower espoused basic principles, yet at times, as in the case of the Gaither committee, his decision-making system generated certain contradictions. In particular, Eisenhower's use of experts suggests that he was not as wedded to democratic principles as he led many to believe. His administration witnessed decision making that was even further removed from public oversight than it was in earlier presidencies. Also, as clearly as he sometimes articulated his views to government agencies, he was unable to define his policies in his second term in a manner that was reassuring to the people. As a result of this failure, he had to make a last-gasp admonition in his farewell address for the people to be vigilant in combating the military-industrial complex.

In the final analysis, how should Eisenhower be judged? He should be seen as a commander in chief who did his best to lead his country through a tumultuous decade. He followed a basic set of values and used a well-organized decision-making system. However, neither his values nor his decision-making system were perfect. He did not always apply his values consistently or articulate his views clearly. On the other hand, his decision-making system did normally provide him thoroughly evaluated advice and an opportunity to devise policies based on his principles. A testament to its effectiveness is Eisenhower's ability to resist the pressures on his administration to spend more on national security programs during his last few years in office. A president without Eisenhower's convictions and organizational capabilities would have been unable to do so.

Introduction

1. In February 1957 a Gallup Poll revealed that 79 percent of those polled supported Eisenhower. By March 1958 only 52 percent supported Eisenhower. See Chester J. Pach, Jr., and Elmo Richardson, *The Presidency of Dwight D. Eisenhower,* rev. ed. (Lawrence: University Press of Kansas, 1991), 175.

2. For U.S. reaction to *Sputnik,* see Robert A. Divine, *The Sputnik Challenge* (New York: Oxford University Press, 1993); and Walter A. McDougall, . . . *the Heavens and the Earth: A Political History of the Space Age* (New York: Basic Books, 1985).

3. U.S. Congress, Joint Committee on Defense Production, *Deterrence and Survival in the Nuclear Age (The "Gaither Report" of 1957)* [hereafter *Gaither Report*] (Washington, D.C.: Government Printing Office [hereafter GPO], 1976), 25.

4. See, e.g., Divine, *Sputnik Challenge,* 40–41, 84, 125–27, 196; Pach and Richardson, *Presidency of Dwight D. Eisenhower,* 173; McDougall, . . . *the Heavens and the Earth,* 151; Stephen E. Ambrose, *Eisenhower: The President,* vol. 2 (New York: Simon and Schuster, 1984), 434–35; John Lewis Gaddis, *Strategies of Containment: A Critical Appraisal of Postwar American National Security Policy* (New York: Oxford University Press, 1982), 185–86; and Samuel P. Huntington, *The Common Defense: Strategic Programs in National Politics* (New York: Columbia University Press, 1961), 111–13.

5. Morton H. Halperin, "The Gaither Committee and the Policy Process," *World Politics* 13, no. 3 (April 1961): 384.

6. Ibid., 373.

7. Unlike Halperin, Kaplan and Herken had access to the Gaither report itself. Most of the report was declassified in 1973 and published by a congressional committee in 1976.

8. Fred Kaplan, *The Wizards of Armageddon* (New York: Simon and Schuster, 1983), 128–30.

9. Ibid., 152.

10. Gregg Herken, *Counsels of War* (New York: Alfred A. Knopf, 1985), xiv. And see Gregg Herken, *Cardinal Choices: Presidential Science Advising from the Atomic Bomb to SDI* (New York: Oxford University Press, 1992).

11. Herken, *Counsels of War,* 118.

12. Peter J. Roman, "American Strategic Nuclear Force Planning, 1957–1960: The Interaction of Politics and Military Planning" (Ph.D. dissertation, University of Wisconsin, Madison, 1992), 2.

13. Ibid., 38. See also p. 43. Arguments similar to those in Roman's dissertation can be found in his more recent book. However, he does not focus nearly as
much on the Gaither committee in his book as in his dissertation. See Peter J. Roman, *Eisenhower and the Missile Gap* (Ithaca: Cornell University Press, 1995). On
his discussion of the Gaither committee, see in particular pp. 66–67.

14. See n. 4 above. See also McGeorge Bundy, *Danger and Survival: Choices
about the Bomb in the First Fifty Years* (New York: Random House, 1988), 335–
37; Desmond Ball, *Politics and Force Levels: The Strategic Missile Program of the
Kennedy Administration* (Berkeley: University of California Press, 1980), 27–30;
Richard A. Aliano, *American Defense Policy from Eisenhower to Kennedy: The Politics
of Changing Military Requirements, 1957–1961* (Athens: Ohio University Press,
1975), 59; and John C. Donovan, *The Cold Warriors: A Policy-Making Elite* (Lexington, Mass.: D.C. Heath, 1974), 130–49. David Rosenberg also used newly declassified documents in examining the Gaither committee, but he really did not add
much to the other arguments. See David A. Rosenberg, "The Origins of Overkill:
Nuclear Weapons and American Strategy, 1945–1960," *International Security* 7 : 4
(Spring 1983): 46–49.

15. Pach and Richardson, *Presidency of Dwight D. Eisenhower,* 238–39. For an
excellent overview of the historiography of the Eisenhower administration, see
Gunter Bischof and Stephen E. Ambrose, *Eisenhower: A Century Assessment* (Baton
Rouge: Louisiana State University Press, 1995), 1–13.

16. See Dwight D. Eisenhower, *Mandate for Change, 1953–1956* (Garden
City, N.Y.: Doubleday, 1963), 446, 488; Robert W. Griffith, "Dwight D. Eisen-
hower and the Corporate Commonwealth," *American Historical Review* 87 : 1
(February 1982): 87–122; John W. Sloan, "The Management and Decision-Mak-
ing Style of President Eisenhower," *Presidential Studies Quarterly* 20 : 2 (Spring
1990): 295–313; R. Gordon Hoxie, "Dwight D. Eisenhower: Bicentennial
Considerations," *Presidential Studies Quarterly* 20 : 2 (Spring 1990): 253–64; Fred
I. Greenstein, *The Hidden-Hand Presidency: Eisenhower as Leader* (New York: Basic
Books, 1982), 100–151; Iwan W. Morgan, *Eisenhower versus 'The Spenders': The
Eisenhower Administration, the Democrats and the Budget, 1953–60* (New York: St.
Martin's Press, 1990); and Douglas Kinnard, *President Eisenhower and Strategy
Management: A Study in Defense Politics* (Lexington: University Press of Kentucky,
1977).

17. Memorandum of Discussion at the 270th Meeting of the NSC, December 9, 1955, Dwight D. Eisenhower Library [hereafter EL], Papers of Dwight D.
Eisenhower [hereafter DDE Papers], NSC Series, Box 7, Folder—270th Meeting
of NSC, December 8, 1955, 4–5. Eisenhower's concern with the impact of defense
spending can be seen as far back as 1945. While Army chief of staff, he wrote in his
diary, "I'm astounded and appalled at the size and scope of plans the [Army] staff
sees as necessary to maintain our security position now and in the future. . . . The

cost is terrific. We'll be merely tilting at windmills unless we can develop something more in line with financial possibilities." See diary entry of Dwight D. Eisenhower, December 12, 1945, in Robert H. Ferrell, ed., *The Eisenhower Diaries* (New York: W. W. Norton, 1981), 136.

18. Eisenhower to Milton Eisenhower, December 3, 1964, EL, Milton S. Eisenhower Papers, 1938–1973, Box 15, Folder—Correspondence, 1964, 2–3.

19. Anna Kasten Nelson, "The 'Top of Policy Hill': President Eisenhower and the National Security Council," *Diplomatic History* 7:4 (Fall 1983): 307–26.

20. The President's News Conference of January 23, 1957, *Public Papers of the Presidents of the United States, Dwight D. Eisenhower* [hereafter *PPP-DDE*], *1957* (GPO, 1958), 74.

21. For the findings of the Senate committee, see U.S. Congress, Senate, Committee on Government Operations, *Organizing for National Security,* Hearings before the Subcommittee on National Policy Machinery (GPO, 1961); and Henry M. Jackson, "Organizing for Security," *Foreign Affairs* 38 (1960): 446–56. For scholars who have relied heavily on the Senate committee's interpretations, see I. M. Destler, "The Presidency and National Security Organization," in Norman A. Graebner, ed., *The National Security* (New York: Oxford University Press, 1986), 230; J. C. Heinlein, *Presidential Staff and National Security Policy* (Cincinnati: Center for the Study of United States Foreign Policy, 1963), 48; Richard A. Melanson and David Mayers, eds., *Reevaluating Eisenhower: American Foreign Policy in the 1950s* (Chicago: University of Illinois Press, 1987), 2; and Huntington, *The Common Defense,* 154.

22. See Anna Kasten Nelson, "The Importance of Foreign Policy Process: Eisenhower and the National Security Council," in Bischof and Ambrose, *Eisenhower: A Century Assessment,* 111–25; Nelson, "The 'Top of Policy Hill,'" 324; Phillip G. Henderson, "Advice and Decision: The Eisenhower National Security Council Reappraised," in R. Gordon Hoxie, *The President and National Security Policy* (New York: Center for the Study of the Presidency, 1984), 155; R. Gordon Hoxie, "The National Security Council," *Presidential Studies Quarterly* 12 (Winter 1982): 109; Greenstein, *The Hidden-Hand Presidency,* 126; and Stanley L. Falk, "The National Security Council under Truman, Eisenhower, and Kennedy," *Political Science Quarterly* 74:3 (1964): 418.

23. Brian Balogh, *Chain Reaction: Expert Debate and Public Participation in American Commercial Nuclear Power, 1945–1975* (New York: Cambridge University Press, 1991), 22, 172; Stuart W. Leslie, *The Cold War and American Science: The Military-Industrial-Academic Complex at MIT and Stanford* (New York: Columbia University Press, 1993); Albert H. Teich and Jill H. Pace, eds., *Science and Technology in the USA* (Essex, UK: Longman House, 1986), 20–22; Aaron L. Friedberg, "Science, the Cold War, and the American State," *Diplomatic History* 20:1 (Winter 1996): 117–18; Robert Gilpin and Christopher Wright, eds.,

Scientists and National Policy-Making (New York: Columbia University Press, 1964); and Michael A. Bernstein and Allen Hunter, "The Cold War and Expert Knowledge: New Essays on the History of the National Security State," *Radical History Review* 63 (1995): 3–4.

24. Herken, *Counsels of War,* 134.

25. Robert Wiebe was one of the first scholars to recognize the growing contradiction between specialization and preserving democratic processes. In his study of the late nineteenth and early twentieth centuries, he argues that leaders came to believe that science and expertise would allow the government to operate efficiently and justly. He concludes that this political theory rested on a perpetual vagueness that was a threat to democracy. Robert H. Wiebe, *The Search for Order 1877–1920* (New York: Hill and Wang, 1967), 159–63.

Chapter 1

1. For his own brief descriptions of these pressures, see Dwight D. Eisenhower, *At Ease: Stories I Tell to Friends* (Doubleday, 1967), 333–35, 377–78.

2. See Stephen E. Ambrose, *Eisenhower,* vol. 2, 17–18; Robert H. Ferrell, *Off the Record: The Private Papers of Harry S. Truman* (New York: Penguin Books, 1980), 264; and David McCullough, *Truman* (New York: Simon & Schuster, 1992), 412–14.

3. George E. Reedy, *The U.S. Senate: Paralysis or a Search for Consensus* (New York: Crown Publishers, 1986), 63.

4. Eisenhower's own recognition of his limited chances of promotion can be seen in Eisenhower, *At Ease,* 240.

5. For a description of Eisenhower's activities between World War II and his presidency, see Eisenhower, *At Ease,* 297–378; and Stephen E. Ambrose, *Eisenhower: Soldier, General of the Army, President-Elect,* vol. 1 (New York: Simon & Schuster, 1983), 433–528.

6. See Sherman Adams, *Firsthand Report: The Story of the Eisenhower Administration* (Westport, Conn.: Greenwood Press, 1961), 155; and Steven Metz, "Eisenhower and the Planning of American Grand Strategy," *Journal of Strategic Studies* 14:1 (March 1991): 49–50.

7. Eisenhower to Swede Hazlett, July 19, 1947, in Robert W. Griffith, ed., *Ike's Letters to a Friend, 1941–1958* (Lawrence: University Press of Kansas, 1984), 40.

8. For descriptions of Eisenhower's childhood and upbringing, see Eisenhower, *At Ease,* 29–198; Kenneth S. Davis, *Soldier of Democracy: A Biography of Dwight Eisenhower* (Garden City, N.Y.: Doubleday, Doran & Company, 1945), 65–98; Bela Kornitzer, *The Great American Heritage: The Story of the Five Eisenhower Brothers* (New York: Farrar, Straus, and Cudahy, 1955), 9–56, 85–98; and Ambrose, *Eisenhower,* vol. 1, 18–42.

9. Kenneth Davis categorizes Eisenhower's beliefs as part of a frontier philoso-

phy. He explains, "The frontiersman, without thinking about it, stood for diverse multiplicity, for individual freedom, for simplicity, particularism, pragmatism." In discussing Eisenhower's early concept of democracy, Davis argues that the future president "had . . . certain underlying principles of action which could be broadly grouped under the Golden Rule, which involved his profound belief in common people and his contempt for selfish egotism and for aristocratic pretensions. There was nothing coldly calculating, nothing relative in his belief in democracy; it was an absolute, instinctively held, upon which all relativities of action must rest." See Davis, *Soldier for Democracy,* 86–87; Kornitzer, *Great American Heritage,* 17, 21, 55–56.

10. Dwight D. Eisenhower, *Crusade in Europe* (Garden City, N.Y.: Doubleday, 1948), 60.

11. Eisenhower to John Eisenhower, April 8, 1943, quoted in Eisenhower, *Crusade in Europe,* 206.

12. Eisenhower to Col. William Lee, October 29, 1942, quoted in Ambrose, *Eisenhower,* vol. 1., 207.

13. See Eisenhower to Georgi Konstantinovich Zhukov, December 6, 1945, and March 13, 1946, in Louis Galambos, ed., *The Papers of Dwight David Eisenhower,* vol. 7, *The Chief of Staff* (Baltimore: Johns Hopkins University Press, 1978), 591, 921.

14. Eisenhower, *Crusade in Europe,* 467–68. Zhukov told Eisenhower, "When we come to a mine field our infantry attacks exactly as if it were not there." Eisenhower's reaction to the comment was that "Americans assess the cost of war in terms of human lives, the Russians in the over-all drain on the nation."

15. Eisenhower explained that his mistrust of the Soviet Union developed from personal experiences and was influenced by messages from James Forrestal during World War II. Eisenhower, *At Ease,* 268, 329–30.

16. Eisenhower, *Crusade in Europe,* 472.

17. Ibid., 476. By January 1946 Eisenhower was circulating a G-2 analysis that concluded, "It is believed that Soviet policy is to increase internal economic and military strength to support expansion, wherever and whenever practicable, in the international field." Galambos, ed., *Papers of Dwight David Eisenhower,* vol. 7, 744n.

18. Dwight D. Eisenhower Diary Entry, September 16, 1947, in Ferrell, ed., *Eisenhower Diaries,* 143.

19. Eisenhower, *Crusade in Europe,* 477. For a discussion of these conversations, see pp. 460–74.

20. See Raymond J. Saulnier, "The Philosophy Underlying Eisenhower's Economic Policies," in Joann P. Krieg, ed., *Dwight D. Eisenhower: Soldier, President, Statesman* (New York: Greenwood Press, 1987), 99–104.

21. Excerpts from Military Sub-Committee of the Appropriations Committee

of the Senate, quoted in Memorandum for the Record, March [?] 1950, EL, DDE Papers, Name Series, Box 7, Folder—DDE Defense Warnings, 1945–51, 8.

22. Eisenhower Diary Entry, January 22, 1952, in Ferrell, ed., *Eisenhower Diaries,* 209. Eisenhower's views on budget deficits might have stemmed from the failure of his father's business in the 1880s due in part to the purchase of too many goods on credit. After this business disaster, Eisenhower's father "had a lifelong dread of debt." See Ambrose, *Eisenhower,* vol. 1, 19; Eisenhower, *At Ease,* 31.

23. Eisenhower Diary Entry, January 22, 1952, in Ferrell, ed., *Eisenhower Diaries,* 210.

24. Eisenhower Diary Entry, May 26, 1946, ibid., 137.

25. Eisenhower Diary Entry, January 22, 1952, ibid., 211.

26. Ibid.

27. Ibid., 213.

28. NSC 68 represented President Truman's strategy to increase defense spending to meet the perceived Soviet threat. It is discussed later in the chapter.

29. See Paul Y. Hammond, "NSC-68: Prologue to Rearmament," in Warner R. Schilling, Paul Y. Hammond, and Glenn H. Snyder, *Strategy, Politics, and Defense Budgets* (New York: Columbia University Press, 1962), 351–58. For exact amounts spent on national security programs, see *The Statistical History of the United States: From Colonial Times to the Present* (New York: Basic Books, 1976), 1124.

30. Dwight D. Eisenhower, "Text of Eisenhower Address on 'Famine or Feast' Defense Policy," in *New York Times,* September 26, 1952, Sec. A, 12.

31. See John W. Sloan, *Eisenhower and the Management of Prosperity* (Lawrence: University of Kansas Press, 1991), 20–47.

32. Ibid., 42.

33. See the title of Eisenhower's presidential memoirs for his first term: *Mandate for Change.*

34. Eisenhower, *Mandate for Change,* 87.

35. Oral History of Andrew J. Goodpaster, Oral History Research Office, Columbia University, 1967, 31.

36. See H. W. Brands, "The Age of Vulnerability: Eisenhower and the National Insecurity State," *American Historical Review* 94:4 (October 1989): 963–89; and Henry M. Jackson, ed., *The National Security Council* (New York: Frederick A. Praeger, 1965).

37. Eisenhower, *Mandate for Change,* 114.

38. See Greenstein, *Hidden-Hand Presidency,* 124–38; and Andrew J. Goodpaster, "Four Presidents and the Conduct of National Security Affairs—Impressions and Highlights," *Journal of International Relations* 2:1 (Spring 1977): 27–28.

39. Pach and Richardson, *Presidency of Dwight D. Eisenhower,* 38.

40. For descriptions of the organization of the Eisenhower White House, see Eisenhower, *Mandate for Change*, 115–20; Pach and Richardson, *Presidency of Dwight D. Eisenhower*, 38–39; and Ambrose, *Eisenhower*, vol. 2, 24–26.

41. Oral History of Dr. Arthur S. Flemming, EL, 1988, 13.

42. On Truman's reluctance to participate actively at NSC meetings prior to 1950, see Samuel R. Williamson, Jr., and Steven L. Rearden, *The Origins of U.S. Nuclear Strategy, 1945–1953* (New York: St. Martin's Press, 1993), 55–56; Anna Kasten Nelson, "President Truman and the Evolution of the National Security Council," *Journal of American History* 72:2 (September 1985): 360–61, 373–78; James S. Lay, Jr., *Organizational History of the National Security Council during the Truman and Eisenhower Administrations* (GPO, 1960), 5, 14–22; and David L. Snead, "United States National Security Policy under Presidents Truman and Eisenhower: The Evolving Role of the National Security Council" (M.A. thesis, Virginia Polytechnic Institute and State University, 1991), 27–29.

43. For some recent analyses of NSC 68, see Ernest R. May, ed., *American Cold War Strategy: Interpreting NSC 68* (Boston: Bedford Books of St. Martin's Press, 1993); Melvyn P. Leffler, *A Preponderance of Power: National Security, the Truman Administration, and the Cold War* (Stanford: Stanford University Press, 1992), 313; and Burton I. Kaufman, *The Korean War: Challenges in Crisis, Credibility, and Command* (New York: Alfred Knopf, 1986), 28.

44. Snead, "United States National Security Policy under Presidents Truman and Eisenhower," 21.

45. Robert Cutler, *No Time for Rest* (Boston: Little, Brown, 1965, 1966), 296.

46. Saki Dockrill, *Eisenhower's New-Look National Security Policy, 1953–61* (New York: St. Martin's Press, 1996), 23–24.

47. Nelson, "President Truman and the Evolution of the National Security Council," 371–78. Prior to the revision of the National Security Act, the NSC's statutory members were the president, the secretary of state, the secretary of defense, the chairman of the National Security Resources Board, and the secretaries of the army, navy, and air force. See 1947 National Security Act, Public Law 253, 80th Congress, July 26, 1947 (61 Stat. 495), reprinted in *United States Statutes at Large*, vol. 61 (GPO, 1948), 495–97.

48. Paul Nitze to Cutler, February 17, 1953, National Archives [hereafter NA], RG 59, Records of the Department of State, S/S—NSC (Miscellaneous) Files, Lot 66D 95, Box 11.

49. "Report by the Special Assistant to the President for National Security Affairs," March 19, 1953, *Papers Related to the Foreign Relations of the United States* [hereafter *FRUS*] *1952–1954*, 2:1 (GPO, 1984), 245–57.

50. Eisenhower also asked the director of the Bureau of the Budget to attend NSC meetings as an informal member. Later, he created the Operations Coordinating Board to supervise the implementation of the NSC's decisions. See Lay,

"Organizational History of the National Security Council," 23–30; and Nelson, "The 'Top of Policy Hill': President Eisenhower and the National Security Council," 308–10.

51. Press Release, March 23, 1953, NA, RG 59, State Department Records, S/S—NSC (Miscellaneous) Files, Lot 66D 95, Box 11, 1. For discussions of the reorganization of Eisenhower's NSC, see Cutler, *No Time For Rest*, 293–313; and Snead, "United States National Security Policy," 36–39.

52. Most scholars, including both supporters and detractors, who have examined Eisenhower's NSC have recognized the importance of these factors. See, e.g., Brands, "Age of Vulnerability," 963–89; Griffith, "Dwight D. Eisenhower and the Corporate Commonwealth," 87–122; John W. Sloan, "The Management and Decision-Making Style of President Eisenhower," 295–313; Morgan, *Eisenhower versus 'The Spenders'*; Huntington, *The Common Defense*; Richard D. Challener, "The National Security Policy from Truman to Eisenhower: Did the 'Hidden Hand' Leadership Make Any Difference," in Graebner, *The National Security*; Aliano, *American Defense Policy from Eisenhower to Kennedy*; and Kaplan, *Wizards of Armageddon*.

53. *Statistical History of the United States*, 1124.

54. See Ambrose, *Eisenhower*, vol. 2, 489. On Eisenhower's desire for more money for defense spending in 1949, see Eisenhower Diary Entry, January 8, 1949, in Ferrell, ed., *Eisenhower Diaries*, 153.

55. Memorandum for the President by the Secretaries of State and Defense and the Director of Mutual Security, January 16, 1953, *FRUS 1952–1954*, 2:1, 211 and 213.

56. Minutes of the 131st Meeting of the National Security Council, February 11, 1953, NA, RG 273, Records of the National Security Council, Folder— 131st Meeting of the NSC.

57. For a discussion of the establishment of Project Solarium, see Snead, "United States National Security Policy under Presidents Truman and Eisenhower," 39–41; Glen H. Snyder, "The 'New Look' of 1953," in Schilling, Hammond, and Snyder, *Strategy, Politics and Defense Budgets*, 407–10; William B. Pickett, "The Eisenhower Solarium Notes," *Society for Historians of American Foreign Relations Newsletter* 16 (June 1985): 1–3; and Dockrill, *Eisenhower's New-Look*, 33–35. While most of these scholars identify the importance of Project Solarium to Eisenhower's deliberations, they generally do not examine the significance of the president's turning to experts outside the government for advice.

58. The members of the directing panel were General James H. Doolittle (chairman), Robert Amory, Jr., Lt. General L. L. Lemnitzer, Dean Rusk, and Admiral Leslie C. Stevens. See Memorandum to the Secretary of State, 5/15/53, *FRUS 1952–1954*, 2:1, 327.

59. Eisenhower assigned each task force one of three specific strategies: con-

tainment, drawing a line in the sand, and rollback, and asked them to develop a national security policy based on that strategy. There was evidently a fourth possibility—alternative D. Although it remains unclear as to what alternative D was, it was based on "the possibility that time is not working in our favor." See Memorandum for the President, undated [June 1953?], NA, RG 273, NSC, Folder—155th Meeting of the NSC, 1. Richard Immerman has found similar evidence related to an alternative D. See Richard H. Immerman, "Confessions of an Eisenhower Revisionist: An Agonizing Reappraisal," *Diplomatic History* 14 : 3 (Summer 1990): 337.

60. Memorandum to the Secretary of State, May 15, 1953, *FRUS 1952–1954,* 2 : 1, 325–26.

61. Snyder, "The 'New Look,'" 408.

62. Task force A consisted of Kennan, Col. C. H. Bonesteel, Rear Adm. H. P. Smith, Col. George Lincoln, C. T. Wood, J. Maury, and Capt. H. S. Sears. Task force B was composed of McCormack, Maj. Gen. J. R. Deane, J. K. Penfield, P. E. Mosely, Calvin Hoover, J. C. Campbell, and Col. E. S. Ligon. Task force C consisted of Conolly, Lt. Gen. L. L. Lemnitzer, G. F. Reinhardt, Col. K. Johnston, Col. A. J. Goodpaster, Leslie Brady, and Col. H. K. Johnson. Memorandum of Discussion at the 157th Meeting of the National Security Council, July 16, 1953, *FRUS 1952–1954,* 2 : 1, 395–96. It remains unclear how and when the members of these task forces were selected. A list of prospective members on May 20, 1953, is remarkably different from the task forces that made presentations to the NSC in July. See Memorandum by the President to the Secretary of State, May 20, 1953, ibid., 350–52.

63. Transcript of "Project Solarium": A Collective Oral History, John Foster Dulles Centennial Conference, Princeton University, 1988, 3. See also George F. Kennan, *Memoirs,* vol. 2 (Boston: Little, Brown, 1972), 182.

64. Paper Prepared by the Directing Panel of Project Solarium, June 1, 1953, *FRUS 1952–1954,* 2 : 1, 361.

65. Notes Taken at the First Plenary Session of Project Solarium, June 23, 1953, ibid., 389.

66. These policies were summarized in NSC 153. See NSC 153/1—"A Report to the National Security Council by the Executive Secretary on Restatement of Basic National Security Policy," June 10, 1953, in Marc Trachtenberg, *The Development of American Strategic Thought: Basic Documents from the Eisenhower and Kennedy Periods, Including the Basic National Security Papers from 1953 to 1959* (New York: Garland Publishing, 1988), 19–33.

67. "A Report to the National Security Council by Task Force 'A' of Project Solarium," July 16, 1953, NA, RG 273, NSC, Folder—157th Meeting of the NSC, 7–8.

68. See Project Solarium Outline, undated [June 1953?], NA, RG 273, NSC, Folder—155th Meeting of the NSC, 7–8.

69. "A Report to the NSC by Task Force 'A,'" I-1, 46, and 56.

70. "A Report to the National Security Council by Task Force 'B' of Project Solarium," July 16, 1953, NA, RG 273, NSC, Folder—157th Meeting of the NSC, 30.

71. "A Report to the National Security Council by Task Force 'C' of Project Solarium," July 16, 1953, NA, RG 273, NSC, Folder—157th Meeting of the NSC, 16.

72. Transcript of "Project Solarium," 22.

73. In her recent study of Eisenhower's New Look, Saki Dockrill describes the evolution of NSC 162/2 in great detail. See Dockrill, *Eisenhower's New-Look,* 35–47. She does not, however, recognize the significance of Eisenhower's using expert consultants to obtain advice.

74. Statement of Policy by the National Security Council, October 30, 1953, *FRUS 1952–1954,* 2:1, 578.

75. Ibid., 582.

76. Williamson and Rearden argue that Eisenhower's "New Look" strategy was simply a continuation of Truman's policies with a few modifications. While true in part, this argument does not sufficiently explain the sharp spending reductions that Eisenhower sought in military programs. Truman might have been a fiscal conservative, as Williamson and Rearden argue, but Eisenhower was much more of one. See Williamson and Rearden, *Origins of U.S. Nuclear Strategy,* 105–7, 148–49, 191–93. For the development of Eisenhower's thinking concerning the New Look, see Samuel F. Wells, "The Origins of Massive Retaliation," *Political Science Quarterly* 96 (Spring 1981): 31–52.

77. War, as defined here, meant a general conflict between the United States and the Soviet Union. Conflicts in peripheral areas of the world, e.g., Korea, were classified differently.

78. Statement of Policy by the National Security Council, October 30, 1953, *FRUS 1952–1954,* 2:1, 585.

79. In an informative analysis of the literature describing Eisenhower's foreign policies and the Third World, Robert McMahon argues that Eisenhower failed to take adequate cognizance of the forces of nationalism in the Third World. Instead, the president viewed revolutions in developing countries as communist-inspired. This view led to policies that ultimately weakened the U.S. position in the Third World. See Robert J. McMahon, "Eisenhower and Third World Nationalism: A Critique of the Revisionists," *Political Science Quarterly* 101 (Fall 1986): 453–73.

80. Statement of Policy by the National Security Council, October 30, 1953, 584.

81. Transcript of "Project Solarium": A Collective Oral Interview, 20.

82. For an excellent analysis of U.S. assessments of Soviet military strength, see John Prados, *The Soviet Threat: U.S. Intelligence Analysis & Russian Military Strength* (New York: Dial Press, 1982).

83. Leffler, *Preponderance of Power,* 96.

84. Draft Memorandum for the President, November 16, 1949, Library of Congress [hereafter LC], Papers of Muir Fairchild, Box 1, Folder—9/30/49–12/7/49, 1.

85. Memorandum by the Chief of Staff, U.S. Air Force to the Joint Chiefs of Staff, 11/16/49, ibid., 5.

86. See NIE 3, "Soviet Capabilities and Intentions," November 15, 1950, NA, RG 263, Records of the Central Intelligence Agency, Box 1—NIE's Regarding Soviet Union 1950–1955, Folder no. 1, 9; NIE 48, "Likelihood of the Deliberate Initiation of Full-Scale War by the USSR against the US and Its Western Allies Prior to the End of 1952," January 18, 1952, ibid., 1; and NIE 64 (Part II), "Probable Soviet Bloc Courses of Action through Mid-1953," December 11, 1952, ibid., 2. For a description of the Soviet Union's reluctance to go to war, see Leffler, *Preponderance of Power,* 488.

87. Memorandum of Discussion at the 148th Meeting of the National Security Council, June 4, 1953, *FRUS 1952–1954,* 2:1, 369. Eisenhower agreed completely with Edwards's assessment. See ibid., 370. For a copy of Edwards's report, see NSC 140/1—Report to the National Security Council by the Special Evaluation Subcommittee of the National Security Council, May 18, 1953, ibid., 328–49.

88. NIE 48, NA, RG 263, CIA, Box 1—NIE's Regarding Soviet Union 1950–1955, Folder no. 1, 2. At the same NSC meeting where Edwards presented his report, CIA Director Allen Dulles concluded that the United States could "not expect any warning of a Soviet 'sneak' attack." Memorandum of Discussion at the 148th NSC Meeting, *FRUS 1952–1954,* 2:1, 369.

89. Memorandum Op-36C/jm, March 18, 1954, in David Alan Rosenberg, "A Smoking Radiating Ruin at the End of Two Hours," *International Security* 6:3 (Winter 1981/82), 26. Any Soviet attack precipitated on these lines would have required the launching of bombers on one-way missions. At that time, the Soviet Union relied on the TU-4 bomber, whose range would not allow two-way missions to the United States without refueling. See SE-36—Soviet Capabilities for Attack on the US through Mid-1955, March 5, 1953, NA, RG 263, CIA, Box 1—NIE's Regarding Soviet Union 1950–1955, Folder no. 1, 2–5.

90. Memorandum Op-36C/jm, March 18, 1954, 24. See also L. Weinstein et al., *The Evolution of U.S. Strategic Command and Control and Warning, 1945–1972* (Arlington, Va.: Institute for Defense Analyses, 1975), 103–4.

91. Memorandum Op-36C/jm, March 18, 1954, 24.

92. NSC 159/4—Statement of Policy by the National Security Council, September 25, 1953, *FRUS 1952–1954,* 2:1, 478.

93. Ibid., 483–85.

94. Memorandum for the NSC, August 21, 1953, RG 218, Records of the Joint Chiefs of Staff, 1951–53 Geographic File, Folder—CCS 381 US (5-23-46)

Sec. 25, 396. See also Kenneth Schaffel, *The Emerging Shield: The Air Force and the Evolution of Continental Air Defense, 1945–1960* (Washington, D.C.: Office of Air Force History, 1991), 193.

95. Magnitude and Imminence of Soviet Air Threat to the United States— 1957, October 30, 1953, RG 218, JCS, 1951–53 Geographic File, Folder—CCS 350.09 USSR (12-19-49) Sec. 5, 1216–18.

96. Ibid., 1217.

97. In 1954 the Soviet Union introduced two new medium- and long-range bombers: TU-16 (codenamed Badger) and M-4 (codenamed Bison). See David A. Brinkley and Andrew W. Hull, *Estimative Intelligence* (Washington, D.C.: Defense Intelligence School, 1979), chap. 3, reprinted in Harold P. Ford, *Estimative Intelligence: The Purposes and Problems of National Intelligence Estimating* (New York: Defense Intelligence College, 1993), 217–18.

98. A. J. Wohlstetter, F. S. Hoffman, R. J. Lutz, and H. S. Rowen, *Selection and Use of Strategic Air Bases* (Santa Monica, Calif.: RAND Corporation, 1963), 227. Although not published until 1963, this report was completed and widely circulated within the government in 1954.

99. Memorandum by the Counselor (Bohlen), March 27, 1952, *FRUS 1952– 1954,* 2:1, 5–6. It must be stressed that Bohlen and most policymakers did not expect the Soviet Union to attack the United States. However, differences did arise among policymakers concerning the risks the Soviet Union would be willing to take to achieve its goals. Regardless, Bohlen's entire statement concerning the assumptions of U.S. policymakers about the Soviet Union is particularly revealing. He argues that "there are certain fundamental features of the Soviet system which are generally uncontested by all analyses." He then explains that

it is generally accepted that the Soviet system:

a. Is a totalitarian system, heavily armed and continuously seeking to increase its military potential, where the power of decision rests entirely in the hands of a small group of men;

b. By the nature of its state structure, reinforced by its ideology, is fundamentally and unappeasably hostile to any society not susceptible to its control;

c. The directing group of the Soviet Government and of international Communism are [*sic*] totally uninhibited by any considerations of a humanitarian, moral, or ethical character which have acted, in history, as restraints upon the use of force.

100. Jack H. Nunn, *The Soviet First Strike Threat: The U.S. Perspective* (New York: Praeger Publishers, 1982), 55. For the importance of the first strike to leading strategic thinkers in the 1950s, see Marc Trachtenberg, *History and Strategy*

(Princeton University Press, 1991), vii; Marc Trachtenberg, "A 'Wasting Asset': American Strategy and the Shifting Nuclear Balance, 1949–1954," *International Security* 13 : 2 (Winter 1988/89): 5–49; and Lawrence Freedman, *The Evolution of Nuclear Strategy* (New York: St. Martin's Press, 1981, 1983), 34.

101. See Stephen E. Ambrose, *Ike's Spies: Eisenhower and the Espionage Establishment* (Garden City, N.Y.: Doubleday, 1981), 253.

102. This assumption can be seen in almost every assessment of the Soviet Union's objectives and capabilities. These assumptions are explained in Brinkley and Hull, *Estimative Intelligence,* 215–16; Scott A. Koch, ed., *Selected Estimates on the Soviet Union, 1950–1959* (Washington, D.C.: Central Intelligence Agency, 1993), xiv; James Meikle Eglin, *Air Defense in the Nuclear Age: The Post-War Development of American and Soviet Strategic Defense Systems* (New York: Garland Publishing, 1988), 272; and Raymond L. Garthoff, *Assessing the Adversary: Estimates by the Eisenhower Administration of Soviet Intentions and Capabilities* (Washington, D.C.: Brookings Institution, 1991), 10.

103. Dr. Lee A. Dubridge to Dr. Arthur S. Flemming, May 24, 1954, EL, DDE Papers, White House Central Files, Subject Series, Box 104, Folder—World War III (1) Confidential File, 1–4. For the best summary of the activities of the Killian committee, see James R. Killian, Jr., *Sputnik, Scientists, and Eisenhower: A Memoir of the First Special Assistant to the President for Science and Technology* (Cambridge, Mass.: MIT Press, 1977), 67–93.

104. In addition to appointing this committee, Eisenhower also established the National Indications Center on July 1 "for the express purpose of 'preventing strategic surprise.'" R. Cargill Hall, "The Eisenhower Administration and the Cold War: Framing American Astronautics to Serve National Security," *Prologue: Quarterly of the National Archives* 27 : 1 (Spring 1995): 61–62.

105. The Report to the President by the Technological Capabilities Panel of the Science Advisory Committee, February 14, 1955 [hereafter Killian Report], in Trachtenberg, *The Development of American Strategic Thought,* 189–90 (in original document).

106. Ibid., iii.

107. The five were Albert Hill, Brockway McMillan, Jerome Wiesner, David Beckler, and Col. Vincent Ford. See Killian Report, 187–88.

108. Killian Report, v.

109. In addition to these three panels, Jerome Wiesner chaired the Communications Working Group, which examined the vulnerability of U.S. communications systems.

110. Killian Report, v.

111. This capability should be viewed as providing two policy options. First, the United States could initiate the use of atomic weapons after a war had begun. Second, the United States could initiate either a preemptive or a preventive war. For

a description of the distinction between preemptive and preventive war, see Freedman, *Evolution of Nuclear Strategy,* 126; and General Thomas S. Power, *Design for Survival* (New York: Coward-McCann, 1964, 1965), 39, 79–84.

112. For Eisenhower's denunciation of preventive war, see *PPP-DDE, 1954* (GPO, 1955), 698. In addition, see Trachtenberg, *History and Strategy,* 132–46; Tami Davis Biddle, "Handling the Soviet Threat: 'Project Control' and the Debate on American Strategy in the Early Cold War Years," *Journal of Strategic Studies* 12 (September 1989): 273–302; Michio Kaku and Daniel Axelrod, *To Win a Nuclear War: The Pentagon's Secret War Plans* (Boston: South End Press, 1987), x–xi, 3, 5; Paul Bracken, *The Command and Control of Nuclear Forces* (New Haven: Yale University Press, 1983), 83–84, 183–84; Weinstein et al., *Evolution of U.S. Strategic Command and Control and Warning,* 101, 201; David Alan Rosenberg, "Toward Armageddon: The Foundations of United States Nuclear Strategy, 1945–1961" (Ph.D. diss., University of Chicago, 1983), 197, 221; and Bundy, *Danger and Survival,* 251–52.

113. Killian Report, 3–4.

114. While U.S. intelligence estimates of Soviet capabilities during the 1950s have become increasingly available over the past few years, there remains considerable ambiguity as to how the U.S. agencies gathered the information they used to make these estimates. For an excellent description of sources of U.S. intelligence and the variety of organizations involved in intelligence gathering and assessment, see Jeffrey Richelson, *The U.S. Intelligence Community* (Cambridge, Mass.: Ballinger Publishing Co., 1985); and Prados, *The Soviet Estimate,* 24–37. For an analysis of the limitations on intelligence, see Brinkley and Hull, *Estimative Intelligence,* 215–22. For an example of the use of aerial overflights (besides the U-2) to acquire intelligence of the Soviet Union, see Robert S. Hopkins III, "An Expanded Understanding of Eisenhower, American Policy, and Overflights," paper presented at the Society of Historians of American Foreign Relations Annual Conference, June 1995.

115. Killian Report, 25.

116. This conclusion is based on the declassified portions of the final Killian report and on published accounts of the activities of the committee.

117. Killian Report, 17.

118. Ibid., 49.

119. See note 116 and Rosenberg, "Toward Armageddon," 221.

120. Killian Report, 37–46.

121. Rosenberg, "The Origins of Overkill: Nuclear Weapons and American Strategy, 1945–1960," 38. See also Bundy, *Danger and Survival,* 325.

122. Dwight D. Eisenhower, *Waging Peace, 1956–1961* (Garden City, N.Y.: Doubleday, 1965), 208. See also Memorandum of Discussion at the 257th Meeting

of the National Security Council, August 4, 1955, *FRUS 1955–1957,* 19 (GPO, 1990), 100–103.

123. Killian to Herbert F. York, May 27, 1976, Massachusetts Institute of Technology [hereafter MIT] Archives, MC 423, James R. Killian Papers, Box 13, Folder—Correspondence L–Z, 2.

124. Donald Welzenbach, "Din Land: Patriot from Polaroid," *Optics and Photonics News* (October 1994): 23.

125. Eisenhower's attempts to balance military spending with economic security are fully detailed in Sloan, *Eisenhower and the Management of Prosperity;* Morgan, *Eisenhower versus 'The Spenders';* and Kinnard, *President Eisenhower and Strategy Management.*

126. See Kenneth W. Thompson, ed., *The Eisenhower Presidency: Eleven Intimate Perspectives of Dwight D. Eisenhower* (New York: University Press of America, 1984), 63–87.

127. For critiques of Eisenhower's NSC and his decision-making process, see Brands, "Age of Vulnerability," 986; Destler, "The Presidency and National Security Organization"; Huntington, *Common Defense,* 154; Heinlein, *Presidential Staff and National Security Policy;* Melanson and Mayers, eds., *Reevaluating Eisenhower;* and Jeri Suri, "America's Search for a Technological Solution to the Arms Race: The Surprise Attack Conference of 1958 and a Challenge for 'Eisenhower Revisionists,'" *Diplomatic History* 21:3 (Summer 1997): 423–31.

128. For more positive analyses of the Eisenhower NSC, see John Prados, *Keepers of the Keys: A History of the National Security Council from Truman to Bush* (New York: William Morrow, 1991); Falk, "The National Security Council under Truman, Eisenhower, and Kennedy"; Nelson, "The Importance of Foreign Policy Process: Eisenhower and the NSC," in Bischof and Ambrose, eds., *Eisenhower: A Centenary;* Nelson, "The 'Top of Policy Hill': President Eisenhower and the National Security Council"; Sloan, "The Management and Decision-Making Style of President Eisenhower"; and Hoxie, "Dwight David Eisenhower: Bicentennial Considerations," 253–264.

Chapter 2

1. Dwight D. Eisenhower to Swede Hazlett, November 18, 1957, in Griffith, ed., *Ike's Letters to a Friend,* 190. Eisenhower makes reference to the same letter in his memoirs to highlight the problems he faced in 1957. See Eisenhower, *Waging Peace,* 226.

2. See Robert A. Divine, *Blowing on the Wind: The Nuclear Test Ban Debate, 1954–1960* (New York: Oxford University Press, 1978), 54; and Allan A. Winkler, *Life under a Cloud: American Anxiety about the Atom* (New York: Oxford University Press, 1993), 84–135. See also Letter to President Eisenhower [from eight

Representatives], June 7, 1957, EL, White House Central Files, Official Files, Box 526, Folder—(3), 2–4.

3. See for example, "Report by the Joint Strategic Plans Committee," August 24, 1951, NA, RG 218, JCS, 1951–1953—Geographic File, CCS 350.09 USSR (12-19-49), Sec. 14, 5.

4. Memorandum of Discussion at the 306th Meeting of the National Security Council, December 20, 1956, *FRUS 1955–1957*, 19, 381.

5. Memorandum of Discussion at the 257th Meeting of the National Security Council, August 4, 1955, ibid., 99.

6. Eisenhower to Governor [Val] Peterson, July 17, 1956, EL, DDE Papers, Cabinet Series, Box 8, Folder—Cabinet Meeting of January 9, 1957 (1), 1–2. See also, Ambrose, *Eisenhower*, vol. 2, 397–401.

7. U.S. Congress, House Military Operations Subcommittee of the Committee on Government Operations, *Civil Defense Plan for National Survival*, 84th Congress, 2nd Session, 1956, 692.

8. For Holifield's views on civil defense and, in particular, shelters, see Thomas J. Kerr, *Civil Defense in the U.S.: Bandaid for a Holocaust* (Boulder, Colo.: Westview Press, 1983), 83–99.

9. For a description of the proposed civil defense legislation, see Kerr, *Civil Defense in the U.S.*, 195.

10. Ibid., 97.

11. See Kerr, *Civil Defense in the U.S.*, 68–70; Divine, *Blowing on the Wind*, 27, 74–75; and Winkler, *Life under a Cloud*, 93–94, 116–17.

12. NSC 5509—Status of United States Programs for National Security as of December 31, 1954, Part 5: The Civil Defense Program, February 1, 1955, NA, RG 273, NSC, Folder—NSC 5509, 9.

13. Civil Defense Legislative Program, December 20, 1956, NA, RG 273, NSC, Folder—NSC 5709 (Background Documents), 2. While it is still unknown whether the Soviet Union was capable of launching missiles from submarines in 1956, both the CIA and SAC reported that the Soviets might have this capability. See Memorandum by the Chief of Staff, U.S. Air Force, for the Joint Chiefs of Staff on Submarine Guided Missile Threat, September 24, 1956, NA RG 218, JCS, CCS 350.09 USSR (12-19-49) Sec. 13, 10–18; and Memorandum for the Secretary of Defense (from Admiral Radford), October 10, 1956, NA RG 218, JCS, CCS 334 Air Defense of North America Ad Hoc Comte (9–2056) Sec. 1, 1–2.

14. For a description of the FCDA's position on shelters, see Kerr, *Civil Defense in the U.S.*, 100–107. For a description of the congressional setting where Holifield's legislation met its fate, see Ambrose, *Eisenhower*, vol. 2, 388–91.

15. "Report of the Federal Civil Defense Administration on a Federal Civil Defense Shelter Program" [hereafter "Federal Civil Defense Shelter Program"], January 17, 1957, EL, WHO, OSANSA, NSC Series, Policy Paper Subseries, Box

21, Folder—NSC 5709, Shelter Program for Civil Defense, A-2. For a description of the NES report, see *FRUS 1955–1957,* 19, 379–81.

16. "Federal Civil Defense Shelter Program," A-2.

17. Ibid., A-3 and A-10.

18. R.C. Conclusions, March 22, 1957, EL, WHO, OSANSA, NSC Series, Briefing Notes Subseries, Box 4, Folder—Civil Defense, 1. See also SNIE 100-5-57, "Probable World Reaction to Certain Civil Defense Programs," March 19, 1957, *FRUS 1955–1957,* 19, 442–45; and Memorandum of Discussion at the 318th Meeting of the National Security Council, April 4, 1957, *FRUS 1955–1957,* 19, 461.

19. "Federal Civil Defense Shelter Program," B-1–B-3.

20. "A Federal Shelter Program for Civil Defense," March 29, 1957, EL, WHO, OSANSA, NSC Series, Policy Paper Subseries, Box 21, Folder—NSC 5709, Shelter Program for Civil Defense, 2. It seems that in developing these questions, which were labeled A to L, the Planning Board may have been influenced by Isidor Rabi, a member of the Science Advisory Committee and future member of the Gaither committee. In a letter to ODM Director Gordon Gray, Rabi wrote:

> There is need for a broadly based study in which personnel protection is examined in relation to the following factors: strategic concepts, including conditions of strategic and tactical warning and the deterrent values of shelters; advances in the types and numbers of nuclear warheads and delivery systems; capabilities of active defenses; the long-range practicability of protecting densely populated urban areas from the effects of blast and cratering; evacuation possibilities; the relative values of blast and fallout protection; the problems of post-attack recovery under continuing atomic harassment; the costs of various types of structural protection and the relationship of dollars invested to types and extent of protection afforded; the possibility of dual purpose construction, including public building programs of school and highway construction; city planning and future patterns of expansion of industry and population; and national construction capabilities under normal and emergency situations.

I quote from Rabi's letter at length because the Gaither committee seems to have examined most of these factors in its study. Dr. Isidor I. Rabi to ODM Director, undated [probably March 1957], quoted in Informal Memorandum for Use at Meeting with Mr. Gaither, June 27, 1957, ibid., Briefing Notes Subseries, Box 8, Folder—Fallout Shelters, 2.

21. Memorandum of Discussion at the 318th Meeting of the National Security Council, April 4, 1957, *FRUS 1955–1957,* 19, 463–64.

22. Among the members of the Science Advisory Committee at the time of

the Gaither study were Lloyd V. Berkner, Hans A. Bethe, Detlev W. Bronk, Hugh L. Dryden, James B. Fisk, Caryl P. Haskins, Albert G. Hill, James R. Killian, Jr., Edwin H. Land, Emanuel R. Piore, Isidor I. Rabi, Herbert Scoville, Jr., Alan T. Waterman, and Jerrold R. Zacharias.

23. J. R. Killian to Herbert F. York, September 9, 1976, MIT Archives, MC 423—Killian Papers, Box 13, Folder—Correspondence L–Z, 2.

24. Eisenhower to Gaither, May 8, 1957, EL, WHO, OSS, Subject Series, Alphabetical Subseries, Box 23, Folder—Science Advisory Committee (1) July '56–May '57, 1.

25. For a complete membership list, see *Gaither Report*, 41–45.

26. See Kaplan, *Wizards of Armageddon*, 128–34; David Callahan, *Dangerous Capabilities: Paul Nitze and the Cold War* (New York: HarperCollins Publishers, 1990), 167–71; and Steven L. Rearden, *The Evolution of American Strategic Doctrine: Paul Nitze and the Soviet Challenge* (Boulder, Colo.: Westview Press, 1984), 41–46.

27. To Directors and Chiefs of the War Department General and Special Staff Divisions and Bureaus and the Commanding Generals of the Major Commands, April 30, 1946, in Galambos, ed., *Papers of Dwight David Eisenhower*, vol. 7, 1046–47.

28. Ibid., 1049.

29. See chap. 1. In most American assessments of the Soviet Union, the Kremlin leaders' intentions were not examined extensively. It was assumed that their intention was world domination.

30. An internal State Department Policy Planning Staff report sheds light on problems of basing policy on preconceptions and assumptions. It concludes that "there is danger that policy may develop unduly on the basis of preconceptions and assumptions." It then explains that after World War II, especially after the advent of long-range bombers and intercontinental missiles, the United States searched for something to blame for its new sense of vulnerability. The report states, "The instinctive, almost visceral reaction of a nation undergoing so disillusioning an experience is to seek an explanation that is psychologically satisfying. Something had gone wrong. The cause, the evil thing must be identified and personified. The Soviet Union became the candidate for *diabolus ex machina* in this situation. It satisfied all requirements. It was evil, powerful, implacable. The cold war was on. Soviet Communism was the enemy." L. W. Fuller, "An Inquiry into United States Policy Respecting the Soviet Union," April 1, 1958, RG 59, State Department, Policy Planning Staff Records, Lot 67D 548, Box 194, Folder—S/P Papers 1958 (January–April), 1, 4.

31. Dwight Macdonald, *The Ford Foundation: The Men and the Millions* (New York: Reynal & Company, 1956), 10.

32. Memorandum for Brig. Gen. Andrew Goodpaster, May 8, 1957, EL,

WHO, OSS, Subject Series, Alphabetical Subseries, Box 23, Folder—Science Advisory Committee (1), 1; and author's interview with Albert Hill, August 14, 1995. For descriptions of the Radiation Laboratory, see John Burchard, *Q.E.D.: M.I.T. in World War II* (New York: John Wiley & Sons, 1948), 215–36; Ivan A. Getting, *All in a Lifetime: Science in the Defense of Democracy* (New York: Vantage Press, 1989), 187–201; and Daniel J. Kevles, *The Physicists: The History of a Scientific Community in Modern America* (Cambridge: Harvard University Press, 1987), 303–8.

33. Eleanora W. Schoenebaum, ed., *Political Profiles: The Eisenhower Years* (New York: Facts on File, 1977), 219.

34. Bruce L. R. Smith, *The RAND Corporation: Case Study of a Nonprofit Advisory Corporation* (Cambridge: Harvard University Press, 1966), 67, 185.

35. Macdonald, *Ford Foundation,* 11.

36. *Report of the Study for the Ford Foundation on Policy and Program* (Detroit: Ford Foundation, 1949), 58.

37. Ibid., 22.

38. Schoenebaum, *Political Profiles: The Eisenhower Years,* 219. For a more in-depth description of Gaither's study for the Ford Foundation, see Macdonald, *Ford Foundation,* 137–40.

39. Eleanora W. Schoenebaum, ed., *Political Profiles: The Truman Years* (New York: Facts on File, 1978), 175–76. For descriptions of some of Foster's activities on the ECA, see Michael J. Hogan, *The Marshall Plan: America, Britain, and the Reconstruction of Western Europe, 1947–1952* (Cambridge: Cambridge University Press, 1987), 222, 283, 388–91; and Sallie Pisani, *The CIA and the Marshall Plan* (Lawrence: University of Kansas Press, 1991), 95–96.

40. Leffler, *Preponderance of Power,* 497–98.

41. Schoenebaum, *Political Profiles: The Eisenhower Years,* 211–12.

42. William Foster to General Curtis LeMay, September 10, 1952, LC, Papers of General Curtis LeMay, Box 72, Folder—Visits to SAC, 1.

43. Schoenebaum, *Political Profiles: The Eisenhower Years,* 212. See Résumé for William Chapman Foster, George C. Marshall Foundation, William Chapman Foster Papers, Box 31, Folder 2.

44. See William C. Foster, "Olin Mathieson Chemical Corporation and Its Role in Defense of the Nation," *Armed Forces Chemical Journal* (November–December 1956), George C. Marshall Foundation, Foster Papers, Box 39, Folder 32.

45. Robert Sprague to General Vandenberg, February 10, 1953, LC, Papers of General Hoyt Vandenberg, Box 31, Folder—S (General), 1–3; Robert C. Sprague Oral History, August 1, 1964, John Foster Dulles Oral History Collection, Princeton University, 2–3.

46. For a summary of Sprague's involvement as an adviser, see Memorandum for the Files, December 9, 1957, EL, WHO, OSANSA, NSC Series, Briefing Notes Subseries, Box 16, Folder—Security Resources Panel, 1.

47. Memorandum for the Secretary of Defense, October 20, 1953, NA, RG 218, JCS, Records of Admiral Arthur Radford, Folder—CJCS 381 (Continental Defense) 1953, 1.

48. Notes for the Commander, November 10, 1953, LC, LeMay Papers, Box B104a, Folder—LeMay Diary no. 5, 1.

49. Memorandum for Adm. Gardner, Gen. Partridge, Gen. Lemnitzer, and Gen. Twining, November 27, 1953, NA, RG 218, JCS, Radford Records, Folder—CJCS 381 (Continental Defense) 1953, 1; Memorandum for Admiral Radford, December 9, 1953, ibid., 1–2; Memorandum for Admiral Radford, December 4, 1953, ibid., 1. In his oral history interview, Sprague reported that he had access to all documents related to U.S. continental defenses except for a report prepared for the JCS on "an assumed air atomic attack by the United States on Russia." Admiral Radford refused to release the report because the JCS had not even had the opportunity to review it. However, Radford did brief Sprague for two hours concerning the content of the document. See Sprague Oral History, 3–4.

50. Memorandum for the Record, December 12, 1953, NA, RG 218, JCS, Radford Records, Folder—CJCS 381 (Continental Defense) 1953, 1–2.

51. "Report on Continental Defense to the Senate Armed Services Committee," March 8, 1954, EL, DDE Papers, Administrative Series, Box 33, Folder—Sprague, Robert C. Material, 1. For a description of the briefing of the Senate Armed Services Committee, see Memorandum for Admiral Arthur Radford, March 26, 1954, NA, RG 218, JCS, Radford Records, Folder—CJCS 381 (Continental Defense) January–March 1954, 1. For a description of Sprague's briefing of both the Joint Atomic Energy Committee and the House Armed Services Committee, see Memorandum for Admiral Arthur Radford, March 30, 1954, ibid., 1–2.

52. "Report on Continental Defense," 2–5. Large portions of this report remain classified.

53. Ibid., 6.

54. Memorandum for the Secretary of Defense, June 23, 1954, NA, RG 218, Radford Records, Folder—CJCS 381 (Continental Defense) June–December 1954, 1. This memorandum discusses a briefing that Sprague presented to Senators Saltonstall, Styles Bridges (R-NH), Harry or Robert [?] Byrd, and Adm. Radford.

55. Ibid., 1.

56. "Report of Robert C. Sprague (NSC Consultant) to the National Security Council on Continental Defense," November 24, 1954, EL, WHO, OSANSA, NSC Series, Subject Subseries, Box 3, Folder—Continental Defense, Study of, by Robert C. Sprague (1953–1954) (12), 1.

57. "Report of Robert C. Sprague (NSC Consultant) to the National Security Council on Continental Defense," June 16, 1955, ibid., Folder—Continental Defense, Study of, by Robert C. Sprague (1955) (3), 3.

58. Memorandum of Discussion at the 252nd Meeting of the National Security Council, June 16, 1955, *FRUS 1955–1957*, 19, 89.

59. Getting, *All in a Lifetime*, 205.

60. Ibid., 192.

61. James R. Killian and A. G. Hill, "For a Continental Defense," *Atlantic* 192:5 (November 1953): 38.

62. James R. Killian, *The Education of a College President: A Memoir* (Cambridge, Mass.: MIT Press, 1985), 74.

63. Killian and Hill, "Continental Defense," 37.

64. Ibid., 40.

65. For a discussion of the creation of the Lincoln Laboratory, see "Draft— Lincoln Laboratory, and the Years 1945–1955," MIT Archives, MC 365—Hill Papers, Box 14, Folder no. 4, 3–5; Schaffel, *Emerging Shield*, 145–56; and Leslie, *The Cold War and American Science*, 32–43.

66. The Lincoln Laboratory researched and developed the SAGE system until 1958, when it turned it over to a nonprofit organization, the MITRE Corporation. See *MITRE: The First Twenty Years, A History of the MITRE Corporation (1958–1978)* (Bedford, Mass.: MITRE Corporation, 1979), 12–16.

67. For a complete list of the different summer study projects, see Special Reports—Studies and Projects, undated [1977], MIT Archives, MC 423—Killian Papers, Box 13, Folder—Backup O–Z, 5.

68. Welzenbach, "Din Land," 22.

69. Killian, *Sputnik, Scientists, and Eisenhower*, 103.

70. "Problems of Air Defense, Final Report of Project Charles," vol. 1, August 1, 1951, 3, quoted in Nunn, *The Soviet Threat*, 118.

71. Schaffel, *Emerging Shield*, 174–75.

72. See chap. 1.

73. Memorandum of a Conference with the President, May 18, 1956, *FRUS 1955–1957*, 19, 303.

74. John Steven Chwat, "The President's Foreign Intelligence Advisory Board: An Historical and Contemporary Analysis (1955–1975)" (Congressional Research Office, 1975), 5.

75. Eisenhower Diary Entry, January 24, 1956, in Ferrell, ed., *Eisenhower Diaries*, 312.

76. Chwat, "The President's Foreign Intelligence Advisory Board," 6. The committee was officially created by executive order 10586, February 8, 1956.

77. Performance of Function of CIA, undated, MIT Archives, MC 423—Killian Papers, Box 36, Folder—President's Foreign Intelligence Advisory Board [7/8], 2.

78. John Ponturo, *Analytical Support for the Joint Chiefs of Staff: The WSEG Experience, 1948–1976* (Arlington, Va.: Institute for Defense Analysis, 1979), x.

79. Joint Chiefs of Staff Decision on JCS 1812/51 on Program of Future Work for WSEG, May 4, 1955, RG 218, JCS, 1957 Decimal File, Folder—CCS 334 WSEG (2-4-48) Sec. 5, i.

80. LeMay to Lt. General S. E. Anderson, December 29, 1955, LC, LeMay Papers, Box B205, Folder—B50703, 1.

81. Memorandum by the Chief of Staff, U.S. Air Force, for the Joint Chiefs of Staff on Submarine Guided Missile Threat, September 24, 1956, NA, RG 218, JCS, Folder—CCS 350.09 USSR (12-19-49) Sec. 13, 10–18.

82. Memorandum for the Secretary of Defense, October 10, 1956, ibid., Folder—CCS 334 Air Defense of North America Ad Hoc Comte (9-20-56) Sec. 1, 1–2. In addition to Hill, the committee consisted of General Carl Spaatz, General Thomas Handy, and Admiral John Ballentine. See Memorandum for General Carl Spaatz, General Thomas Handy, Admiral John Ballentine, and Dr. Albert Hill, November 7, 1956, ibid., 1.

83. "Report of the Joint Chiefs of Staff Ad Hoc Committee on Air Defense," June 30, 1957, quoted in Note by the Secretaries of the Joint Chiefs of Staff on Briefing Presented to the Joint Chiefs of Staff on Levels of Defense Effectiveness, October 18, 1957, ibid., Folder—CCS 381 US (5-23-46) Sec. 89 RB, 2395.

84. Ponturo, *Analytical Support for the Joint Chiefs of Staff,* xv.

85. McCormack also had an extensive background in strategic matters. For instance, he served as the director of task force B of Project Solarium. See chap. 1.

86. Ponturo, *Analytical Support for the Joint Chiefs of Staff,* 164–65.

87. See the influence of the 1952 Project East River in Memorandum for President Eisenhower, April 10, 1953, EL, DDE Papers, Miscellaneous Series, Box 4, Folder—President's Advisory Committee on Government Organization—Government Reorganization Civil Defense, 2.

88. For a description of the 1952 Project East River, see Schaffel, *Emerging Shield,* 172–91.

89. "Military Measures Precedent to a Manageable Civil Defense, Part IIA of the Report of Project East River," June 26, 1952, 63, quoted in Joseph T. Jockel, *No Boundaries Upstairs: Canada, the United States, and the Origins of North American Air Defense, 1945–1958* (Vancouver: University of British Columbia Press, 1987), 28.

90. *Project East River: Reduction of Urban Vulnerability,* part 5 (New York: Associated Universities, 1952), 60a.

91. "1955 Review of the Report of Project East River," October 17, 1955, NA, RG 218, JCS, Folder—CCS 384.51 (10-31-46) sec. 10 BP Planning for Civil Defense of U.S., iii.

92. Ibid., 2.

93. Ibid., 5.

94. See "1955 Review of the Report of Project East River," 7, 15.

95. *Civil Defense Plan for National Survival,* 83.

96. Ibid., 97.

97. *Civil Defense Plan for National Survival,* 215.

98. Ibid., 671.

99. Memorandum for JCS, January 26, 1953, NA, RG 218, JCS, 1951–1953 Geographical File, Folder—CCS 381 US (5-23-46) sec. 23, 1. In addition to Kelly, the committee consisted of Walker Cisler, the president of Detroit Edison Company; S. C. Hollister, dean of engineering at Cornell University; F. L. Hoyde, president of Purdue University; C. C. Lauritsen, physics professor at the California Institute for Technology; Arthur E. Raymond, vice president of Douglas Aircraft Company; and R. E. Wilson, chairman of Standard Oil Company.

100. Robert J. Watson, *History of the Joint Chiefs of Staff*, vol. 5, *The Joint Chiefs of Staff and National Policy, 1953–1954,* (GPO, 1986), 119–20. For a description of the Kelly Report, see Schaffel, *Emerging Shield,* 185–90.

101. See Watson, *History of the Joint Chiefs of Staff,* vol. 5, 126–27.

102. Memorandum for the JCS, July 28, 1953, NA, RG 218, JCS, 1951–1953 Geographical File, Folder—CCS 381 US (5-23-46) sec. 24, 1. In addition to Baxter, the committee consisted of James Black, president of Pacific Gas and Electric Company; Alan Gregg, vice president of the Rockefeller Foundation; David McDonald, president of the United States Steel Workers of America; and Arthur Page, former vice president of AT&T.

103. Minutes of the 163rd Meeting of the National Security Council, September 24, 1953, NA, RG 273, NSC, Folder—Minutes of the 163rd Meeting, 1.

104. Thomas A. Strum, *The USAF Scientific Advisory Board: Its First Twenty Years, 1944–1964* (GPO, 1967), 45. Mervin Kelly, a future Gaither committee member, also served on this board from 1951 to 1957.

105. Herbert F. York, *Making Weapons, Talking Peace: A Physicist's Odyssey from Hiroshima to Geneva* (New York: Basic Books, 1987), 88.

106. James H. Doolittle, "A Program for World Peace," address at Georgetown University, April 30, 1949, in Eugene M. Emme, ed., *The Impact of Air Power: National Security and World Politics,* (Princeton, N.J.: D. Van Nostrand, 1959), 800.

107. Minutes of Air Force Science Advisory Board Meeting, November 3, 1949, quoted in Strum, *The USAF Scientific Advisory Board,* 33–34.

108. Charter for Doolittle Committee, July 13, 1954, EL, WHO, OSS, Subject Series, Alphabetical Subseries, Box 12, Folder—Doolittle Committee (July 1954–February 1955), 1.

109. Wayne G. Jackson, "Allen Welsh Dulles as Director of Central Intelligence, 26 February 1953–29 November 1961," vol. 4—Congressional Oversight and Internal Administration, NA, RG 263, CIA, Box—Allen Welsh Dulles as Director of Central Intelligence Agency, 26 February 1953–29 November 1961, Folder—Volume no. 4, 112.

110. Eisenhower Diary Entry, in Ferrell, ed., *Eisenhower Diaries,* 284.

111. Press Release—The White House, October 19, 1954, EL, White House Central Files, Official Files, Box 320, Folder—Task Force to Investigate CIA, 1.

112. Quoted in U.S. Congress, Senate, "Final Report of the Select Committee

to Study Governmental Operations with Respect to Intelligence Activities," 94th Congress, 2nd Session, 1975, 52–53n.

113. Paul Nitze, *From Hiroshima to Glasnost: At the Center of Decision* (New York: Grove Weidenfeld, 1989), 167.

114. Nitze to Colonel G. A. Lincoln, January 30, 1961, United States Military Academy [hereafter USMA], George A. Lincoln Collection, Subject Files—Names, Box 194, Folder—Nitze, Paul, 1956–61, 1.

115. Roger H. Nye, "George A. Lincoln: Architect in National Security," undated, USMA, Lincoln Collection, Personal Papers, Box 1, Folder—Lincoln, George A., 3. A shorter version of this essay was published in Colonel Amos A. Jordan, Jr., ed., *Issues of National Security in the 1970s: Essays Presented to Colonel George A. Lincoln on His Sixtieth Birthday* (New York: Frederick A. Praeger, 1967). See also Ray S. Cline, *United States Army in World War II: The War Department, Washington Command Post: The Operations Division* (Washington, D.C.: Office of the Chief of Military History, Department of the Army, 1951), 194, 299–300, 329–30.

116. Nye, "George A. Lincoln."

117. Leffler, *Preponderance of Power*, 29.

118. Quoted in Cline, *Washington Command Post*, 330.

119. For examples of the collaboration between Eisenhower and Lincoln after the war, see Galambos, ed., *Papers of Dwight David Eisenhower*, vol. 7, 575n, 577–78n, 761n, 850n, 931n, 961n.

120. Eisenhower to Milton Eisenhower, April 6, 1963, EL, Milton S. Eisenhower Papers, 1938–1973, Box 15, Folder—Correspondence—1963, 2.

121. Eisenhower to Lincoln, undated, quoted in Nye, "George A. Lincoln," 1.

122. Quoted in Nye, "George A. Lincoln," 8.

123. George A. Lincoln, *Economics of National Security: Managing America's Resources for Defense,* 2nd ed. (Englewood Cliffs, N.J.: Prentice-Hall, 1954), 24.

124. For a description of Project Solarium, see chap. 1. For a description of the Rockefeller study group, also known as the Quantico II Panel, see *FRUS 1955–1957,* 19, 153–54.

125. Nye, "George A. Lincoln," 11.

126. Colonel G. A. Lincoln and Lt. Colonel Amos A. Jordan, Jr., "Technology and the Changing Nature of General War," *Military Review* 36 (May 1957): 13.

127. Ibid., 7.

128. Herken, *Counsels of War*, 17; Rearden, *Evolution of American Strategic Doctrine*, 2–4; *United States Strategic Bombing Survey: Summary Report (Pacific War)* (GPO, 1946). The summary report, which Nitze helped write, reached several conclusions that influenced his later writings. It stressed the importance of maintaining offensive retaliatory power, building continental defenses, developing and implementing civil defense plans, preserving technological superiority, and increasing intelligence capabilities. See *Summary Report,* 29–32.

129. See chap. 1.

130. For descriptions of the controversial dismissal of Nitze, see Emmet John Hughes, *The Ordeal of Power: A Political Memoir of the Eisenhower Years* (New York: Atheneum, 1963), 120–21; and Callahan, *Dangerous Capabilities,* 150–52.

131. Memorandum by Nitze and Savage, May 6, 1953, *FRUS 1952–1954,* 2, 322.

132. Paul Nitze, "Critique of Dulles' 'Massive Retaliation' Speech," in Kenneth W. Thompson and Steven L. Rearden, eds., *Paul H. Nitze on National Security and Arms Control* (Lanham, Md.: University Press of America, 1990), 41; and Rearden, *Evolution of American Strategic Doctrine,* 37–38.

133. Nitze, *From Hiroshima to Glasnost,* 165.

134. Callahan, *Dangerous Capabilities,* 160.

135. Paul Nitze, "Atoms, Strategy and Policy," *Foreign Affairs* 34:2 (January 1956): 198.

136. Paul Nitze, "Limited Wars or Massive Retaliation?" *The Reporter* 17 (September 5, 1957): 41.

137. Ibid.

138. Winkler, *Life under a Cloud,* 84–85.

139. Eisenhower, *Waging Peace,* 220.

140. For summaries of the impact of World War II on the relationship between experts and the federal government, see Balogh, *Chain Reaction,* 4–13, 21–23; Kevles, *The Physicists,* 302–67; Friedberg, "Science, the Cold War, and the American State," 108–9; Leslie, *The Cold War and American Science,* 6–7; Ralph E. Lapp, *The New Priesthood: The Scientific Elite and the Uses of Power* (New York: Harper & Row, 1965), 39–86; and Robert Gilpin, "Introduction: Natural Scientists in Policy-Making," in Gilpin and Wright, eds., *Scientists and National Policy-Making,* 3–6.

141. See Balogh, *Chain Reaction;* Leslie, *The Cold War and American Science;* Lapp, *The New Priesthood,* 12–15; and Friedberg, "Science, the Cold War, and the American State," 107–118.

142. Farewell Radio and Television Address to the American People by President Eisenhower, January 17, 1961, in Robert L. Branyan and Lawrence H. Larsen, eds., *The Eisenhower Administration 1953–1961: A Documentary History* (New York: Random House, 1971), 1375–76.

143. Herken, *Counsels of War,* 133.

Chapter 3

1. In this argument, I am accepting the main premise of one of the seminal works on Eisenhower's national security programs. Samuel Huntington argues, "Military policy cannot be separated from foreign policy, fiscal policy, and domestic policy." See Huntington, *Common Defense,* x-xi.

2. Morgan, *Eisenhower versus 'The Spenders,'* ix.

3. *Statistical History of the United States,* 1123–24.

4. Ibid., 1105. Eisenhower had to make significant reductions in the FY 1954 budget that he inherited from Truman in order to have only a $5.3 billion deficit. Truman's original budget would have produced a $10 billion deficit. See Iwan W. Morgan, "Eisenhower and the Balanced Budget," in Shirley Anne Warshaw, ed., *Reexamining the Eisenhower Presidency* (Westport, Conn.: Greenwood Press, 1993), 125.

5. Eisenhower, *Waging Peace,* 129.

6. Pach and Richardson, *Presidency of Dwight D. Eisenhower,* 168.

7. Eisenhower, *Waging Peace,* 129.

8. See Morgan, *Eisenhower versus 'The Spenders,'* 84; Thomas A. Gaskin, "Senator Lyndon B. Johnson, the Eisenhower Administration, and U.S. Foreign Policy, 1957–60," *Presidential Studies Quarterly* 24:2 (Spring 1994): 341; Robert A. Divine, *Since 1945: Politics and Diplomacy in Recent American History,* 3rd ed. (New York: Alfred A. Knopf, 1985), 78–80; and Kinnard, *President Eisenhower and Strategy Management,* 67.

9. See Eisenhower, *Waging Peace,* 130; and Morgan, *Eisenhower versus 'The Spenders,'* 84.

10. Morgan, *Eisenhower versus 'The Spenders,'* 84–88. See also Ambrose, *Eisenhower,* vol. 2, 390; Pach and Richardson, *Presidency of Dwight D. Eisenhower,* 168; and Edward A. Kolodziej, *The Uncommon Defense and Congress, 1945–1963* (Columbus: Ohio State University Press, 1966), 245–52.

11. Charles H. Donnelly, *United States Defense Policies in 1957* (GPO, 1958), 83.

12. Morgan, *Eisenhower versus 'The Spenders,'* 88. The House Appropriations Committee justified its cuts by arguing that "the nature and extent of a military threat against the United States and its allies appears, in certain respects, to have somewhat abated." Quoted in Donnelly, *United States Defense Policies in 1957,* 83.

13. Letter to the Speaker of the House of Representatives on the 1958 Budget, April 18, 1957, in *PPP-DDE, 1957,* 304.

14. Ibid., 305.

15. Eisenhower's chairman of the CEA, Raymond Saulnier, made this announcement at a cabinet meeting on May 3, 1957. Quoted in Sloan, *Eisenhower and the Management of Prosperity,* 143–44.

16. Ibid., 144; Morgan, *Eisenhower versus 'The Spenders,'* 94.

17. The figures are reported in Eisenhower, *Waging Peace,* 305; Morgan, *Eisenhower versus 'The Spenders,'* 93–94; and Sloan, *Eisenhower and the Management of Prosperity,* 144–45.

18. For descriptions of Eisenhower's reaction to the recession, see Eisenhower, *Waging Peace,* 305–10; Morgan, *Eisenhower versus 'The Spenders,'* 93–98; and Sloan, *Eisenhower and the Management of Prosperity,* 143–51.

19. Eisenhower to Arthur Burns, March 12, 1958, in Eisenhower, *Waging Peace,* 309.

20. Pach and Richardson, *Presidency of Dwight D. Eisenhower,* 176–77.

21. The best study of Eisenhower's civil rights policies remains Robert Frederick Burk, *The Eisenhower Administration and Black Civil Rights* (Knoxville: University of Tennessee Press, 1984). For an excellent roundtable discussion of civil rights in the 1950s involving some of the Eisenhower administration's key participants, see Shirley Anne Warshaw, ed., *The Eisenhower Legacy: Discussions of Presidential Leadership* (Silver Springs, Md.: Bartleby Press, 1992), 63–88.

22. Eisenhower, *Waging Peace,* 171.

23. See Pach and Richardson, *Presidency of Dwight D. Eisenhower,* 146; and Burk, *The Eisenhower Administration and Black Civil Rights,* 208–17.

24. Eisenhower, *Waging Peace,* 159–62.

25. Harvard Sitkoff reports, "In 1960, only one-sixth of one percent of the black students in the South went to a desegregated school." Harvard Sitkoff, *The Struggle for Black Equality, 1954–1992,* rev. ed. (New York: Hill and Wang, 1993), 36.

26. *Brown v. Board of Education,* 349 U.S. 294, 75 S.Ct. 753, 99 L.ED. 1083 (1955), in Roland D. Rotunda, *Modern Constitutional Law: Cases and Notes,* 3rd ed. (St. Paul: West Publishing Co., 1989), 495. This case is often referred to as *Brown II,* as it was the followup case to the original *Brown* decision. The question before the Supreme Court was what was an appropriate time frame for desegregation.

27. For a description of the Little Rock crisis, see James C. Duram, *A Moderate among Extremists: Dwight D. Eisenhower and the School Desegregation Crisis* (Chicago: Nelson-Hall, 1981), 144; Eisenhower, *Waging Peace,* 162–75; and Diary Entry of the President, October 8, 1957, in Ferrell, ed., *Eisenhower Diaries,* 347–48.

28. For an excellent description of the tensions at the school, see Elizabeth Huckaby, *Crisis at Central High, Little Rock, 1957–58* (Baton Rouge: Louisiana State University Press, 1980), 39. See also Burk, *The Eisenhower Administration and Black Civil Rights,* 185–86.

29. Statement by the President Regarding Occurrences at Central High School in Little Rock, September 23, 1957, in *PPP-DDE, 1957,* 689.

30. Radio and Television Address to the American People on the Situation in Little Rock, September 24, 1957, ibid., 690–92.

31. Ibid., 694.

32. For U.S. reactions to *Sputnik,* see Divine, *The Sputnik Challenge;* McDougall, . . . *the Heavens and the Earth.*

33. See Memorandum for Mr. Victor Cooley, Acting Director ODM, October 8, 1957, EL, WHO, OSAST, Box 3, Folder—Space October 1957–October 1959, 1.

34. "Into Space: Man's Awesome Adventure," *Newsweek* 50:16 (October 14, 1957): 37.

35. Quoted in McDougall, . . . *the Heavens and the Earth,* 145.

36. George H. Gallup, *The Gallup Poll,* vol. 2 (New York: Random House, 1972), 1521.

37. U.S. Congress, Senate, *Inquiry into Satellite and Missile Programs,* Hearings before the Preparedness Investigating Subcommittee of the Committee on Armed Services, 85th Congress, 1st and 2nd Sessions, 1957–1958, 342.

38. Donnelly, *United States Defense Policies in 1957,* 1.

39. See Eisenhower, *Waging Peace,* 211–12; McDougall, . . . *the Heavens and the Earth,* 146–50; and Divine, *Sputnik Challenge,* xiv, 7–8, 16–17.

40. Memorandum for the President, October 7, 1957, EL, WHO, OSANSA, NSC Series, Briefing Notes Subseries, Box 7, Folder—Earth Satellites, 4. Quarles had resigned as secretary of the Air Force earlier in the year to become the deputy secretary of defense.

41. Conference in the President's Office, October 8, 1957, ibid., 1.

42. Memorandum for the President, October 7, 1957, ibid., 6.

43. Memorandum of Conference with the President, October 8, 1957, EL, DDE Papers, DDE Series, Box 27, Folder—October 1957 Staff Notes (2), 1. At this 5:00 p.m. meeting, Eisenhower had Detlev Bronk, the chairman of the National Science Foundation, read the statement and offer suggestions. Bronk approved the statement with only a few revisions.

44. Statement by the President, October 9, 1957, EL, WHO, OSS, Subject Series, Alphabetical Subseries, Box 23, Folder—Satellites [October 1957–February 1960] (1), 2. Two of Eisenhower's principal critics, Drew Pearson and Jack Anderson, call his response to *Sputnik* "Operation Soothing Syrup." Drew Pearson and Jack Anderson, *U.S.A.—Second-Class Power?* (New York: Simon and Schuster, 1958), 5.

45. See Divine, *Sputnik Challenge,* 7–8.

46. Quoted in McDougall, . . . *the Heavens and the Earth,* 154.

47. Divine, *Sputnik Challenge,* 73–74.

48. Legislative Leadership Meeting, January 7, 1958, EL, DDE Papers, Legislative Meeting Series, Box 3, Folder—Legislative Minutes 1958 (1) January–February, 1.

49. Divine, *Sputnik Challenge,* viii. See also Bundy, *Danger and Survival,* 341–42.

50. John Foster Dulles, "The Evolution of Foreign Policy," *Department of State Bulletin* 30:271 (January 25, 1954): 108.

51. Ibid.

52. See John S. Duffield, *Power Rules: The Evolution of NATO's Conventional Force Posture* (Stanford: Stanford University Press, 1995), 124–30.

53. Memorandum of Discussion at the 204th Meeting of the National Security Council, June 14, 1954, *FRUS 1952–1954,* 2, 690.

54. Dwight D. Eisenhower to Swede Hazlett, November 11, 1945 in Griffith, ed., *Ike's Letters to a Friend,* 29.

55. Memorandum of a Conference with the President, March 30, 1956, *FRUS 1955–1957,* 19, 281. See also Memorandum for General Nathan F. Twining, February 4, 1956, LC, Twining Papers, Box 92, Folder—1956 White House, 3; Memorandum of a Conference with the President, April 5, 1956, *FRUS 1955–1957,* 19, 286, 289.

56. Memorandum of a Conference with the President, April 5, 1956, *FRUS 1955–1957,* 19, 287.

57. See A. J. Bacevich, *The Pentomic Era: The U.S. Army between Korea and Vietnam* (Washington, D.C.: National Defense University Press, 1986), 42–46.

58. "Air Power and National Security," from the Air Power Subcommittee on the Air Force of the Senate Committee on Armed Services, January 25, 1957, 85th Congress, 1st Session, reprinted in Emme, ed., *The Impact of Air Power,* 704.

59. See Freedman, *Evolution of Nuclear Strategy,* 95.

60. Rosenberg, "The Origins of Overkill: Nuclear Weapons and American Strategy, 1945–1960," 69.

61. Ibid., 66.

62. Ibid., 16–17, 23.

63. See Oral History Interview with Lyman L. Lemnitzer, OH no. 301, Oral History Research Office, Columbia University, 1973, 56. Lemnitzer stated that from 1957 to 1960, "We in the armed forces were probably having the greatest controversy that existed among the services, in my time at least, and that had to do with the role of the various services in the Strategic Bombing area."

64. For succinct definitions of both counterforce and countercity strategies, see Huntington, *Common Defense,* 103.

65. Rosenberg, "Origins of Overkill," 51–55.

66. See Diary Entry of the President, January 23, 1956, reprinted in Kaku and Axelrod, *To Win a Nuclear War,* 105; Trachtenberg, *History and Strategy,* 132; and David Alan Rosenberg, "U.S. Nuclear War Planning, 1945–1960," in Desmond Ball and Jeffrey Richelson, eds., *Strategic Nuclear Testing* (Ithaca: Cornell University Press, 1986), 44. An Air Force study in 1953–54 called Project Control sheds light on the widespread consideration of aggressive policies by the United States against the Soviet Union. The plan called for the United States to gain control of the Soviet air space and force the Kremlin to change its policies. See Biddle, "Handling the Soviet Threat," 273–302.

67. For a counterforce strategy to work, the enemy's offensive striking power would have to be hit before it could be launched. See Rosenberg, "Origins of Overkill," 63.

68. LeMay to Gen. Hoyt S. Vandenberg, December 12, 1949, LC, LeMay Papers, Box B195, Folder—B311, 3.

69. General Curtis LeMay, "The Strategic Air Command: Question Period," lecture given at the National War College, January 28, 1954, LC, LeMay Papers, Box B204, Folder—B-33815, 1.

70. Memorandum to the Chief of Staff–Enclosure D, September 30, 1957, LC, Thomas D. White Papers, Box 6, Folder—General White–McConnell Report, 2.

71. See "5 November 1957," LC, Thomas D. White Papers, Box 6, Folder—Conference 4 November 1957, 5–6; and "6 November 1957," ibid., 1–3.

72. See Herken, *Counsels of War,* 99; Kaplan, *Wizards of Armageddon,* 185–200; and Kinnard, *President Eisenhower and Strategy Management,* 42–46.

73. For excellent bibliographies of the writings concerning limited war strategies, see Morton H. Halperin, *Limited War: An Essay on the Development of the Theory and an Annotated Bibliography* (Cambridge, Mass.: Center for International Affairs, Harvard University, 1962); and *Bibliography on Limited War,* Pamphlet 20-60, Department of the Army, February 1958.

74. Oral History of Andrew Goodpaster, no. 477, EL, 1982, 30.

75. See Henry Cabot Lodge to the President, July 25, 1957, EL, DDE Papers, Administrative Series, Box 23, Folder—Kissinger Book; "Synopsis 'Nuclear Weapons and Foreign Policy' by Henry A. Kissinger," ibid.; Memorandum for the Acting Secretary of State, July 31, 1957, EL, DDE Diary Series, Box 25, Folder—July 1957–DDE Dictation; and "Transcript of Remarks by Henry A. Kissinger Before the Board of the Research Institute of America" [September 1957?], DDE Records, White House Central Files, Subject Series, Box 7, Folder—Atomic Energy & the Bomb (10).

76. Freedman, *Evolution of Nuclear Strategy,* 113. See also John Baylis, "Anthony Buzzard," in John Baylis and John Garnett, eds., *Makers of Nuclear Strategy* (London: Pinter Publishers, 1991).

77. Rear Admiral Sir Anthony W. Buzzard, "Massive Retaliation and Graduated Deterrence," *World Politics* 8:2 (January 1956): 229.

78. Ibid., 230.

79. "Paper by Rear Admiral Sir Anthony Buzzard," June 19, 1957, USMA, Box 63A, Folder no. 10—Gaither Committee, 1957, 1.

80. For a good short summary of Kissinger's strategic ideas, see Lawrence Freedman, "Henry Kissinger," in Baylis and Garnett, eds., *Makers of Nuclear Strategy.*

81. Henry A. Kissinger, *Nuclear Weapons and Foreign Policy* (New York: Harper & Brothers, 1957), 156–57.

82. Ibid., 145.

83. Ibid.

84. Robert Endicott Osgood, *Limited War: The Challenge to American Strategy* (Chicago: University of Chicago Press, 1957), 26.

85. Memorandum for the President, August 7, 1957, EL, WHO, OSANSA, NSC Series, Briefing Notes Subseries, Box 12, Folder—Limited War (2) 1957–61, 1.

86. Ibid.

87. R. McClintock, "A National Doctrine for Limited War," October 4, 1957, NA, RG 59, Records of the State Department, Policy Planning Staff Records, 1957–61, Lot 67D 548, Box 121, Folder—Military and Naval Policy, 2.

88. Ibid., 6–7.

89. Ibid., 7.

90. John Foster Dulles, "Challenge and Response in United States Policy," *Foreign Affairs* 36 : 1 (October 1957): 31.

91. Ibid., 31. Duffield reports that as early as November 1954, Secretary of State Dulles argued that the United States and NATO needed to maintain flexibility in their military forces. Duffield, *Power Rules,* 114.

92. Bacevich, *Pentomic Era,* 48.

93. Science Advisory Board Meeting on Limited War on December 4, 5, and 6 Tentative Agenda, November 5, 1957, LC, Twining Papers, Box 6, Folder—Diary of CJCS 8/15/57 to 12/31/57, 1–2. Among the military leaders making presentations were General Lemnitzer, Army vice chief of staff; Admiral Burke, chief of Naval Operations; General White, Air Force chief of staff; and General Power, SAC commander in chief.

94. Summary of Major Strategic Considerations for the 1960–70 ERA, January 22, 1958, NA, RG 59, State Department Records, Policy Planning Staff Records (1957–61), Lot 67D 548, Box 121, Folder—Military and Naval Policy, 1.

Chapter 4

1. For descriptions of deterrence theory in the Eisenhower administration, see Freedman, *Evolution of Nuclear Strategy,* 81–89; and Deborah Welch Larson, "Deterrence Theory and the Cold War," *Radical History Review* 63 (Fall 1995): 86–95.

2. Diary Entry by the President's Press Secretary (Hagerty), January 3, 1955, *FRUS 1955–1957,* 19, 4.

3. Diary—Donald Quarles, Wednesday, June 19, 1957, EL, Donald Quarles Papers, Box 1, Folder—Untitled [5/1/57–12/31/57], 1.

4. Memorandum for the President, July 10, 1957, EL, WHO, OSS, Subject Series, Department of Defense Subseries, Box 6, Folder—Military Planning, 1958–1961 (1), 6.

5. Robert Cutler's Personal Notes, June 20, 1957, EL, OSANSA, OCB Series, Subject Subseries, Box 3, Folder File—June 1957 (4), 1.

6. Ibid.

7. For a list of those who attended this meeting, see Memorandum for File,

June 28, 1957, EL, NSC Series, Briefing Notes Subseries, Box 8, Folder—Fallout Shelters (3), 1.

8. Informal Memorandum for Use at Meeting with Mr. Gaither, June 25, 1957, ibid., 3–4.

9. Fred Kaplan argues that Albert Wohlstetter persuaded Gaither to expand the scope of the committee's study. After meeting with Wohlstetter, "Gaither was talking about something potentially larger—a Presidentially appointed commission, packed with prominent names, that might change the whole focus of the Eisenhower Administration's skimpy and unimaginative defense policies." Kaplan, *Wizards of Armageddon*, 128. See also Herken, *Counsels*, 114.

10. Cutler, *No Time for Rest*, 355. Unfortunately, our understanding of the establishment of the Gaither committee remains restricted. At least four documents remain either classified or lost: three memoranda sent to the Steering Committee in July and an additional memorandum entitled "Purpose and Scope of Study." See To whom it may concern from H. R. Gaither, Jr., Marshall Foundation, Foster Papers, Box 34, Folder 1, 1.

11. Quoted in Winkler, *Life under a Cloud*, 119.

12. William C. Foster, "Search for Survival," June 1958, EL, WHO, OSS, Subject Series, Alphabetical Subseries, Box 13, Folder—Foster, William C. May–July 1958 (1), 1. Foster further explained why the committee asked to expand its study. "The reasoning," he wrote, "was simply: We had come together to study the best means of protecting America's civil population from nuclear extinction in case of attack. But we knew our military strategy was based on the assumption that any defense is worthless unless it has absolute capability of returning an attack. And when you return an attack, you are then on the offensive. Defense alone as a national policy is an invitation to oblivion. Offensive power is key to defense." Ibid., 4. See also Nitze, *From Hiroshima to Glasnost*, 166.

13. Memorandum for File, June 28, 1957, EL, WHO, NSC Series, Briefing Notes Subseries, Box 8, Folder—Fallout Shelters (3), 1–2.

14. See Cutler to H. Rowan Gaither, June 18, 1957, EL, WHO, OSANSA, OCB Series, Subject Subseries, Box 3, Folder—June 1957 (4), 1; Passive Panel—Preliminary Roster as of July 11, 1957, ibid., 1–2; and Group Visiting President, July 16, 1957, ibid., NSC Series, Briefing Notes Subseries, Box 16, Folder—Security Resources Panel, 2. The Institute for Defense Analyses (IDA) played a particularly important role in organizing the Gaither committee. IDA paid all of the committee members except Gaither and Sprague. Under the provisions for establishing the Gaither committee, IDA was granted $300,000 to organize and pay the advisers. Gaither and Sprague were paid separately as consultants to the Office of Defense Mobilization.

15. *Gaither Report*, 30.

16. These issues can be inferred from a summary of the subcommittee's con-

clusions. While most of its comments remain classified, the report's Table of Contents indicates the main objectives of the subcommittee. See Bonus Reports, undated, Marshall Foundation, Foster Papers, Box 31, Folder 2, 1.

17. Ibid., 2.

18. Ibid., 2–3; and Memorandum to Dr. William C. Foster, August 9, 1957, Foster Papers, Box 31, Folder 1, 1–4.

19. Memorandum for Mr. H. Rowan Gaither, Jr., August 19, 1957, ibid.

20. William Foster's records indicate that he participated in briefings, meetings, luncheons, and/or dinners on more than forty days between August and November 1957. See WCF Appointment Books 1957, Foster Papers, Box 44, Folder 1; Foster Calendar, August–November 1957, Box 43, Folder 6; Security Resources Panel Schedule of Briefings for Steering Committee, September 3, 1957, Box 30, Folder 19; Navy Presentation for Gaither Panel, August 13, 1957, Box 31, Folder 2; and 15–16 September 1957 The Commander in Chief Welcomes the Security Resources Panel to Headquarters Strategic Air Command, Box 3, Folder 3.

21. Outline for Advisory Committee, Foster Papers, Box 31, Folder 1.

22. Some Questions Suggested by Trend in the Technological Equation, undated [August–September 1957?], ibid., Folder 2, 1–2.

23. Some Questions Suggested by Trend in the Technological Equation—Summary of Certain Conclusions, ibid., 8–9.

24. Informal Memorandum for Use at Meeting with Mr. Gaither, June 25, 1957, 3–4. See also Prados, *Soviet Threat*, 68–69.

25. Document List, undated [1957], Marshall Foundation, Foster Papers, Box 31, Folder 2, 1–2.

26. See Foster, "Search for Survival," 1–2; and Memorandum for James S. Lay, Jr., December 24, 1957, NA, RG 273, NSC, Folder—NSC 5724 (background documents), 1.

27. Very little information exists on the proceedings of the Gaither committee between its establishment in May and the presentation of its report to the NSC in November. I have been unable to determine why that is the case. I have had only limited success in obtaining the declassification of documents. For the various archival sources that I have examined, see the bibliography.

28. See Memorandum for the Deputy Secretary of Defense, July 31, 1957, NA, RG 218, JCS, CCS 381 US (5-23-46) Sec. 84 RB, 1; and Col. Robert H. Warren to Gaither, August 16, 1957, ibid.

29. Memorandum for the Secretary of Defense, July 11, 1957, NA, RG 218, JCS, CCS 384.51 (10-31-46) Sec. 14, 1. Unfortunately, information related to these briefings remains unavailable.

30. Foster, "Search for Survival," 7.

31. For the agenda of briefing, see 15–16 September 1957 The Commander

in Chief Welcomes the Security Resources Panel to Headquarters Strategic Air Command, Marshall Foundation, Foster Papers, Box 3, Folder 3.

32. Carroll L. Zimmerman, *Insider at SAC: Operations Analysis under General LeMay* (Manhattan, Kans.: Sunflower University Press, 1988), 115. See also Kaplan, *Wizards of Armageddon*, 132.

33. Zimmerman, *Insider at SAC*, 114. See also Gaither to LeMay, August 26, 1957, LC, LeMay Papers, Box B107, Folder—Personal Correspondence July–December 1957, 1.

34. I have to thank Robert Hopkins for providing me a copy of a government records transmittal form that identifies some of the Air Force's briefings and meetings during the summer and fall of 1957. He found the form at the National Security Archive. At the time of this writing, my request for the declassification of this information is still pending. See Transmittal of Government Records, Ac. 61-A1449, RG 341, Records of Hq USAF. The records are still under Air Force custody.

35. General Curtis E. LeMay, "Strategic Air Command and World Peace," reprinted in Emme, *Air Power*, 668.

36. Ibid., 670.

37. General Curtis E. LeMay, "The Operational Side of Air Offense," remarks to the USAF Scientific Advisory Board, May 21, 1957, LC, LeMay Papers, Box B206, Folder—B60725, 2–3.

38. Ibid., 3.

39. Ibid., 6.

40. Kaplan, *Wizards of Armageddon*, 132–34. See also Hopkins, "An Expanded Understanding of Eisenhower, American Policy, and Overflights," 6–9; and Richard H. Hahn and Joseph P. Harahan, eds., "U.S. Strategic Air Power, 1948–1962," *International Security* 12 : 4 (Spring 1988): 78–95.

41. White to Sprague, September 23, 1957, LC, White Papers, Box 7, Folder—White House, 1. See also Sprague to White, September 18, 1957, ibid., 1.

42. Letter from White to Sprague, September 23, 1957, 1–2.

43. Statement by the Commandant of the Marine Corps to Gaither Committee, September 25, 1957, USMA, Lincoln Papers, Box 63A, Folder 10—Gaither Committee 1957, 1.

44. [Col. George Lincoln and Paul Nitze], "Limited Military Operations," undated [December 1957], EL, WHO, OSANSA, Special Assistant Series, Subject Subseries, Box 11, Folder—SRP, 10–11.

45. The presentation to the Army Policy Council occurred at the same time as the Army's presentation to the Gaither committee. I do not know if they are related.

46. [General Lyman Lemnitzer], "The Philosophy of Limited War," Briefing for Army Policy Council, September 9, 1957, RG 59, State Department, PPS Records, Lot 67D 548, Box 121, Folder—Military and Naval Policy, 13.

47. Address by General Lyman L. Lemnitzer, December 4, 1957, LC, White Papers, Box 18, Folder—Science Advisory Board, 14.

48. Memorandum by the Chief of Staff, U.S. Air Force on Ballistic Missile Defense, September 4, 1957, NA, RG 218, JCS, 1957 Geographic File, CCS 381 US (5-23-46) Sec. 85, 2334–35. For other examples of the Air Force's support of a ballistic missile defense system, see Memorandum by the Chief of Staff, November 14, 1957, ibid., CCS 381 US (5-23-46) Sec. 89, 1; and Department of Air Force Decision, September 19, 1957, LC, White Papers, Box 5, Folder—1957 Chairman of Staff Decisions, 1.

49. Memorandum by the Chief of Staff U.S. Army, September 15, 1957, RG 218, JCS, 1957 Geographic File, CCS 381 US (5-23-46) Sec. 89, 2.

50. Navy Presentation for Gaither Panel, August 13, 1957, Marshall Foundation, Foster Papers, Box 31, Folder 2.

51. R. McClintock, "A National Doctrine for Limited War," October 4, 1957, NA, RG 59, State Department, PPS Records, Lot 67D 548, Box 121, Folder—Military and Naval Policy, 2.

52. Ibid., 7. At a meeting in October, the Gaither committee and PPS discussed the committee's tentative conclusions. See Memorandum of Conversation of Meeting, October 1, 1957, ibid., Box 117, Folder—Civil Defense, 1–2.

53. Informal Memorandum for Use at Meeting with Mr. Gaither, June 25, 1957, EL, WHO, OSANSA, NSC Series, Briefing Notes Subseries, Box 8, Folder—Fallout Shelters, 3–4. At this point, I have been unable to locate any records that state what happened at these briefings.

54. Document List, undated [1957], Marshall Foundation, Foster Papers, Box 31, Folder 2, 1–2.

55. See NIE 11-4-57, November 12, 1957, *FRUS 1955–1957*, 19, 665.

56. See NIE 100-7-55, November 1, 1955, ibid., 134.

57. See SNIE 100-5-57, March 19, 1957, ibid., 442–45.

58. For descriptions of the process used in developing an NIE, see Sherman Kent, "The Law and Custom of the National Intelligence Estimate: An Examination of the Theory and Some Recollections Concerning the Practice of the Art," in Donald P. Steury, ed., *Sherman Kent and the Board of National Estimates* (Washington, D.C.: Center for the Study of Intelligence, Central Intelligence Agency, 1994), 56–115; and Freedman, *US Intelligence*, 32–41.

59. NIE 11-4-54, "Soviet Capabilities and Probable Courses of Action Through Mid-1959," NA, RG 263, Records of the Central Intelligence Agency, NIE's 1950–1992, Box 2, Folder 66, 34.

60. SNIE 12-2-56, "Probable Developments in Eastern Europe and Implications for Soviet Policy," October 30, 1956, reprinted in Scott A. Koch, *Selected Estimates on the Soviet Union, 1950–1959* (Washington, D.C.: Central Intelligence Agency, 1993), 3.

61. NIE 11-4-57, November 12, 1957, *FRUS 1955–1957,* 19, 665. See also NIE 100-7-55, "World Situation and Trends," November 1, 1955, ibid., 134.

62. SNIE 11-8-54, "Probable Warning of Soviet Attack on the US Through Mid-1957," September 14, 1954, NA, RG 263, CIA, NIE's 1950–1992, Box 2, Folder 66, 2–3.

63. NIE 11-6-55, "Probable Intelligence Warning of Soviet Attack on the US Through Mid-1958," July 1, 1955, ibid., 13.

64. NIE 11-4-57, *FRUS 1955–1957,* 19, 671. By mid-1957, intelligence estimates of Soviet bomber production were shrinking remarkably. See Freedman, *US Intelligence,* 66–67; Prados, *The Soviet Estimate,* 43–50; and Ford, *Estimative Intelligence,* 217–22.

65. Comparison of Estimated US-USSR Missile Operational Capability, January 5, 1958, EL, WHO, OSANSA, NSC Series, Briefing Notes Subseries, Box 16, Folder—Security Resources Panel, 1. This estimate was probably part of NIE 11-4-57 or SNIE 11-10-57. After reading this estimate, one member of the State Department's Bureau of Intelligence and Research exclaimed, "We must, then, reckon that in one year the United States may well, with absolutely no direct defense, confront a Russian capability for shattering devastation of the homeland." The ICBM Threat to the United States, December 23, 1957, NA, RG 59, State Department, Records of the Intelligence Bureau, Office of the Director, 1949–1959, Box 9, Folder—S/P, 1. Another member of the Office of Intelligence Research and Analysis called the report "Doom." See Memo from R. P. Joyce to Mr. A. Evans, January 6, 1958, ibid., Box 10, Folder—ICBM, 1.

66. SNIE 100-5-57, "Probable World Reaction to Certain Civil Defense Programs," March 19, 1957, *FRUS 1955–1957,* 19, 444.

67. Ibid., 445.

68. Kent, "Law and Custom of the National Intelligence Estimate," 81.

69. U.S. Congress, Senate, "Report of the Subcommittee on the Air Force of the Committee on Armed Services" (GPO, 1957), 57. See also Prados, *The Soviet Estimate,* 43–46; and Freedman, *US Intelligence,* 67.

70. NSC 5511—A Net Evaluation Subcommittee, February 14, 1955, in *FRUS 1955–1957,* 19, 56.

71. See Memorandum for the Record by the President's Special Assistant for National Security Affairs, January 23, 1956, ibid., 190.

72. Memorandum of Discussion at the 263rd Meeting of the National Security Council, October 27, 1955, ibid., 127. There was no Plan B as far as I can tell.

73. Ibid., 128.

74. Diary Entry By the President, January 23, 1956, *FRUS 1955–1957,* 187.

75. Ibid., 187–88. Whether the United States launched a preemptive or a retaliatory strike, it would use the same types of forces. In 1956 these forces consisted

of medium- and long-range bombers. The main difference between the two is that if the United States allowed the Soviet Union to attack first, a sufficient number of U.S. bombers and runways would have to survive to permit a retaliatory strike.

76. Memorandum of Discussion at 306th Meeting of the NSC, December 20, 1956, ibid., 380.

77. See Nitze, *From Hiroshima to Glasnost,* 167; Handwritten Notes by Killian [undated], MIT Archives, MC 423—Killian Papers, Box 25, Folder—Greenstein, 1; and Herbert F. York, "The White House Years (1957–1961)," ibid., Box 66, Folder—Correspondence, XYZ, 1965–87, 42.

78. York, "White House Years," 42.

79. See chap. 1 and also Herbert F. York and G. Allen Greb, "Strategic Reconnaissance," *Bulletin of the Atomic Scientists* (April 1977): 33–42. Dino Brugioni argues that General Doolittle also had access to the U-2 photographs. See Dino A. Brugioni, *Eyeball to Eyeball: The Inside Story of the Cuban Missile Crisis* (New York: Random House, 1991), 32.

80. Office of Research and Reports, "Visual-Talent Coverage of the USSR in Relation to Soviet ICBM Deployment, January 1959–June 1960," July 11, 1960, reprinted in Kevin C. Ruffner, ed., *Corona: America's First Satellite Program* (Washington, D.C.: Central Intelligence Agency, 1995), 106. See also CIA/NPIC, Photographic Intelligence Report, "Chronological Development of the Kapustin Yar/Vladimirovka and Tyuratam Missile Test Centers, USSR, 1957–1963," November 1963, reprinted in Ruffner, *Corona,* 191–96; Jeffrey Richelson, *American Espionage and the Soviet Target* (New York: William Morrow, 1987), 146; and Garthoff, *Assessing the Adversary,* 41–42.

81. Henry M. Narducci, *Strategic Air Command and the Alert Program* (Office of the Historian, Headquarters SAC, Offutt Air Force Base, NB, 1988), 1. A memorandum sent to Eisenhower presented even more pessimistic numbers. It said that only 134 out of SAC's 1,654 heavy and medium bombers would be able to take off with two hours' warning. See Memorandum for the President, October 25, 1957, EL, WHO, OSANSA, NSC Series, Briefing Notes Subseries, Box 16, Folder—Security Resources Panel, 1–2.

82. Memorandum of Discussion at the 292nd Meeting of the National Security Council, August 9, 1956, *FRUS 1955–1957,* 19, 339–41. The Gaither committee definitely got to see a copy of the report presented by Lindsay. See Transmittal of Government Records, AC-A1449, RG 341, Records of the Headquarters USAF. The report is still in Air Force custody.

83. Memorandum of Discussion at the 292nd NSC Meeting, August 9, 1956, *FRUS 1955–1957,* 19, 339–40. See also *Alert Operations and the Strategic Air Command, 1957–1991* (Office of the Historian, Headquarters SAC, Offutt Air Force Base, NE, 1991), 4–5.

84. The Gaither Committee definitely examined this report, officially called the Report of the JCS Ad Hoc Committee on the Air Defense of North America. The report remains classified.

85. See Memorandum by the Chief of Staff, U.S. Air Force for the Joint Chiefs of Staff on Submarine Guided Missile Threat, September 24, 1956, NA, RG 218, JCS, CCS 350.09 USSR (12-19-49) Sec. 13, 10–18; and Memorandum for the Secretary of Defense (from Admiral Radford), October 10, 1956, ibid., CCS 334 Air Defense of North America Ad Hoc Comte (9-20-56), Sec. 1, 1–2.

86. Memorandum for: Spaatz, Handy, Ballentine, and Hill, November 7, 1956, ibid., 1.

87. "Report of the Joint Chiefs of Staff Ad Hoc Committee on Air Defense," June 30, 1957, quoted in Note by the Secretaries to the Joint Chiefs of Staff on Briefing Presented to the Joint Chiefs of Staff on Levels of Defense Effectiveness, October 18, 1957, ibid., CCS 381 US (5-23-46) Sec. 89 RB, 2395.

88. William Lee, "Soviet Nuclear Targeting Strategy," in Desmond Ball and Jeffrey Richelson, eds., *Strategic Nuclear Targeting* (Ithaca: Cornell University Press, 1986), 86. For the JCS assessment of the attack strategies the Soviet Union might employ in an attack against the United States, see Request for Assistance in Determination of the Soviet Atomic Threat Against North America in 1960, January 9, 1957, RG 218, JCS, 1957 Geographic File, CCS 381 US (5-23-46) Sec. 75, 2106–25.

89. Notes to the Secretaries of the Joint Chiefs of Staff on Briefing Presented to the Joint Chiefs of Staff on Levels of Defense Effectiveness, November 12, 1957, ibid., CCS 381 US (5-23-46) Sec. 89 RB, 2391.

90. Ibid., 2391–92.

91. NSC 5606—Continental Defense, June 5, 1956, NA, RG 273, NSC, Folder—NSC 5606, 2.

92. Ibid., 4.

93. Ibid., 15–18. In the part of the NSC meeting on NSC 5606, "Mr. Sprague commented on the vital importance that SAC be in a position to get the required percentage of SAC planes off bases and in the air within the estimated warning time of Russian attack." Memorandum of Discussion at the 288th Meeting of the NSC, June 15, 1956, *FRUS 1955–1957,* 19, 328.

94. See Wm. F. Vandercook, "Making the Very Best of the Worst: The 'Human Effects of Nuclear Weapons' Report of 1956," *International Security* 11:1 (Summer 1986): 184–95.

95. "The Human Effects of Nuclear Weapons Development," November 21, 1956, WHO, OSANSA, NSC Series, Briefing Notes Subseries, Box 9, Folder—Human Effects of Nuclear Weapons Development, 9.

96. Ibid.

97. Ibid., 13. Operation Alert, the Eisenhower administration's annual test of its civil defense programs, reached similar conclusions in 1957. See Operation Alert 1957—Final Exercise Progress and Evaluation Report, July 19, 1957, EL, DDE Papers, Cabinet Series, Box 9, Folder—Special Cabinet Meeting on Operation Alert—July 19, 1957, 2.

98. NSC 5720—Status of National Security Programs on June 30, 1957, Part 5—Civil Defense Program, EL, WHO, OSANSA, NSC Series, Status of Projects Subseries, Box 7, Folder—NSC 5720 (5), 19.

99. Ibid., 3.

100. See Memorandum for Gaither, Director Security Resources Panel, ODM, Science Advisory Committee, July 23, 1957, EL, WHO, OSANSA, NSC Series, Briefing Notes Subseries, Box 16, Folder—Security Resources Panel, 1–2; and Memorandum for Mr. Smith, October 18, 1957, NA, RG 59, State Department, PPS Records, Lot 67D 548, Box 194, Folder—S/P Papers 1958 (January–April) (from William Leonhart), 1.

101. Memorandum for Mr. Smith, (Attachment 1), October 18, 1957, ibid., 1.

102. Ibid., 2.

103. Ibid.

104. Memorandum for Mr. Smith, (Attachment 2), October 18, 1957, ibid., 1.

105. Ibid.

106. Memorandum for Mr. Smith, (Attachment 3), October 18, 1957, ibid., 1.

107. Ibid., 1.

108. For a complete bibliography of the sources used by the Passive Defense subcommittee, see Security Resources Panel, Volume 2—"Passive Defense," November 27, 1957, EL, WHO, NSC Staff: Papers, 1948–1961, Executive Secretary Subject File Series, Box 16, Folder—Security Resources Panel, vol. 2 (2), 88–100.

109. Kaplan, *Wizards of Armageddon,* 129–30. See also R-322-RC, *Report on a Study of Non-Military Defense,* July 1, 1958, RAND Corporation. Kahn was responsible for writing this report.

110. Smith, *RAND Corporation,* 212.

111. A. J. Wohlstetter, F. S. Hoffman, R. J. Lutz, and H. S. Rowen, *Selection and Use of Strategic Air Bases R-266* (Santa Monica, Calif.: RAND Corporation, 1963), 375–83.

112. Smith, *RAND Corporation,* 213. See also Memorandum for Director of Plans, April 6, 1955, NA, RG 218, JCS, Radford Records, Folder—381 (1955), 1–4.

113. For a discussion of R-290, see Kaplan, *Wizards,* 117–21.

114. "Interview with Dr. Ellis A. Johnson Who Directed the Top-Secret Johns Hopkins Report," *U.S. News and World Report* 44:5 (January 31, 1958): 50.

115. Ibid., 54.

116. Ibid., 53.

117. *Prospect for America: The Rockefeller Panel Reports* (Garden City, N.J.: Doubleday & Company, 1961), xv-xxvi.

118. Handwritten note to Bill Foster, August 27, 1957, Marshall Foundation, Foster Papers, Box 31, Folder 3, 1.

119. Gerhard Colm and Manuel Holzner, "General Economic Feasibility of National Security Programs," undated [1957], ibid., 8–9.

120. Ibid., 20. These conclusions had a distinctly partisan flair. The same author presented another study to Paul Nitze, who later passed it to Foster and Sprague. It argued:

> Although for a time it was denied, it is now transparently clear that the reductions in our military strength over the last five years and the failures to initiate or accelerate new national security programs are a consequence of the Republican Administration's national economic policy or lack of it. Our national security outlays are not determined by national security needs and requirements. They are curbed by the erroneous economic assumption that the nation cannot afford to provide more for our security or the political desire to reduce the percentage of our national income devoted to national security so that the Republican Party can place its political trademark on tax reduction. (Memorandum to Messrs. Foster and Baxter, October 1, 1957, Marshall Foundation, Foster Papers, Box 30, Folder 19, 1–2.)

121. Mr. Nitze's Proposal for a Suave Plan, October 7, 1957, ibid., 1.

122. Ibid., 2.

123. Memorandum for Mr. Sprague, Mr. Foster, Security Resources Panel, October 21, 1957 (from G. A. Lincoln), USMA, Lincoln Papers, Box 63A, Folder 10—Gaither Committee 1957, 1.

124. Kissinger, *Nuclear Weapons and Foreign Policy*, 96.

125. Ibid., 274.

126. Ibid., 427.

127. Transcript of NBC Briefing Session 13: "Has U.S. Complacency Given Leadership to the Soviets?" June 17, 1958, EL, WHO, OSANSA, NSC Series, Briefing Notes Subseries, Box 8, Folder—Fallout Shelters, 7.

128. Ibid. 6.

129. *Inquiry into Satellite*, 1805.

130. November 6, 1957—Afternoon, LC, White Papers, Box 6, Folder—Conference November 4, 1957, 1; Gen. E. E. Partridge to Gen. Doolittle, November 8, 1957, LC, Doolittle Papers, Box 3, Folder—Gen. E. E. Partridge, 1; and Doolittle to Partridge, November 12, 1957, ibid., 1.

131. *Inquiry into Satellite,* 112.

132. Ibid., 113.

133. Ibid., 127.

134. [Lincoln and Nitze], "Limited Military Operations," 9.

135. Ibid., 8.

136. Ibid., 10.

137. J. Corson and L. Carulli, "Effective Organization for Military Defense," November 18, 1957, EL, WHO, OSAST, Box 6, Folder—Department of Defense (1957) (1), 1.

138. Ibid., 8.

139. [J. B. Fisk], "Efficiency and Results in U.S. Military Technology," October 1957, ibid., Series 1: Alphabetical Series, Subseries B: non-Top Secret File, Box 6, Folder—Department of Defense (1957) (1), 1.

140. Ibid., 5.

141. *Organizing for National Security,* 82.

142. Memorandum for Arthur S. Flemming, December 13, 1956, EL, WHO, OSAST, Box 13, Folder—OCDM and Civil Defense, December 1956–October 1960 (1), 1.

143. Foster, "Search for Survival," 18.

144. Hill to Sprague, September 28, 1957, MIT Archives, MC 365—Hill Papers, Box 37, Folder 4, enclosure.

145. For the meetings involving Foster, see WCF Appointment Books 1957, Marshall Foundation, Foster Papers, Box 44, Folder 1; and Foster Calendar, August–November 1957, ibid., Box 43, Folder 6.

146. Herken, *Counsels to the President,* 114. This quote and a similar one, "I felt as though I was spending ten hours a day staring straight into hell," have been attributed in separate sources to Robert Lovett, Foster, and Sprague. See Prados, *Soviet Estimate,* 70.

147. Foster, "Search for Survival," 5.

148. Parts of each volume are classified. Vol. 1, on active defense and SAC vulnerability, is especially restricted. For a declassified Table of Contents to all three volumes, see Bonus Report, undated [November 1957], Marshall Foundation, Foster Papers, Box 31, Folder 2, 1–3.

149. Security Resources Panel, vol. 1—"Active Defense and SAC Vulnerability," November 27, 1957, EL, WHO, NSC Staff Executive Secretary Subject File Series, Box 15, Folder—Security Resources Panel, vol. 1 (2), B-7.

150. Ibid., B-12.

151. Sherman Kent argues, "To the normal difficulties of piercing Soviet secrecy in even the most mundane of matters we confronted two exceptional ones. The Soviets redoubled their efforts to conceal the nature of their forces in being and

made far greater endeavors to obscure their plans for future changes in the scale and nature of the strategic attack and strategic defense forces. Basically our task was not only to identify and enumerate the operational forces of the principal strategic weapons systems but also to project the probable size and deployment of such forces, three, five and sometimes ten or more years in the future. These flights of fancy into the outer reaches of the unknowable were forced upon us by the exigencies of our planners." See Kent, "Law and Custom of the National Intelligence Estimate," 113.

152. York, "The White House Years," 42–43.

153. Security Resources Panel, vol. 1—"Active Defense and SAC Vulnerability," November 27, 1957, EL, WHO, NSC Staff Executive Secretary Subject File Series, Box 15, Folder—Security Resources Panel, vol. 1 (7), D-97.

154. Nitze, *From Hiroshima to Glasnost,* 167.

155. Security Resources Panel, vol. 1—"Active Defense and SAC Vulnerability," November 27, 1957, EL, WHO, NSC Staff Executive Secretary Subject File Series, Box 15, Folder—Security Resources Panel, vol. 1 (5), D-6.

156. Ibid., D-1.

157. Ibid., D-4–D-5.

158. Ibid., Folder—Security Resources Panel, vol. 1 (6), D-72.

159. Security Resources Panel, vol. 2—"Passive Defense," November 27, 1957, EL, WHO, NSC Staff Executive Secretary Subject File Series, Box 16, Folder—Security Resources Panel, vol. 2 (1), 2.

160. Ibid., Folder—Security Resources Panel, vol. 2 (2), 71.

161. Ibid., 80–81.

162. Ibid., Folder—Security Resources Panel, vol. 2 (1), 46.

163. Security Resources Panel, vol. 2—"Passive Defense," November 27, 1957, EL, WHO, NSC Staff Executive Secretary Subject File Series, Box 16, Folder—Security Resources Panel, vol. 2 (1), 45.

164. Ibid., 74.

165. Most of this volume was based on information provided by the Evaluation Quantitative Assessments subcommittee. For an indication of some of the subcommittee's work, see Memorandum for Mr. H. Rowan Gaither, Jr., August 19, 1957, Marshall Foundation, Foster Papers, Box 31, Folder 1, 1–4.

166. Security Resources Panel, vol. 3—"Economic, Social and Political," November 27, 1957, EL, WHO, NSC Staff Executive Secretary Subject File Series, Box 16, Folder—Security Resources Panel, vol. 3 (1), 14–15.

167. Project Assignments, undated [late September–early October 1957], Marshall Foundation, Foster Papers, Box 30, Folder 19, 1. See also Agenda, September 24, 1957, ibid., 1–2.

168. See Nitze, *From Hiroshima to Glasnost,* 167; and Kaplan, *Wizards,* 136.

169. Nitze, *From Hiroshima to Glasnost*, 167. See also Killian, *Sputnik*, 97–98. Kaplan stresses the importance of Nitze in writing the final report. While Nitze did help write the report, the evidence does not support Kaplan's view that Nitze played an important role in shaping the committee's final conclusions. See Kaplan, *Wizards*, 136–41.

170. Security Resources Panel Advisor's Notes for Conference, November 4, 1957, EL, WHO, OSS, Subject Series, Alphabetical Subseries, Box 13, Folder—Gaither Report November 1957–December 1958 (1), 2–3.

171. Presentation by the Security Resources Panel to the National Security Council, November 7, 1957, ibid., 1.

172. *Gaither Report*, 1.

173. For the timetable the committee used in making its recommendations, see *Gaither Report*, 15–17.

174. Memo for General Whisenand, November 5, 1957, LC, Twining Papers, Box 6, Folder—Diary of CJCS, August 15, 1957 to December 31, 1957, 1.

175. Memorandum of Conference with the President, November 7, 1957, EL, WHO, OSS, Subject Series, Department of Defense Subseries, Box 6, Folder—Military Planning, 1958–1961 (3), 1–2.

176. Sprague Oral History, 31.

177. Appointments, November 9, 1957, EL, DDE Papers, Ann Whitman Diary Series, Box 9, Folder—November 1957, A. C. W. Diary (2), 1. These three committee members remain unidentified. In a conversation with Secretary of State Dulles, "Sprague argued that for the next two and a half years [1958–1960], the U.S. position vis-à-vis the Soviet Union will be at its strongest, and that during this period we can knock out the Soviet Union's military capability without taking a similar blow from the Soviet Union." Memorandum of Conversation, January 3, 1958, EL, Dulles Papers, General Correspondence Series, Box 1, Folder—Memoranda of Conversation—General—S (1), 1.

178. See Eglin, *Air Defense in the Nuclear Age*, 272.

179. Jervis, "Deterrence and Perception," 4.

180. Arnold L. Horelick and Myron Rush, *Strategic Power and Soviet Foreign Policy* (Chicago: University of Chicago Press, 1965, 1966), 36.

181. *Pravda*, October 11, 1957, reprinted in Horelick and Rush, *Strategic Power and Soviet Foreign Policy*, 43.

182. Excerpt from *Pravda*, September 8, 1957, translated and quoted in Memorandum for the Steering Committee, October 1957, EL, WHO, OSAST, Series 1: Alphabetical Series, Subseries B non-Top Secret File, Box 6, Folder—Department of Defense (1957) (1), 1–2. See also McDougall, *... the Heavens and the Earth*, 237; Vladislav Zubok and Constantine Pleshakov, *Inside the Kremlin's Cold War: From Stalin to Khrushchev* (Cambridge: Harvard University Press, 1996),

192–94; Bundy, *Danger and Survival*, 416; and R. Craig Nation, *Black Earth, Red Star: A History of Soviet Security Policy, 1917–1991* (Ithaca: Cornell University Press, 1992), 213.

Chapter 5

1. Dwight D. Eisenhower to B. G. Chynoweth, July 15, 1954, quoted in Duram, *Moderate among Extremists,* 54.

2. Untitled Paper by Paul Nitze, [January 1958], EL, WHO, OSAST, Box 14, Folder—SRP June 1957–November 1960, 1.

3. Ibid., 10.

4. Ibid., 4.

5. Ibid., 9. Nitze defined quick reaction capabilities as those forces which had to be launched as soon as a Soviet attack was detected. These forces would have included land-based ballistic missiles and aircraft. Delayed reaction capabilities were those forces that did not have to be launched immediately. Nitze concluded that submarine-launched missiles and bombers after they were in the air offered these capabilities.

6. Comments by R.C. [Robert Cutler] on W. C. Foster article, May 29, 1958, EL, WHO, NSC Series, Briefing Notes Subseries, Box 8, Folder—Fallout Shelters (2), 1.

7. *Newsweek* found that "Most Americans are in favor of a crash program to put the U.S. ahead in the missile race. . . . There was concern but no panic. Rather Americans seemed to have suffered a severe blow to their pride. They weren't used to being second best, and they wanted to catch up. Above all, they understood that catching up might well be a matter of survival." "The U.S., Ike, and Sputnik," *Newsweek,* 50:18 (October 28, 1957), 30. See also "The Moon's Meaning," ibid., 50:16 (October 14, 1957), 39.

8. Robert Holtz, "Why Mr. President?," *Aviation Week* 67:16 (October 21, 1957), 21.

9. Ibid., "Intelligence Without Leadership," *Aviation Week* 67:17 (October 28, 1957), 21.

10. American Institute of Public Opinion, November 24, 1957, reprinted in Hazel Gaudet Erskine, ed., "The Polls: Defense, Peace, and Space," *The Public Opinion Quarterly* 25:3 (Fall 1961), 483.

11. "U.S. Satellite—A Myth Exploded," *U.S. News & World Report* 43:24 (December 13, 1957), 31.

12. "The Changing Mood in America," ibid., 43:25 (December 20, 1957), 43.

13. Nevil Shute, *On the Beach* (New York: William Morrow and Company, Inc., 1957), 225.

14. See Horelick and Rush, *Strategic Power and Soviet Foreign Policy,* 36; Mc-

Dougall, . . . *the Heavens and the Earth,* 237; Zubok and Pleshakov, *Inside the Kremlin's Cold War,* 192–94; Bundy, *Danger and Survival,* 416; and Nation, *Black Earth, Red Star,* 213.

15. *Pravda,* November 19, 1957, in Horelick and Rush, *Strategic Power and Soviet Foreign Policy,* 48.

16. *Pravda,* November 29, 1957, ibid., 44–45.

17. "What Congress Hears: We'd Better Get Busy," *Newsweek* 50:26 (December 23, 1957), 15.

18. George A. Almond, "Public Opinion Polls and the Development of American Public Opinion," *The Public Opinion Quarterly* 24:4 (Winter 1960), 567.

19. Memorandum of Conference with the President, November 4, 1957, EL, WHO, OSS, Subject Series, Alphabetical Subseries, Box 23, Folder—Science Advisory Committee (3) [November 1957–April 1956], 2.

20. Dwight D. Eisenhower, "Science in National Security," November 7, 1957, reprinted in *The Department of State Bulletin* 37:961 (November 25, 1957), 821.

21. Ibid., "Our Future Security," November 13, 1957, reprinted in *The Department of State Bulletin* 37:962 (December 2, 1957), 868.

22. Ibid., 869.

23. Record of Actions by the National Security Council at its 343rd Meeting, November 7, 1957, EL, WHO, OSS, Subject Series, Alphabetical Subseries, Box 19, Folder—NSC—Record of Actions, 1957 (7), 2–3.

24. Decision of JCS 2101/284, December 4, 1957, NA, RG 218, JCS, 1957 Geographic File, CCS 381 US (1-31-50) Sec. 73, 2539.

25. Ibid., 2539.

26. Ibid., 2545.

27. Ibid., 2540.

28. Ibid., 2544.

29. Ibid., 2541–42.

30. Ibid., 2543.

31. Ibid., 2546.

32. "Comments and Recommendations on Report to the President by the Security Resources Panel of the ODM Science Advisory Committee," December 16, 1957, EL, WHO, OSANSA, NSC Series, Policy Papers Subseries, Box 22, Folder—Gaither Report, Defense-1.

33. Ibid., Defense-8.

34. Ibid., Defense-5.

35. Ibid., Defense-11.

36. Ibid., Defense-13–14.

37. Ibid., Defense-19.

38. Ibid., State-1.

39. Ibid., Budget-3.

40. Ibid., CEA-1–CEA-2.

41. Ibid., Treasury-3–Treasury-4.

42. Ibid., CIA-1.

43. Ibid., FCDA-1–FCDA-5.

44. See Memorandum from the Secretary of Defense (Wilson) to the President, July 10, 1957, *FRUS 1955–1957,* 19, 540–46; Memorandum of a Conference with the President, July 10, 1957, ibid., 547–48; and Memorandum of Discussion at the 332nd Meeting of the National Security Council, July 25, 1957, ibid., 556–63.

45. See for example World Gallup Poll, October 27, 1957, reprinted in Erskine, ed., "The Polls: Defense, Peace, and Space," 486.

46. Memorandum of Conversation with the President, November 11, 1957, EL, WHO, OSS, Subject Series, Department of Defense Subseries, Box 2, Folder—Budget, Military (6) (September 1957–January 1959), 3.

47. Ibid., 3.

48. Memorandum of Conference with the President, November 22, 1957, ibid., 1.

49. Memorandum of Conference with the President, December 5, 1957, ibid., 2.

50. Informal Notes, November 22, 1957, EL, WHO, OSANSA, Special Assistant Series, Chronological Subseries, Box 5, Folder—November 1957 (2), 1. See also Memorandum for the Secretary of Defense, November 17, 1957, LC, Twining Papers, Box 105, Folder—Memos., November 1957, 1.

51. Memorandum of Conference with the President, December 5, 1957, ibid., OSS, Subject Series, Department of Defense Subseries, Box 2, Folder—Budget, Military (6) (September 1957–January 1959), 1.

52. Status of the Gaither Report, [December 1957], ibid., OSANSA, NSC Series, Briefing Notes Subseries, Box 16, Folder—Security Resources Panel, 1. See also J. R. Killian, Jr. to Donald Quarles, November 30, 1957, ibid., OSAST, Series 1: Alphabetical Series, Subseries B: non-Top Secret File, Box 6, Folder—Department of Defense (1957) (1), 2; Notes on Dr. Killian's Aide Memoire, November 30, 1957, ibid., 1–2; Memorandum for Dr. Killian, [late 1957], ibid., 1–5.

53. Notes, November 23, 1957, ibid., OSANSA, NSC Series, Briefing Notes Subseries, Box 16, Folder—Security Resources Panel, 1.

54. For an example of one of the leaks, see Robert A. Hawkins to Senator Leverett Saltonstall, December 2, 1957, ibid., OSAST, Box 4, Folder—SRP June 1957–November 1960, 1. Hawkins served on the Gaither study group that examined anti-ICBM missile defenses. Robert Lovett wrote Foster in November, "I noticed the expected leak yesterday—I can't believe it can do anything but good to make the knowledge of the report a matter of public record." Dear Beulah & Bill

[Foster], November 24, 1957, Marshall Foundation, Foster Papers, Box 30, Folder 17, 2.

55. Arthur Krock quoted Foster in a newspaper article. See Krock, "A Clue to the Top-Secret N.S.C. Report," *New York Times,* December 20, 1957, 1. Foster may have made this statement, but it is not in the written record of his speech. See William C. Foster, "West Point Speech," [December 4, 1957], Marshall Foundation, Foster Papers, Box 34, Folder 20, 1–12.

56. Krock, "A Clue to the Top-Secret N.S.C. Report," 1.

57. William Foster to Killian, October 31, 1975, MIT Archives, MC 423—Killian Papers, Box 13, Folder—JRK Book—Correspondence A–K, 1.

58. Foster to Lincoln, November 26, 1957, USMA, Lincoln Papers, Box 63A, Folder 10—Gaither Committee 1957, 1.

59. Memorandum, [November 1957], EL, WHO, OSS, Subject Series, Alphabetical Subseries, Box 13, Folder—Gaither Report (November 1957–January 1958) (1), 1.

60. A Draft Statement of Objectives, [Late November/Early December 1957], Marshall Foundation, Foster Papers, Box 30, Folder 18, 1–7.

61. [Untitled list of names], EL, WHO, OSS, Subject Series, Alphabetical Subseries, Box 13, Folder—Gaither Report (November 1957–January 1958) (1), 1.

62. Robert F. Whitney, "President Backs 'Alert' Advocates," *New York Times,* December 12, 1957, 11. For other newspaper reports on the dinner, see ibid., December 11, 1957, 8; and ibid., December 13, 1957, 26. For descriptions of the dinner based on interviews with some of the participants, see Halperin, "The Gaither Committee and the Policy Process," 374; and Kaplan, 152–53.

63. Chalmer Roberts, "Enormous Arms Outlay Is Held Vital to Survival," *Washington Post,* December 20, 1957, Sec. A, pp. 1, 19. Roberts was not the first to write about the Gaither report, but his article provided the most in-depth description and discussion of it. For early articles, see the *New York Herald Tribune,* November, 23, 1957, 1; and *Aviation Week* 67:22, December 2, 1957, 28.

64. Interview XII with George E. Reedy, December 21, 1983, LBJ Oral History Foundation, AC 84-54, 1.

65. *Inquiry into Satellite,* 2038. See also ibid., 923–24; Senator Lyndon B. Johnson to the President, December 4, 1957, EL, White House Central Files, Official File, Box 676, Folder—OF 133-R, 1; Killian to Foster, October 24, 1975, MIT Archives, MC 423—Killian Papers, Box 13, Folder—JRK Book—Correspondence A–K, 1–2; and Minutes of Telephone Conversation between JFD and LBJ, December 23, 1957, EL, John Foster Dulles Papers, Telephone Call Series, Box 7, Folder—Minutes of Telephone Conversations—General, November 1, 1957–December 27, 1957, 1. See also Divine, *Sputnik Challenge,* 78.

66. *Inquiry into Satellite,* 1340. For examples of other requests, see Senator Joseph S. Clark to the President, December 17, 1957, EL, White House Central

Files, Official File, Box 676, Folder—OF 133-R, 1; Henry C. Kittredge to [Sherman] Adams, December 29, 1957, ibid., 1; General Robert E. Wood (ret.) to Eisenhower, December 30, 1957, ibid., 1; and Holifield to Eisenhower, January 6, 1958, ibid., 1.

67. See Notes of Meeting , November 7, 1957, ibid., OSS, Subject Series, Alphabetical Subseries, Box 13, Folder—Gaither Report November 1957–December 1958 (1), 1; and Memorandum for J. Patrick Coyne, November 19, 1957, NA, RG 273, NSC, Folder—NSC 5724, 1–2.

68. See Jim Fisk to Killian, December 19, 1957, EL, U.S. President's Science Advisory Committee Papers, Correspondence—B (1), Box 6, Folder—Correspondence—F, 1; Kaplan, *Wizards of Armageddon,* 152–53; and Sprague to Killian, August 24, 1972, MIT Archives, MC 423—Killian Papers, Box 13, Folder—Correspondence L–Z, 1.

69. "Secret Service," *Newsweek* 51 : 1 (January 6, 1958), 35.

70. Handwritten Notes by Killian, [undated], MIT Archives, MC 423—Killian Papers, Box 25, Folder—Greenstein, 1.

71. See political cartoon in "Perils, Problems, The Job Ahead," *Newsweek* 51 : 2 (January 13, 1958).

72. Memorandum of Conversation with the President, December 26, 1957, EL, Papers of John Foster Dulles and Christian A. Herter, 1953–1961, White House Memoranda Series, Chronological Subseries, Box 5, File—Meetings with the President, 1957 (1) [November–December], 1.

73. Telephone Conversation between JFD and Nixon, January 8, 1958, EL, JFD Papers, Telephone Call Series; Box 8, Folder—Memorandum of Telephone Conversations General January 2, 1958–March 31, 1958 (4), 1.

74. Adams to Kittredge, January 6, 1958, ibid., Records of Bryce Harlow, Box 6, Folder—Gaither Report—A Summary, 1. This letter was written by Cutler.

75. Draft Letter to Mr. Gaither, January 9, 1958, EL, WHO, OSS, Subject Series, Alphabetical Subseries, Box 13, Folder—Gaither Report November 1957–January 1958 (3), 1.

76. Gaither to Killian, January 14, 1958, ibid., OSAST, Box 14, Folder—SRP June 1957–November 1960, 1.

77. Eisenhower to LBJ, January 21, 1958, EL, WHO, OSANSA, NSC Series, Administration Series, Box 4, Folder—NSC Agenda and Minutes—1960, 1.

78. Annual Message to the Congress on the State of the Union, January 9, 1958, *PPP-DDE, 1958,* 3.

79. Ibid., 7–13.

80. Annual Budget Message to the Congress, January 13, 1958, ibid., 17–18.

81. Ibid., 19.

82. Memorandum for the Record, January 27, 1958, EL, WHO, NSC Staff,

Special File Series, Box 3, Folder—Gaither Report, 2–3. In comparison to these figures, the Gaither committee recommended adding $450 million for alert and dispersal programs, $190 million for early warning, $700 million accelerating IRBMs, ICBMs, and SLBMs, and $130 million for air defense to the FY 1959 budget. *Gaither Report,* 34.

83. Memorandum for the Record, January 27, 1958, EL, WHO, NSC Staff, Special File Series, Box 3, Folder—Gaither Report, 1.

84. See footnote 65 in chapter 4.

85. Memorandum of Discussion at the 350th NSC Meeting, January 6, 1958, EL, DDE Papers, NSC Series, Box 9, Folder—350th Meeting of the NSC, 17.

86. "Comments and Recommendations," December 16, 1957, Defense-14.

87. Memorandum for the Record, February 25, 1958, EL, WHO, OSANSA, NSC Series, Briefing Notes Subseries, Box 16, Folder—Security Resources Panel, 1.

88. Ibid., 2.

89. Memorandum for the Secretary of Defense, Appendix A, March 19, 1958, LC, Twining Papers, Box 105, Folder—Memos 13-31 MR 1958, 1.

90. "Report by Joint Strategic Plans Committee to the Joint Chiefs of Staff," March 24, 1958, NA, RG 218, JCS, 1958 Geographic File, CCS 381 US (1-31-50) Sec. 76, 2665.

91. "Report by Joint Strategic Plans Committee to the Joint Chiefs of Staff," March 26, 1958, NA, RG 218, JCS, 1958 Geographic File, CCS 381 US (1-31-50) Sec. 76, 2670–73. See also Ponturo, *Analytical Support,* 166–67.

92. Memorandum of Discussion at the 363rd Meeting of the NSC, April 24, 1958, EL, DDE Papers, NSC Series, Box 10, Folder—363rd Meeting of NSC, April 24, 1958, 2.

93. Ibid., 4.

94. Ibid., 6.

95. Eisenhower, *Waging Peace,* 222. At the NSC meeting in January 1958, Eisenhower asserted that he considered "money expended on improving the early warning system and the dispersal of SAC bases to be money well spent." Discussion at the 350th NSC Meeting, January 6, 1958, EL, DDE Papers, NSC Series, Box 9, Folder—350th Meeting of the NSC 18. See also Memorandum for General LeMay, January 20, 1958, LC, White Papers, Box 15, Folder—Chief of Staff Signed Memos January 1958–December 1958, 1.

96. Memorandum for General Cutler, April 23, 1958, EL, WHO, OSANSA, NSC Series, Briefing Notes Subseries, Box 16, Folder—Security Resources Panel, 1–2.

97. Nunn, *The Soviet First Strike Threat,* 159.

98. Memorandum for the Record, January 31, 1958, NA, RG 51, Records of the Office of Management and Budget, General Budgetary Administration, Subject

Files, Series 51.14a—Subject Files for the National Military Establishment and Department of Defense, 1953–1961, Box 3, Folder—Defense Department Air Defense Programs, 2.

99. "Supplemental Report on Items in Security Resources Panel Report," March [?] 1958, EL, WHO, OSANSA, NSC Series, Policy Papers Subseries, Box 22, Folder—Gaither Report, 3.

100. Memorandum for the Secretary of Defense, March 21, 1958, NA, RG 218, JCS, 1958—Geographic File, CCS 381 US (1-31-50) Sec. 76 RB, 4.

101. Power to White, October 22, 1958, LC, White Papers, Box 19, Folder—Top Secret Files #4, 1.

102. Hopkins, J.C., and Sheldon A. Goldberg, *The Development of Strategic Air Command, 1946–1986 (The Fortieth Anniversary History)* (Offutt Air Force Base, Nebraska: Office of the Historian, SAC, 1986), 101.

103. Statement of Secretary of Defense Neil McElroy Before the Preparedness Investigating Subcommittee of the Senate Committee on Armed Services, February 26, 1958, EL, WHO, OSS, Subject Series, Department of Defense Subseries, Box 1, Folder—Department of Defense Vol. 2 (5) February 1958, 8.

104. *Inquiry into Satellite*, 2324.

105. "Supplemental Report on Items in Security Resources Panel Report," March [?] 1958, EL, WHO, OSANSA, NSC Series, Policy Papers Subseries, Box 22, Folder—Gaither Report, 4; Memorandum for the Secretary of Defense, March 21, 1958, RG 218, JCS, 1958—Geographic File, CCS 381 US (1-31-50) Sec. 76 RB, 3; and Memorandum for the Secretary of Defense/SAC Alert Status, March 28, 1958, LC, Twining Papers, Box 105, Folder—Memos 13-31 MR 1958, 1.

106. "Report by the Joint Strategic Plans Committee to the Joint Chiefs of Staff on Provision of Blast Shelters at SAC Bases," February 19, 1958, NA, RG 218, JCS, 1958 Geographic File, CCS 381 US (1-31-50) Sec. 75, 2585.

107. Memorandum for the Record, January 31, 1958, NA, RG 51, Office of Management and Budget Records, General Budgetary Administration, Subject Files, Series 51.14a—Subject Files for the National Military Establishment and Department of Defense, 1953–1961, Box 3, Folder—Defense Department Air Defense Programs, 2.

108. Note by the Secretaries to the Joint Chiefs of Staff on SAC Alert Warning Times (Appendix), January 21, 1958, NA, RG 218, JCS, 1958 Geographic File, CCS 381 US (5-23-46) Sec. 92, 2511.

109. Ibid., 2511–12.

110. NSC 5802/1—U.S. Policy on Continental Defense, February 19, 1958, NA, RG 273, NSC, Folder—NSC 5802, 3.

111. Memorandum of Discussion at the 350th NSC Meeting, January 6,

1958, EL, DDE Papers, NSC Series, Box 9, Folder—350th Meeting of the NSC, 16.

112. "Supplemental Report on Items in Security Resources Panel Report," March [?] 1958, EL, WHO, OSANSA, NSC Series, Policy Papers Subseries, Box 22, Folder—Gaither Report, 1; and Memorandum by the Director, Joint Staff to the Joint Chief of Staff, January 21, 1958, NA, JCS, RG 218, JCS, 1958 Geographic File, CCS 381 US (1-31-50) Sec. 74 RB, 2565a.

113. "Report by the Joint Strategic Plans Committee to the Joint Chiefs of Staff," March 3, 1958, NA, RG 218, JCS, 1958 Geographic File, CCS 381 US (1-31-50) Sec. 75 RB, 2605.

114. Memorandum for the Secretary of Defense (Area Defense Against ICBMs), March 31, 1958, LC, Twining Papers, Box 105, Folder—Memos 13-31 MR 1958, 2.

115. Memorandum for the Secretary of Defense (BMEWS), March 28, 1958, ibid., 1. See also "Report by the Joint Strategic Plans Committee to the Joint Chiefs of Staff," March 24, 1958, NA, RG 218, JCS, 1958 Geographic File, CCS 381 US (1-31-50) Sec. 76, 2655.

116. "Report to the Underseas Warfare Advisory Panel to the Subcommittee on Military Applications of the Joint Committee on Atomic Energy," Joint Committee on Atomic Energy, U.S. Congress, August 1958, 5.

117. Statement of Secretary of Defense Neil McElroy Before the Preparedness Investigating Subcommittee of the Senate Committee on Armed Services, February 26, 1958, EL, WHO, OSS, Subject Series, Department of Defense Subseries, Box 1, Folder—Department of Defense Vol. 2 (5) February 1958, 4.

118. "Supplemental Report on Items in Security Resources Panel Report," March [?] 1958, EL, WHO, OSANSA, NSC Series, Policy Papers Subseries, Box 22, Folder—Gaither Report, 7.

119. Report by the Deputy Director for Strategic Plans, July 17, 1958, NA, RG 218 JCS, 1958 Geographic File, CCS 381 US (91-31-50) Sec. 78, 2751.

120. Raymond L. Garthoff, "Air Power and Soviet Strategy," *Air University Quarterly* (Fall 1957), reprinted in Emme, *Air Power,* 538.

121. General Nathan F. Twining, *Neither Liberty Nor Safety: A Hard Look at U.S. Military Policy and Strategy* (New York: Holt, Rinehart and Winston, 1966), 105.

122. Memorandum to the Secretary of State, January 4, 1958, NA, RG 59, State Department, PPS Records, Lot 67D 548, Box 194, Folder—S/P Papers 1958 (January–April), 4–5.

123. Memorandum of Discussion at the 352nd Meeting of the NSC, January 22, 1958, EL, DDE Papers, NSC Series, Box 9, Folder—352nd Meeting of NSC (January 22, 1958), 2.

124. Ibid., 2.

125. Memorandum for the Executive Secretary of the National Security Council, March 5, 1958, NA, RG 273, NSC, Folder—NSC 5724 (background documents), 2.

126. Ibid., 1–3.

127. Memorandum of the Discussion at the 364th Meeting of the NSC, May 1, 1958, EL, DDE Papers, NSC Series, Box 10, Folder—364th Meeting of NSC, May 1, 1958, 3.

128. Ibid., 5.

129. Memorandum for Record, May 9, 1958, EL, WHO, OSS, Subject Series, Alphabetical Subseries, Box 21, Folder—Nuclear Exchange (September 1957–June 1958) (3), 1.

130. Ibid., 3.

131. Memorandum of the Discussion at the 364th Meeting of the NSC, May 1, 1958, EL, DDE Papers, NSC Series, Box 10, Folder—364th Meeting of NSC, May 1, 1958, 4.

132. Ibid., 4.

133. Ibid., 7.

134. Ibid., 10.

135. Ibid., 10.

136. Conference, June 17, 1958, EL, WHO, OSS, Subject Series, Alphabetical Subseries, Box 21, Folder—Nuclear Exchange (September 1957–June 1958) (3), 1. See also Memorandum for the National Security Council, June 18, 1958, NA RG 59, State Department/OCB and NSC, 1947–63, Lot 63D 95, Box #111, 2.

137. Memorandum for the Secretary of State and Secretary of Defense, July 2, 1958, NA, RG 273, NSC, NSC 5724 (Background Docs.), 5.

138. Dwight D. Eisenhower, "Annual Message to the Congress on the State of the Union," January 9, 1958, *PPP-DDE, 1958,* 7.

139. Eisenhower, *Waging Peace,* 244.

140. Ibid., 247–48. See also Chris Donnelly, *United States Defense Policies in 1958* (GPO, 1959), 48–50.

141. Brian L. Duchin, " 'The Most Spectacular Legislative Battle of the Year': President Eisenhower and the 1958 Reorganization of the Department of Defense," *Presidential Studies Quarterly* 24:2 (Spring 1994), 254.

142. See ibid., 248–53.

143. Duchin, " 'The Most Spectacular Legislative Battle of the Year,' " 256–57.

144. Sprague Oral History, 23.

145. Memorandum of Conversation with the President, December 26, 1957, EL, JFD Papers, White House Memoranda Series, Chronological Subseries, Box 5, File—Meetings with the President, 1957 (1) [November–December], 1. The sec-

retary's view did not represent the consensus of opinions of officials in the State Department. Its PPS recommended the initiation of the shelter program. See Memorandum for Mr. Gerard Smith, December 5, 1957, NA, RG 59, PPS Records, Lot 67D 548, Box 194, Folder—S/P Papers 1958 (January–April), 1; Memorandum for Mr. Smith, December 6, 1957, ibid., 1; Memorandum for Mr. Gerard Smith, December 7, 1957, ibid., 1; Memorandum for Mr. Smith [from Christian Herter], December 9, 1957, ibid., 1; and Minutes of Telephone Conversation between Dulles and Secretary Anderson, December 27, 1957, JFD Papers, Telephone Call Series, Box 7, Folder—Memorandum of Telephone Conversation—General, November 1, 1957–December 27, 1957 (1), 1.

146. See Killian, *Sputnik, Scientists, and Eisenhower,* 97–98; Kaplan, *Wizards of Armageddon,* 185; and Telephone Conversation between Dulles and Allen Dulles, November 18, 1957, JFD Papers, Telephone Call Series, Box 7, Folder—Memorandum of Telephone Conversation, General, November 1, 1957–December 27, 1957, 1. For a description of the origins of the animosity between Dulles and Nitze, see Hughes, *The Ordeal of Power,* 120–21; and Callahan, *Dangerous Capabilities,* 150–52.

147. Memorandum of Discussion at the 351st NSC Meeting, January 16, 1958, EL, DDE Papers, NSC Series, Box 9, Folder—351st Meeting of NSC, January 16, 1958, 2.

148. Ibid., 6–11.

149. Ibid., 8.

150. Ibid., 11–12.

151. Ibid., 4.

152. Memorandum for General Robert Cutler, February 11, 1958, EL, WHO, OSAST, Box 14, Folder—SRP June 1957–November 1960, 1.

153. Memorandum for General Cutler, February 14, 1958, EL, WHO, OSANSA, NSC Series, Briefing Notes Subseries, Box 8, Folder—Fallout Shelters, 1.

154. Sprague to Killian, February 28, 1958, EL, WHO, OSAST, Box 13, Folder—OCDM and Civil Defense, December 1956–October 1960 (1), 1. Sprague sent a copy of the same letter to Cutler on March 19.

155. Ibid., 2.

156. Cutler to Sprague, March 19, 1958, EL, WHO, OSANSA, NSC Series, Briefing Notes Subseries, Box 8, Folder—Fallout Shelters, 1; and Memorandum of Discussion at the 360th Meeting of the NSC, March 27, 1958, EL, DDE Papers, NSC Series, Box 10, Folder—360th Meeting of the NSC, March 27, 1958, 8.

157. Ibid., 3.

158. Ibid., 10.

159. [Untitled], March 28, 1958—R.C., EL, WHO, OSANSA, NSC Series, Briefing Notes Subseries, Box 8, Folder—Fallout Shelters, 1.

160. Record of Actions by the NSC at its 360th Meeting, March 27, 1958, EL, DDE Papers, NSC Series, Box 2, Folder—Record of Actions by NSC 1958 (1) Action nos. 1839–1893, 2–3.

161. Ambrose, *Eisenhower*, v. 2, 435. See also Gaddis, *Strategies of Containment*, 185–88.

162. See Divine, *Sputnik Challenge*, 127.

163. Memorandum of Discussion at the 363rd Meeting of the NSC, April 24, 1958, EL, DDE Papers, NSC Series, Box 10, Folder—363rd Meeting of NSC, April 24, 1958, 6.

164. Memorandum for the Secretary of Defense, March 12, 1958, LC, Twining Papers, Box 105, Folder—Memos MR 1958 1–12, 1.

165. Eisenhower to Richard L. Simon, April 4, 1956, MIT Archives, MC 423—Killian Papers, Box 25, Folder—Greenstein, 1. See also Memorandum for the Secretary of Defense, March 12, 1958, LC, Twining Papers, Box 105, Folder—Memos MR 1958 1–12, 2.

166. Duchin, "'The Most Spectacular Legislative Battle of the Year,'" 256–57.

167. Comments by R. C. on W. C. Foster article, May 29, 1958, EL, WHO, OSANSA, NSC Series, Briefing Notes Subseries, Box 8, Folder—Fallout Shelters (2), 2.

168. Memorandum of Discussion at the 356th Meeting of the NSC, February 28, 1958, EL, DDE Papers, NSC Series, Box 9, Folder—356th Meeting of the NSC, February 27, 1958, 11.

Chapter 6

1. See n. 4 in the introduction.

2. For an excellent recent discussion of the Surprise Attack Conference, see Suri, "America's Search for a Technological Solution to the Arms Race."

3. Statement of the Senate Democratic Caucus on The Current Status of the Strategic Air Force by Senator Stuart Symington, January 7, 1958, LC, White Papers, Box 17, Folder—Congressional (M–Z), 6.

4. Roman, *Eisenhower and the Missile Gap*, 33.

5. Zubok and Pleshakov, *Inside the Kremlin's Cold War*, 192–93.

6. Adam B. Ulam, *Expansion and Coexistence: The History of Soviet Foreign Policy, 1917–67* (New York: Frederick A. Praeger Publishers, 1968), 613–21; and Dockrill, *Eisenhower's New-Look*, 236–51.

7. The best account of the first few months of the 1958 Berlin crisis is William Burr, "Avoiding the Slippery Slope: The Eisenhower Administration and the Berlin Crisis, November 1958–January 1959," *Diplomatic History* 18:2 (Spring 1994): 177–205. See also Zubok and Pleshakov, *Inside the Kremlin's Cold War*, 194–99; and Ulam, *Expansion and Coexistence*, 619–20.

8. Obviously, the debate over national security issues was only one of the many areas of difference between Kennedy and Nixon.

9. See Chalmer Roberts, "Kennedy Names Policy Group To Prepare Program If He Wins," *The Washington Post,* August 31, 1960.

10. Memorandum of Conference with the President, February 6, 1958, quoted in Nunn, *The Soviet First Strike Threat,* 188.

11. See Robert Cutler to Admiral Arthur W. Radford, July 9, 1958, EL, WHO, OSANSA, NSC Series, Briefing Notes Subseries, Box 8, Folder—Fallout Shelters, 2.

12. The influence of satellite intelligence on intelligence estimates will be discussed more fully later in the chapter.

13. See Horelick and Rush, *Strategic Power and Soviet Foreign Policy,* 35–70.

14. Memorandum of Discussion at the 363rd Meeting of the NSC, April 24, 1958, EL, DDE Papers, NSC Series, Box 10, Folder—363rd Meeting of NSC, April 24, 1958, 5.

15. *Gaither Report,* 34.

16. See Neufeld, *Ballistic Missiles,* 190; and Roman, *Eisenhower and the Missile Gap,* 179.

17. See Neufeld, *Ballistic Missiles,* 184; and Roman, *Eisenhower and the Missile Gap,* 197.

18. Roman, *Eisenhower and the Missile Gap,* 150–51 and 187. By the time Eisenhower left office, he had deployed twelve Atlas ICBMs and launched two Polaris submarines carrying a total of thirty-two SLBMs. See Desmond Ball, "The Development of the SIOP, 1960–1983," in Ball and Richelson, *Strategic Nuclear Targeting,* 57.

19. Roman, *Eisenhower and the Missile Gap,* 184.

20. Ibid., 190.

21. Neufeld, *Ballistic Missiles,* 224–26.

22. Ibid., 232.

23. *Alert Operations and the Strategic Air Command, 1957–1991* (Offutt Air Force Base, Neb.: Office of the Historian, Headquarters Strategic Air Command, 1991), 77. See also, Peter J. Roman, "Strategic Bombers over the Missile Horizon," *Journal of Strategic Studies* 18 (March 1995): 200–210.

24. Memorandum for the National Security Council, June 18, 1958, NA, RG 59, State Department, Records of the OCB and NSC, 1947–63, Lot 66D 95, Box 111, 2.

25. "Final Report of the Task Group on Limited War, Defense Science Board," September 1, 1958, NA, RG 359, Office of Science and Technology, Subject Files, 1957–62, Box 58, Folder—Limited War—Army, 3.

26. Ibid., 6.

27. Memorandum of Meeting with the President, August 25, 1960, EL,

WHO, OSS, Subject Series, Alphabetical Subseries, Box 23, Folder—Science Advisory Committee (6) July 1959–August 1960, 2.

28. Ibid., 4–5.

29. See Memorandum for the Special Assistant to the President for National Security Affairs, September 28, 1960, NA, RG 273, NSC, Folder—NSC 5724 (Background Documents), 1; and Memorandum for the Acting Secretary, October 5, 1960, NA, RG 59, Records of the OCB and NSC, 1947–63, Lot 66D 95, Box 111, 1.

30. See Memorandum for the Special Assistant to the President for National Security Affairs, September 28, 1960, NA, RG 273, NSC, Folder—NSC 5724 (Background Documents), 1–3.

31. Memorandum for the Acting Secretary, October 5, 1960, NA, RG 59, Records of the OCB and NSC, 1947–63, Lot 66D 95, Box 111, 2.

32. Memorandum of Conversation, September 27, 1960, ibid., 3.

33. "U.S. and Allied Capabilities for Limited Military Operations to July 1, 1962," excerpt quoted in Memorandum for the Secretary of Defense—Appendix, December 9, 1960, EL, WHO, OSANSA, NSC Series, Subject Subseries, Box 5, Folder—Limited Military Operations, Appendix—1.

34. Memorandum for the Acting Secretary, October 5, 1960, NA, RG 59, State Department, OCB and NSC Records, Lot 66D 95, Box 111, 1.

35. Memorandum of Conversation, September 27, 1960, NA, RG 59, State Department, OCB and NSC Records, Lot 66D 95, Box 111, 2.

36. Memorandum for the Secretary of Defense—Appendix, December 9, 1960, EL, WHO, OSANSA, NSC Series, Subject Subseries, Box 5, Folder—Limited Military Operations, 1.

37. Ibid., 3–4.

38. Maxwell D. Taylor, *The Uncertain Trumpet* (New York: Harper & Brothers, Publishers, 1959, 1960), 5.

39. Ibid., 6–7 and 136–64. See also A. J. Bacevich, *The Pentomic Era: The U.S. Army between Korea and Vietnam* (Washington, D.C.: National Defense University Press, 1986), 44.

40. Paul Nitze, "An Alternative Nuclear Policy as a Base for Negotiations," in *East-West Negotiations,* 2nd edition (Washington, D.C.: The Washington Center for Foreign Policy Research, 1959), reprinted in Kenneth W. Thompson and Steven L. Rearden, eds., *Paul H. Nitze on National Security and Arms Control* (Lanham, MD: University Press of America, Inc., 1990), 140.

41. Ibid., 105–6.

42. Eisenhower was well aware of these specific studies criticizing his limited war forces. See Memorandum of Meeting with the President, August 25, 1960, EL, WHO, OSS, Subject Series, Alphabetical Subseries, Box 23, Folder—Science Advisory Committee (6) July 1959–August 1960.

43. See ibid., 5–6.

44. Roman, *Eisenhower and the Missile Gap*, 82; Charles H. Donnelly, *United States Defense Policies in 1958* (GPO, 1959), 12–17; Charles H. Donnelly, *United States Defense Policies in 1959* (GPO, 1960), 18–20; and Charles H. Donnelly, *United States Defense Policies in 1960* (GPO, 1961), 23–24.

45. Memorandum to the Secretary [of State], July 10, 1958, NA, RG 59, State Department, PPS Records, Lot 67D 548, Box 194, Folder—S/P Papers 1958 (January–April), 2.

46. Memorandum of Discussion at the 390th Meeting of the NSC, December 11, 1958, EL, DDE Papers, NSC Series, Box 10, Folder—390th Meeting of the NSC, December 11, 1958, 3.

47. NSC 5807/2—Measures to Carry Out the Concept of Shelter, December 24, 1958, EL, WHO, OSANSA, NSC Series, Policy Papers Subseries, Box 24, Folder—Shelter Program, 1–6.

48. See for example, Memorandum to the Secretary, October 6, 1960, NA, RG 59, State Department, PPS Records, Lot 67D 548, Box 194, Folder—S/P Papers 1958 (January–April), 1–2.

49. See Gallup, *Gallup Poll*, v. 3, 1671; and Kerr, *Civil Defense in the United States*, 115.

50. See Kerr, *Civil Defense in the United States*, 114; and Winkler, *Life under a Cloud*, 120.

51. See Donald P. Steury, ed., *Intentions and Capabilities: Estimates on Soviet Strategic Forces, 1950–1983* (Washington, D.C.: Center for the Study of Intelligence, Central Intelligence Agency, 1996), xii; and Nunn, *The Soviet First Strike Threat*, 173.

52. Bottome, *The Missile Gap*, 66.

53. See Robert J. Watson, "The Eisenhower Administration and the Missile Gap, 1958–1960," paper presented at the 1996 Annual Meeting of the Society for Military History, Washington, D.C., 1996; Roman, *Eisenhower and the Missile Gap*, 138–39; and Bottome, *The Missile Gap*, 115–46.

54. Stuart Symington to the President, August 29, 1958, EL, DDE Papers, Harlow Records, Box 2, Folder—[Missiles] Sen. Stuart Symington, 1958, 6.

55. *Inquiry into Satellite*, 2469.

56. Prados, *The Soviet Estimate*, 79.

57. NIE 11-5-58, "Soviet Capabilities in Guided Missiles and Space Vehicles," [December 1958?], reprinted in Steury, ed., *Intentions and Capabilities*, 67–68. See also NIE 11-4-58 which contained similar estimates. See Roman, *Eisenhower and the Missile Gap*, 40.

58. NIE 11-8-59, "Soviet Capabilities for Strategic Attack Through Mid-1964," February 9, 1960, reprinted in Steury, ed., *Intentions and Capabilities*, 75. See also descriptions of NIE 11-4-59 in Prados, *The Soviet Estimate*, 89; and Roman, *Eisenhower and the Missile Gap*, 43.

59. NIE 11-8-60, "Soviet Capabilities for Long Range Attack Through Mid-

1965," August 1, 1960, reprinted in Steury, ed., *Intentions and Capabilities*, 3. See also Prados, *The Soviet Estimate*, 89.

60. York and Greb, "Strategic Reconnaissance," 36.

61. U.S. Congress, Senate, Joint Hearings before the Preparedness Investigating Subcommittee of the Committee on Armed Services and the Committee on Aeronautical and Space Activities, *Missile and Space Activities*, 86th Congress, 1st session, 1958, 15–16.

62. Oral History of James H. Douglas, Oral History Research Office, Columbia University, 1973, 15.

63. U.S. Congress, Senate, *Executive Sessions of the Senate Foreign Relations Committee*, Vol. X (GPO, 1980), 63.

64. *Pravda*, May 9, 1959, reprinted in McDougall, . . . *the Heavens and the Earth*, 240.

65. The exaggeration of Soviet missile capabilities by intelligence analysts was not realized until the advent of the Corona satellite program beginning in 1960. See Kenneth E. Greer, "Corona," *Studies in Intelligence*, Supplement, 17 (Spring 1973), reprinted in Ruffner, ed., *Corona*, 24 and 38. For the impact of satellite photography on intelligence estimates, see NIE 11-8/1-6, "Strength and Deployment of Soviet Long Range Ballistic Missile Forces," September 21, 1961, printed in Ruffner, ed., *Corona*, 127–55.

66. Interview XI with George E. Reedy, December 20, 1983, LBJ Oral History Project, 41–42.

67. See Divine, *Sputnik Challenge*, 177; and Roy E. Linklider, "The Missile Gap Controversy," *Political Science Quarterly* 85:4 (December 1970), 615.

68. Robert Amory, Jr. Oral History, February 9, 1966, John F. Kennedy Library [hereafter JFK Library], 87.

69. *Inquiry into Satellite*, 2447.

70. "Speech to the Senate on the Missile Gap by John F. Kennedy," August 14, 1958, reprinted in Senator John F. Kennedy, *The Strategy of Peace* (New York: Harper & Brothers, 1960), 40.

71. Ibid., 37–38. Kennedy made similar arguments in a book review of General James Gavin's *War and Peace in the Space Age* (1958). See Senator John F. Kennedy, "General Gavin Sounds the Alarm," *The Reporter* 19:7 (October 30, 1958), 35.

72. Interview with [John F.] Kennedy by Philip Deane, undated [March 1959?], JFK Library, Pre-Presidential Papers, Senate Files, General Files, 1953–1960, Folder—President's Office Files—Defense, 1.

73. Callahan, *Dangerous Capabilities*, 185–92. See also Roberts, "Kennedy Names Policy Group To Prepare Program If He Wins," *The Washington Post*, August 31, 1960.

74. Ibid., 187–89.

75. Senate Speech by John Kennedy on American Defense Policy, February 29, 1960, reprinted in Branyan and Larsen, eds., *The Eisenhower Administration*, 1233–35.

76. Ibid., 1228.

77. "Speech to the American Legion by John F. Kennedy," October 1960, quoted in "Kennedy on National Defense," *Aviation Week and Space Technology* 73:17 (October 24, 1960), 21.

78. Robert A. Divine, *Foreign Policy and U.S. Presidential Elections: 1952/ 1960* (New York: New Viewpoints, 1974), 242.

79. Bundy, *Danger and Survival*, 349.

80. James N. Giglio, *The Presidency of John F. Kennedy* (Lawrence, KA: University Press of Kansas, 1991), 18.

81. Ambrose, *Eisenhower*, v. 2, 604.

82. Jean Edward Smith, "Kennedy and Defense," *Air University Review* 18:3 (March–April 1967), 48. See also Bundy, *Danger and Survival*, 352; and Gaddis, *Strategies of Containment*, 203, 215, and 227–28.

83. See Ball, *Politics and Force Levels*, 23; and Herken, *Cardinal Choices*, 127–45.

84. See The President's News Conference of February 1, 1961, in *Public Papers of the Presidents of the United States, John Fitzgerald Kennedy*, [hereafter *PPP, JFK*] *1961* (GPO, 1964), 40.

85. See Michael Brower, "Nuclear Strategy of the Kennedy Administration," *Bulletin of the Atomic Scientists* 18:8 (October 1962): 34–41.

86. Ball, *Politics and Force Levels*, 50–1.

87. Ruffner, ed., *Corona*, xiii. See also Kenneth E. Greer, "Corona," *Studies in Intelligence*, Supplement, 17 (Spring 1973): 1–37, reprinted in ibid., 22–26.

88. Herken, *Counsels of War*, 140.

89. For the impact of satellite photography on intelligence estimates, see NIE 11-8/1-61, "Strength and Deployment of Soviet Long Range Ballistic Missile Forces," September 21, 1961, printed in Ruffner, ed., *Corona*, 127–55.

90. See Kolodziej, *Uncommon Defense and Congress*, 390–92; and Giglio, *Presidency of John F. Kennedy*, 46.

91. Ball, *Politics and Force Levels*, 114–16.

92. Ibid., 50–51.

93. John F. Kennedy, "A Democrat Looks at Foreign Policy," *Foreign Affairs* 36:1 (October 1957), 48.

94. Oral History of Herbert York, JFK Library, June 16, 1964, 11.

95. Kolodziej, *Uncommon Defense and Congress*, 328.

96. Ibid., 385–89.

97. John F. Kennedy, "Urgent National Needs: Address of the President of the United States," May 25, 1961, quoted in Kerr, *Civil Defense in the U.S.*, 118.

98. John F. Kennedy, "Radio and Television Report to the American People on the Berlin Crisis," July 25, 1961, quoted in Kerr, *Civil Defense in the U.S.,* 119.

99. Kerr, *Civil Defense in the U.S.,* 120.

100. See Winkler, *Life under a Cloud,* 12–30; Kaplan, *Wizards of Armageddon,* 309–14; Arthur M. Schlesinger, Jr., *A Thousand Days: John F. Kennedy in the White House* (Boston: Houghton Mifflin Company, 1965), 747–49; and Stanley L. Newman, "Civil Defense and the Congress: Quiet Reversal," *Bulletin of the Atomic Scientists* 18:9 (November 1962), 35.

101. Kerr, *Civil Defense in the U.S.,* 126–31; Giglio, *Presidency of John F. Kennedy,* 82; and Kaplan, *Wizards of Armageddon,* 314.

102. See Bundy, *Danger and Survival,* 355–56; Winkler, *Life under a Cloud,* 128–32; and Newman, "Civil Defense and the Congress," 33–37.

103. Memorandum of Discussion at the 453rd Meeting of the NSC, July 25, 1960, quoted in Roman, *Eisenhower and the Missile Gap,* 189.

104. Memorandum of Meeting with the President, August 25, 1960, EL, OSS, Subject Series, Alphabetical Subseries, Box 23, Folder, Science Advisory Committee (6) July 1959–August 1960, 5–6. See also Roman, *Eisenhower and the Missile Gap,* 189–90.

105. A similar argument can be found in Dockrill, *Eisenhower's New-Look,* 277–78; and Divine, *Sputnik Challenge,* viii.

106. Bernard J. Firestone, "Defense Policy as a Form of Arms Control: Nuclear Force Posture and Strategy under John F. Kennedy," in Paul Harper and Joann P. Krieg, eds., *John F. Kennedy: The Promise Revisited* (New York: Greenwood Press, 1988), 58. See also Alan Wolfe, *America's Impasse: The Rise and Fall of the Politics of Growth* (New York: Pantheon Books, 1981), 124–25.

107. *Statistical History of the United States,* 1123 and 1141.

108. The President's News Conference of April 3, 1963, in *PPP, JFK, 1963,* 308.

Conclusion

1. See for example Griffith, "Dwight D. Eisenhower and the Corporate Commonwealth," 87–122; Sloan, "The Management and Decision-Making of President Eisenhower," 295–331; and Greenstein, *Hidden-Hand Presidency,* 100–51.

2. Eisenhower, *Waging Peace,* 712.

3. For Eisenhower's use of experts, see Griffith, "Dwight D. Eisenhower and the Corporate Commonwealth," 87–122; Kaplan, *Wizards of Armageddon,* 11–247; Herken, *Cardinal Choices,* 69–123; and Herken, *Counsels of War,* 102–34.

4. For assessments of the Gaither committee's lack of influence, see Ambrose, *Eisenhower,* v. 2, 434–35; and Gaddis, *Strategies of Containment,* 185–86.

5. See McDougall, . . . *Heavens and the Earth,* 7–8; Divine, *The Sputnik Challenge,* vii and xiii-xviii.

6. See Bottome, *The Missile Gap*, 37–61 and 115–46.

7. *Organizing for National Security*, 55.

8. Ibid., 293 and 294.

9. Eisenhower, *Waging Peace*, 221.

10. Both the Rockefeller Panel Report and Johns Hopkins Report reached conclusions similar to those of the Gaither committee. See chapter 4.

11. See Roman, "American Strategic Nuclear Force Planning," 38.

12. For the role of perceptions in decision making, see Jervis, "Deterrence and Perception;" and David L. Snead, "Eisenhower, the Gaither Committee, and Intelligence Assessment: The Problem of Equating Capabilities with Intentions," paper presented at the 1996 Annual Meeting of the Society for Military History, Washington, D.C., April 1996. For discussion of the exaggerations of Soviet capabilities and intentions by intelligence analysts, see Roman, *Eisenhower and the Missile Gap*, 30–47; Prados, *Soviet Estimate*, 57–126; Freedman, *US Intelligence and the Soviet Strategic Threat*, 67–80; and Steury, *Intentions and Capabilities*, 5–7 and 55–57.

13. Dwight D. Eisenhower to Swede Hazlett, February 26, 1958, in Griffith, *Ike's Letters to a Friend*, 199.

14. Eisenhower, *Waging Peace*, 220.

15. Greenstein, *Hidden-Hand Presidency*, 58–65 and 80–92.

16. In his recent study of the 1958 Surprise Attack Conference, Jeremi Suri reaches similar conclusions concerning the weaknesses in Eisenhower's "hidden-hand" decision-making system in planning for arms control talks. He argues that Eisenhower failed to adopt a flexible negotiating posture with the Soviet Union in part because he received conflicting recommendations from his advisers. Instead of adopting a flexible approach to negotiations, as Suri argues the president should have done, Eisenhower adopted a rigid position representing the one area where a consensus could be reached by his advisers and foreign allies. See Suri, "America's Search for a Technological Solution to the Arms Race," 423–37. While Suri's assessment has merit, he does overestimate the degree of flexibility Eisenhower possessed in making his policy and underemphasizes the challenges posed by the accelerating technological capabilities of both superpowers to relatively inexperienced arms control negotiators.

17. It was not until the early 1960s that U.S. intelligence estimates fully recognized the deficiencies in Soviet missile technology. See NIE 11-8/1-61, "Strength and Deployment of Soviet Long Range Ballistic Missile Forces," September 21, 1961, printed in Ruffner, ed., *Corona*, 127–55; and Steury, ed., *Intentions and Capabilities*, 121–38.

18. Rosenberg, "Origins of Overkill," 8, 44, and 65–66.

Primary Sources

Dwight D. Eisenhower Library
Arthur F. Burns Papers
Council of Economic Advisors, Office of: Records, 1953–1961
Dwight D. Eisenhower Papers as the President of the United States, 1953–1961
  (Ann Whitman File)
    Administrative Series
    Ann Whitman Diary Series
    Cabinet Series
    Dulles-Herter Series
    Dwight D. Eisenhower Diary Series
    Legislative Meeting Series
    Miscellaneous Series
    Name Series
    NSC Series
    U.S. President's Science Advisory Committee: Records, 1957–61
Milton S. Eisenhower Papers
Bryce N. Harlow Papers
Neil H. McElroy Papers
Donald A. Quarles Papers
White House Central Files
White House Office Files
  Office of the Staff Secretary
    Cabinet Series
    Legislative Meeting Series
    Subject Series
  Office of the Special Assistant for National Security Affairs: Records, 1952–1961
    NSC Series
    OCB Series
    Special Assistant Series
  Office of the Special Assistant for Science and Technology
  NSC Staff
    Executive Secretary Subject File Series

John Fitzgerald Kennedy Library
Pre-Presidential Papers

George C. Marshall Foundation
William Chapman Foster Papers

Library of Congress
Joseph and Stewart Alsop Papers
Lloyd Berkner Papers
James Doolittle Papers
Muir Fairchild Papers
Curtis LeMay Papers
Isidor I. Rabi Papers
Nathan F. Twining Papers
Hoyt Vandenberg Papers
Thomas D. White Papers

Massachusetts Institute of Technology Archives
Albert G. Hill Papers
James R. Killian Papers

National Archives of the United States
Record Group 51—Bureau of the Budget
Record Group 56—Department of Treasury
Record Group 59—Department of State
Record Group 218—Joint Chiefs of Staff
Record Group 263—Central Intelligence Agency
Record Group 273—National Security Council
Record Group 304—Office of Defense Mobilization
Record Group 330—Department of Defense
Record Group 359—Office of Science and Technology

United States Military Academy Special Collections
Robert Cutler Papers
George A. Lincoln Papers

Government Publications
Alert Operations and the Strategic Air Command, 1957–1991. Offutt Air Force Base, Neb.: Office of the Historian, Headquarters SAC, 1991.
Cline, Ray S. *United States Army in World War II: The War Department, Washington Command Post, The Operations Division.* Washington, D.C.: Office of the Chief of Military History, Department of the Army, 1951.
Condit, Kenneth W. *History of the Joint Chiefs of Staff: The Joint Chiefs of Staff and*

National Policy, 1955–1956. Volume 6. Government Printing Office [hereafter GPO], 1992.

Donnelly, Charles H. *United States Defense Policies in 1957*. GPO, 1958.

———. *United States Defense Policies in 1958*. GPO, 1959.

———. *United States Defense Policies in 1959*. GPO, 1960.

———. *United States Defense Policies in 1960*. GPO, 1961.

———. *United States Defense Policies in 1961*. GPO, 1962.

———. *United States Defense Policies in 1962*. GPO, 1963.

Galambos, Louis, ed. *The Papers of Dwight D. Eisenhower*. Volumes 1–13. Baltimore: Johns Hopkins University Press.

Hopkins, J.C., and Sheldon A. Goldberg. *The Development of Strategic Air Command, 1946–1986 (The Fortieth Anniversary History)*. Offutt Air Force Base, Neb.: Office of the Historian, Headquarters SAC, 1986.

Koch, Scott A., ed. *Selected Estimates on the Soviet Union, 1950–1959*. Washington, D.C.: Center for the Study of Intelligence, Central Intelligence Agency, 1993.

Kreis, John F. *Air Warfare and Air Base Air Defense 1914–1973*. Washington, D.C.: GPO, 1988.

Lay, James S., Jr. *Organizational History of the National Security Council during the Truman and Eisenhower Administrations*. GPO, 1960.

Narducci, Henry M. *Strategic Air Command and the Alert Program*. Offutt Air Force Base, Neb.: Office of the Historian, Headquarters SAC, 1988.

Neufeld, Jacob. *The Development of Ballistic Missiles in the United States Air Force 1945–1960*. Washington, D.C.: Office of Air Force History, United States Air Force, 1990.

Protection in the Nuclear Age. Washington, D.C.: Federal Emergency Agency, 1985.

Public Papers of the Presidents of the United States: Dwight D. Eisenhower, GPO.

Public Papers of the Presidents of the United States: John Fitzgerald Kennedy, GPO.

Ruffner, Kevin C., ed. *Corona: America's First Satellite Program*. Washington, D.C.: Center for the Study of Intelligence, Central Intelligence Agency, 1995.

Schaffel, Kenneth. *The Emerging Shield: The Air Force and the Evolution of Continental Air Defense, 1945–1960*. Washington, D.C.: Office of Air Force History, 1991.

Steury, Donald P., ed. *Intentions and Capabilities: Estimates on Soviet Strategic Forces, 1950–1983*. Washington, D.C.: Center for the Study of Intelligence, Central Intelligence Agency, 1996.

———. *Sherman Kent and the Board of National Estimates*. Washington, D.C.: Center for the Study of Intelligence, Central Intelligence Agency, 1994.

Strum, Thomas A. *The USAF Scientific Advisory Board: Its First Twenty Years, 1944–1964*. GPO, 1967.

U.S. Congress. Joint Committee on Defense Production. *Deterrence and Survival in the Nuclear Age (The "Gaither Report" of 1957)*. 94th Congress, 2nd Session. GPO, 1976.

———. Committee on Government Operations. Subcommittee on National Policy Machinery of the Committee on Government Operations. *Organizing for National Security*. 86th Congress, 2nd Session. 1961.

———. House Military Operations Subcommittee of the Committee on Government Operations. *Civil Defense Plan for National Survival*, 84th Congress, 2nd Session, 1956.

———. Subcommittee on Military Operations. *New Civil Defense Legislation*. 85th Congress, 1st Session. 1957.

———. Senate. Committee on Foreign Relations. Subcommittee on Arms Control, Oceans, International Operations and Environment. *United States and Soviet Civil Defense Programs*. 97th Congress, 2nd Session. 1982.

———. Senate. Committee on Armed Services. Preparedness Investigating Subcommittee. *Inquiry into Satellite and Missile Programs*. 85th Congress, 1st and 2nd Sessions. 1957–1958.

———. Senate. Joint Hearings before the Preparedness Investigating Subcommittee of the Committee on Armed Services and the Committee on Aeronautical and Space Activities. *Missile and Space Activities*. 86th Congress, 1st Session, 1958.

———. Executive Sessions of the Senate Foreign Relations Committee. Volume X. 1958.

U.S. Department of State. *Foreign Relations of the United States, 1955–1957*. Volume 19. GPO, 1990.

———. *Foreign Relations of the United States, 1950*. Volume 1. GPO, 1977.

———. *Foreign Relations of the United States, 1952–1954*. Volume 2. GPO, 1984.

———. *Bulletin*. GPO, 1957.

United States Statutes at Large. Volume 61. GPO, 1948.

United States Strategic Bombing Survey: Summary Report (Pacific War). GPO, 1946.

Watson, Robert J. *History of the Joint Chiefs of Staff: The Joint Chiefs of Staff and National Policy, 1953–1954*, v. 5. GPO, 1986.

Diaries and Memoirs

Adams, Sherman. *Firsthand Report: The Story of the Eisenhower Administration*. Westport, Conn.: Greenwood Press, Publishers, 1961.

Alsop, Joseph, and Stewart Alsop. *The Reporter's Trade*. New York: Reynal & Company, 1958.

Cutler, Robert. *No Time for Rest*. Boston: Little, Brown and Company, 1965, 1966.

Doolittle, James H. *I Could Never Be So Lucky Again.* New York: Bantam Books, 1991.

Eisenhower, Dwight D. *At Ease: Stories I Tell to Friends.* Garden City, N.Y.: Doubleday & Company, Inc., 1967.

———. *Waging Peace, 1956–1961.* Garden City, N.Y.: Doubleday & Company, Inc., 1965.

———. *Mandate for Change.* Garden City, N.Y.: Doubleday & Company, Inc., 1963.

———. *Crusade in Europe.* Garden City, N.Y.: Doubleday & Company, Inc., 1948.

Ferrell, Robert, ed. *The Eisenhower Diaries.* New York: Norton, 1981.

———. *Off the Record: The Private Papers of Harry S. Truman.* New York: Penguin Books, 1980.

Getting, Ivan A. *All in a Lifetime: Science in the Defense of Democracy.* New York: Vantage Press, 1989.

Griffin, Robert W., ed. *Ike's Letters to a Friend, 1941–1958.* Lawrence: University Press of Kansas, 1984.

Hughes, Emmet John. *The Ordeal of Power: A Political Memoir of the Eisenhower Years.* New York: Atheneum, 1963.

Kennan, George F. *Memoirs.* Volume 2. Boston: Little, Brown and Company, 1972.

Kennedy, Senator John F. *The Strategy of Peace.* New York: Harper & Brothers, 1960.

Killian, James R., Jr. *Sputnik, Scientists, and Eisenhower: A Memoir of the First Special Assistant to the President for Science and Technology.* Cambridge, MA: MIT Press, 1977.

———. *The Education of the College President: A Memoir.* Cambridge, MA: MIT Press, 1985.

Kistiakowsky, George B. *A Scientist at the White House: The Private Diary of President Eisenhower's Special Assistant for Science and Technology.* Cambridge: Harvard University, 1976.

Nitze, Paul H. *From Hiroshima to Glasnost: At the Center of Decision.* New York: Grove Weidenfeld, 1988.

Roberts, Chalmer M. *First Rough Draft: A Journalist's Journal of Our Times.* New York: Praeger Publishers, 1973.

Taylor, Maxwell D. *The Uncertain Trumpet.* New York: Harper & Brothers, 1959, 1960.

———. *Swords and Plowshares.* New York: W. W. Norton & Company, Inc., 1972.

Twining, General Nathan F. *Neither Liberty Nor Safety: A Hard Look at U.S. Military Policy and Strategy.* New York: Holt, Rinehart and Winston, 1966.

Wiesner, Jerome B. *Where Science and Politics Meet.* New York: McGraw-Hill Book Company, 1965.

York, Herbert. *Race to Oblivion: A Participant's View of the Arms Race.* New York: Simon and Schuster, 1970.

————. *Making Weapons, Talking Peace: A Physicist's Odyssey from Hiroshima to Geneva.* New York: Basic Books, Inc., Publishers, 1987.

Miscellaneous (Document Collections, Foundation Reports, etc.)

Branyan, Robert L., and Lawrence H. Larsen, eds. *The Eisenhower Administration 1953–1961: A Documentary History.* New York: Random House, Inc., 1971.

Civil Defense: Project Harbor Summary Report. Washington, D.C.: National Academy of Sciences-National Research Council, 1964.

Galambos, Louis, *et al. The Papers of Dwight David Eisenhower.* Baltimore, MD: Johns Hopkins University Press.

Gallup, George H. *The Gallup Poll,* volume 2. New York: Random House, 1972.

Howard, Nathaniel R., ed. *The Basic Papers of George M. Humphrey.* Cleveland: Western Reserve Historical Society, 1965.

Pamphlet 20-60: *Bibliography on Limited War.* Headquarters, Department of Army, February 1958.

Project Rand: Close-In Fallout. R-309 (September 30, 1957). Santa Monica, Calif.: Rand Corporation, 1958.

Prospect of America: The Rockefeller Panel Reports. Garden City, N.Y.: Doubleday & Company, Inc., 1961.

Report of Project East River. New York: Associated Universities, Inc., 1952.

Report of the Study for the Ford Foundation on Policy and Program. Detroit, Mich.: The Ford Foundation, 1949.

Report on a Study of Non-Military Defense. R-322-RC (July 1, 1958). Santa Monica, Calif.: Rand Corporation, 1958.

Rotunda, Roland D., ed. *Modern Constitutional Law: Cases and Notes.* 3rd ed. St. Paul: West Publishing Co., 1989.

The Ford Foundation Annual Report, 1958. New York: Ford Foundation, 1958.

The Statistical History of the United States: From Colonial Times to the Present. New York: Basic Books, Inc., 1976.

Trachtenberg, Marc. *The Development of American Strategic Thought: Basic Documents from the Eisenhower and Kennedy Periods, Including the Basic National Security Papers from 1953 to 1959.* New York: Garland Publishing, 1988.

Newspapers/Journals
Army-Navy-Air Force Journal
Aviation Week
New York Herald Tribune
New York Times
Newsweek

Studies in Intelligence
U.S. News & World Report
Washington Post

Oral Histories and Interviews
Dillon Anderson Oral History, Dwight D. Eisenhower Library, Abilene, Kansas
Robert Armory, Jr. Oral History, John Fitzgerald Kennedy Library, Boston, Massachusetts
Hans Bethe Oral History, Eisenhower Library
Richard M. Bissell, Jr. Oral History, Eisenhower Library
Robert R. Bowie Oral History, Eisenhower Library
Charles A. Coolidge Oral History, Eisenhower Library
James H. Douglas Oral History, Eisenhower Library
Arthur S. Fleming Oral History, Eisenhower Library
William B. Franke Oral History, Eisenhower Library
Thomas S. Gates, Jr. Oral History, Eisenhower Library
Andrew J. Goodpaster Oral History, Columbia University, New York City
Charles A. Halleck Oral History, Eisenhower Library
Bryce N. Harlow Oral History, Eisenhower Library
Leo A. Hoegh Oral History, Eisenhower Library
Katherine G. Howard Oral History, Eisenhower Library
Kenneth B. Keating Oral History, Eisenhower Library
George Kistiakowsky Oral History, Eisenhower Library
William F. Knowland Oral History, Eisenhower Library
Lyman L. Lemnitzer Oral History, Columbia University
John J. McCloy Oral History, Eisenhower Library
John A. McCone Oral History, Eisenhower Library
Neil McElroy Oral History, Eisenhower Library
Robert E. Merriman Oral History, Eisenhower Library
Lauris Norstad Oral History, Eisenhower Library
John S. Patterson Oral History, Eisenhower Library
George E. Reedy Oral History, Lyndon Baines Johnson Library, Austin, Texas
Leverett Saltonstall Oral History, Johnson Library
Raymond J. Saulnier Oral History, Columbia University
Gerard C. Smith Oral History, Eisenhower Library
Mansfield D. Sprague Oral History, Eisenhower Library
Robert C. Sprague Oral History, Princeton, New Jersey
Charles Thomas Oral History, Eisenhower Library
Thor C. Tollefson Oral History, Eisenhower Library
Nathan F. Twining Oral History, Eisenhower Library
Herbert York Oral History, Kennedy Library

Secondary Sources

Books

Alexander, Charles C. *Holding the Line: The Eisenhower Era, 1952–1961.* Bloomington: Indiana University Press, 1975.

Aliano, Richard A. *American Defense Policy from Eisenhower to Kennedy: The Politics of Changing Military Requirements, 1957–1961.* Athens: Ohio University Press, 1975.

Ambrose, Stephen E. *Eisenhower,* Volume 1: *Soldier, General of the Army, President-Elect, 1890–1952.* New York: Simon and Schuster, 1983.

———. *Eisenhower,* Volume 2: *The President.* New York: Simon and Schuster, 1984.

———. *Ike's Spies: Eisenhower and the Espionage Establishment.* Garden City, New York: Doubleday & Company, Inc., 1981.

Armacost, Michael H. *The Politics of Weapons Innovation: The Thor-Jupiter Controversy.* New York: Columbia University Press, 1969.

Bacevich, A. J. *The Pentomic Era: The U.S. Army Between Korea and Vietnam.* Washington, D.C.: National Defense University Press, 1986.

Ball, Desmond. *Politics and Force Levels: The Strategic Missile Program of the Kennedy Administration.* Berkeley: University of California Press, 1980.

Ball, Desmond, and Jeffrey Richelson, eds. *Strategic Nuclear Targeting.* Ithaca, N.Y.: Cornell University Press, 1986.

Balogh, Brian. *Chain Reaction: Expert Debate and Public Participation in American Commercial Nuclear Power, 1945–1975.* New York: Cambridge University Press, 1991.

Baylis, John, and John Garnett, eds. *Makers of Nuclear Strategy.* London: Pinter Publishers, 1991.

Beard, Edmund. *Developing the ICBM: A Study in Bureaucratic Politics.* New York: Columbia University Press, 1976.

Beschloss, Michael R. *Mayday The U-2 Affair: The Untold Story of the Greatest U.S.-U.S.S.R. Spy Scandal.* New York: Harper & Row Publishers, 1986.

Bird, Kai. *The Chairman: John J. McCloy, and the Making of the American Establishment.* New York: Simon & Schuster, 1992.

Bischof, Gunter, and Stephen E. Ambrose, eds. *Eisenhower: A Centenary Assessment.* Baton Rouge: Louisiana State University Press, 1995.

Bottome, Edgar M. *The Missile Gap: A Study of the Formulation of Military and Political Policy.* Rutherford, N.J.: Fairleigh Dickinson University Press, 1971.

Bracken, Paul. *The Command and Control of Nuclear Forces.* New Haven, Conn.: Yale University Press, 1983.

Branch, Taylor. *Parting the Waters: America in the King Years, 1954–63.* New York: Simon & Schuster, 1988.

Brendon, Piers. *IKE: His Life and Times*. New York: Harper & Row, Publishers, 1986.

Brinkley, David A., and Andrew W. Hull. *Estimative Intelligence*. Washington, D.C.: Defense Intelligence School, 1979.

Brodie, Bernard. *Strategy in the Missile Age*. Princeton, N.J.: Princeton University Press, 1959.

Brugioni, Dino A. *Eyeball to Eyeball: The Inside Story of the Cuban Missile Crisis*. New York: Random House, 1991.

Bundy, McGeorge. *Danger and Survival: Choices about the Bomb in the First Fifty Years*. New York: Random House, 1988.

Burchand, John. *Q.E.D.: M.I.T. in World War II*. New York: John Wiley & Sons, Inc., 1948.

Burk, Robert Frederick. *The Eisenhower Administration and Black Civil Rights*. Knoxville: University of Tennessee Press, 1984.

Burrows, William E. *Deep Black: Space Espionage and National Security*. New York: Random House, 1986.

Callahan, David. *Dangerous Capabilities: Paul Nitze and the Cold War*. New York: HarperCollins Publishers, 1990.

Chayes, Abram, and Jerome B. Wiesner, eds. *ABM: An Evaluation of the Decision to Deploy an Antiballistic Missile System*. New York: Harper & Row, 1969.

Coffey, Thomas M. *The Turbulent Life of General Curtis LeMay*. New York: Crown Publishers, Inc., 1986.

Cook, Blanche Wiesen. *The Declassified Eisenhower: A Divided Legacy*. Garden City, N.Y.: Doubleday & Company, Inc., 1981.

Davis, Kenneth S. *Soldier of Democracy: A Biography of Dwight Eisenhower*. Garden City, N.Y.: Doubleday, Doran & Company, Inc., 1945.

Divine, Robert A. *The Sputnik Challenge*. New York: Oxford University Press, 1993.

——. *Eisenhower and the Cold War*. New York: Oxford University Press, 1981.

——. *Blowing on the Wind: The Nuclear Test Ban Debate, 1954–1960*. New York: Oxford University Press, 1978.

——. *Since 1945: Politics and Diplomacy in Recent American History*. 3rd ed. New York: Alfred A. Knopf, 1985.

——. *Foreign Policy and U.S. Presidential Elections: 1952/1960*. New York: New Viewpoints, 1974.

Dockrill, Saki. *Eisenhower's New-Look National Security Policy, 1953–61*. New York: St. Martin's Press, Inc., 1996.

Donovan, John C. *The Cold Warriors: A Policy-Making Elite*. Lexington, Mass.: D.C. Heath and Company, 1974.

Duffield, John S. *Power Rules: The Evolution of NATO's Conventional Force Posture*. Stanford, Calif.: Stanford University Press, 1995.

Duram, James C. *A Moderate among Extremists: Dwight D. Eisenhower and the School Desegregation Crisis.* Chicago: Nelson-Hall, Inc., 1981.

Eglin, James Meikle. *Air Defense in the Nuclear Age: The Post-War Development of American and Soviet Strategic Defense Systems.* New York: Garland Publishing, Inc., 1988.

Emme, Eugene M., ed. *The Impact of Air Power: National Security and World Politics.* Princeton, N.J.: D. Van Nostrand Company, Inc., 1959.

Ford, Harold P. *Estimative Intelligence: The Purposes and Problems of National Intelligence Estimating.* New York: Defense Intelligence College, 1993.

Freedman, Lawrence. *US Intelligence and the Soviet Strategic Threat.* London: MacMillan Press, 1977, 1986.

———. *The Evolution of Nuclear Strategy.* New York: St. Martin's Press, 1983.

Gaddis, John Lewis. *Strategies of Containment: A Critical Appraisal of Postwar American National Security Policy.* New York: Oxford University Press, 1982.

Garthoff, Raymond L. *Assessing the Adversary: Estimates by the Eisenhower Administration of Soviet Intentions and Capabilities.* Washington, D.C.: Brookings Institution, 1991.

———. *Soviet Strategy in the Nuclear Age.* New York: Frederick A. Praeger, Publishers, 1958.

Gaston, James C., ed. *Grand Strategy and the Decisionmaking Process.* Washington, D.C.: National Defense University Press, 1991.

Giglio, James N. *John F. Kennedy: A Bibliography.* Westport, Conn.: Greenwood Press, 1995.

———. *The Presidency of John F. Kennedy.* Lawrence: University Press of Kansas, 1991.

Gilpin, Robert. *American Scientists and Nuclear Weapons Policy.* Princeton, N.J.: Princeton University Press, 1962.

———, and Christopher Wright, eds. *Scientists and National Policy-Making.* New York: Columbia University Press, 1964.

Golden, William T., ed. *Science and Technology Advice to the President, Congress, and Judiciary.* New York: Pergamon Press, 1988.

———. *Science Advice to the President.* New York: Pergamon Press, 1980.

Goure, Leon. *War Survival in Soviet Strategy: USSR Civil Defense.* University of Miami Center for Advance International Studies, 1976.

Graebner, Norman A., ed. *The National Security: Its Theory and Practice, 1945–1960.* New York: Oxford University Press, 1986.

Greenstein, Fred I. *The Hidden-Hand Presidency: Eisenhower as Leader.* New York: Basic Books, Inc., Publishers, 1982.

Halperin, Morton H. *National Security Policy-Making: Analyses, Cases, and Proposals.* Lexington, Mass.: Lexington Books, 1975.

———. *Limited War: An Essay on the Development of the Theory and An Annotated Bibliography.* Cambridge, Mass.: Center for International Affairs, 1962.

Harper, Paul, and Joann P. Krieg, eds. *John F. Kennedy: The Promise Revisited.* New York: Greenwood Press, 1988.

Heinlein, J.C. *Presidential Staff and National Security Policy.* Cincinnati: Center of the Study of United States Foreign Policy, 1963.

Herken, Gregg. *Cardinal Choices: Presidential Science Advising from the Atomic Bomb to SDI.* New York: Oxford University Press, 1992.

———. *Counsels of War.* New York: Alfred A. Knopf, 1985.

Hilsman, Roger. *The Politics of Policy Making in Defense and Foreign Affairs.* New York: Harper & Row, Publishers, 1971.

Hitch, Charles J. *Decision-Making for Defense.* Berkeley: University of California Press, 1965.

Hogan, Michael J. *The Marshall Plan: America, Britain, and the Reconstruction of Western Europe, 1947–1952.* Cambridge: Cambridge University Press, 1987.

Horelick, Arnold L., and Myron Rush. *Strategic Power and Soviet Foreign Policy.* Chicago: University of Chicago Press, 1965, 1966.

Hoxie, R. Gordon. *The Presidency and National Security Policy.* New York: Center for the Study of the Presidency, 1984.

Huckaby, Elizabeth. *Crisis at Central High, Little Rock, 1957–58.* Baton Rouge: Louisiana State University Press, 1980.

Huntington, Samuel P. *The Common Defense: Strategic Programs in National Politics.* New York: Columbia University Press, 1961.

Immerman, Richard H. *The CIA in Guatemala: The Foreign Policy of Intervention.* Austin: University of Texas Press, 1982.

Jackson, Henry M., ed. *The National Security Council.* New York: Frederick A. Praeger, 1965.

Jockel, Joseph T. *No Boundaries Upstairs: Canada, the United States, and the Origins of North American Air Defense, 1945–1958.* Vancouver: University of British Columbia Press, 1987.

Jordan, Colonel Amos A., Jr., ed. *Issues of National Security in the 1970s: Essays Presented to Colonel George A. Lincoln on His Sixtieth Birthday.* New York: Frederick A. Praeger, 1967.

Kahn, Herman. *On Thermonuclear War.* Princeton, N.J.: Princeton University Press, 1960.

Kaku, Michio, and Daniel Axelrod. *To Win a Nuclear War: The Pentagon's Secret War Plans.* Boston: South End Press, 1987.

Kaplan, Fred. *The Wizards of Armageddon.* New York: Simon & Schuster, 1983.

Kaufman, Burton I. *The Korean War: Challenges in Crisis, Credibility, and Command.* New York: Alfred Knopf, 1986.

Kerr, Thomas J. *Civil Defense in the U.S.: Bandaid for a Holocaust?* Boulder, Colo.: Westview Press, 1983.

Kevles, Daniel J. *The Physicists: The History of a Scientific Community in Modern America.* Cambridge, Mass.: Harvard University Press, 1987.

Kinnard, Douglas. *President Eisenhower and Strategy Management: A Study in Defense Politics.* Lexington: University Press of Kentucky, 1977.

Kissinger, Henry A. *Nuclear Weapons and Foreign Policy.* New York: Harper & Brothers, 1957.

Knorr, Klaus. *Passive Defense for Atomic War.* Princeton University, Center for International Studies, 1954.

Kolodziej, Edward A. *The Common Defense and Congress, 1945–1963.* Columbus: Ohio State University Press, 1966.

Kornitzer, Bela. *The Great American Heritage: The Story of the Five Eisenhower Brothers.* New York: Farrar, Straus, and Cudahy, 1955.

Krieg, Joann P., ed. *Dwight D. Eisenhower: Soldier, President, Statesman.* New York: Greenwood Press, 1987.

LaFeber, Walter. *The American Age: United States Foreign Policy at Home and Abroad since 1750.* New York: W. W. Norton & Co., 1989.

Lapp, Ralph E. *The New Priesthood: The Scientific Elite and the Uses of Power.* New York: Harper & Row, 1965.

Larsen, Arthur. *A Republican Looks at His Party.* New York: Harper & Brothers, 1956.

Leffler, Melvyn P. *A Preponderance of Power: National Security, the Truman Administration, and the Cold War.* Stanford, Calif.: Stanford University Press, 1992.

Leslie, Stuart W. *The Cold War and American Science: The Military-Industrial-Academic Complex at MIT and Stanford.* New York: Columbia University Press, 1993.

Lincoln, George A. *Economics of National Security: Managing America's Resources for Defense,* 2nd ed. Englewood Cliffs, N.J.: Prentice-Hall, Inc., 1954.

MacDonald, Dwight. *The Ford Foundation: The Men and the Millions.* New York: Reynal & Company, 1956.

Manno, Jack. *Arming the Heavens: The Hidden Military Agenda for Space, 1945–1995.* New York: Dodd, Mead & Company, 1984.

May, Ernest J., ed. *American Cold War Strategy: Interpreting NSC 68.* Boston: Bedford Books of St. Martin's Press, 1993.

McCormick, Thomas J. *America's Half-Century: United States Foreign Policy in the Cold War.* Baltimore: John Hopkins University Press, 1989.

McCullough, David. *Truman.* New York: Simon & Schuster, 1992.

McDougall, Walter A. *. . . the Heavens and the Earth: A Political History of the Space Age.* New York: Basic Books, Inc., 1985.

Melanson, Richard A., and David Mayers, ed. *Reevaluating Eisenhower: American Foreign Policy in the 1950s.* Chicago: University of Illinois Press, 1987.

Miller, Merle. *Lyndon: An Oral Biography.* New York: Ballentine Books, 1980.

MITRE: The First Twenty Years, A History of the MITRE Corporation (1958–1978). Bedford, Mass.: The MITRE Corporation, 1979.

Morgan, Iwan W. *Eisenhower Versus 'The Spenders': The Eisenhower Administration, the Democrats and the Budget, 1953–60.* New York: St. Martin's Press, 1990.

Nation, R. Craig. *Black Earth, Red Star: A History of Soviet Security Policy, 1917–1991.* Ithaca, N.Y.: Cornell University Press, 1992.

Neustadt, Richard E. *Presidential Power: The Politics of Leadership.* New York: John Wiley & Sons, Inc., 1960.

Newhouse, John. *War and Peace in the Nuclear Age.* New York: Alfred A. Knopf, 1989.

Nunn, Jack H. *The Soviet First Strike Threat: The U.S. Perspective.* New York: Praeger Publishers, 1982.

Osgood, Robert Endicott. *Limited War: The Challenge to American Strategy.* Chicago: University of Chicago Press, 1957.

Pach, Chester J., Jr., and Elmo Richardson. *The Presidency of Dwight D. Eisenhower.* Revised edition. Lawrence: University Press of Kansas, 1991.

Paret, Peter, ed. *Makers of Modern Strategy from Machiavelli to the Nuclear Age.* Princeton University Press, 1986.

Pearson, Drew, and Jack Anderson. *U.S.A.—Second-Class Power?* New York: Simon & Schuster, 1958.

Pisani, Sallie. *The CIA and the Marshall Plan.* Lawrence: University Press of Kansas, 1991.

Ponturo, John. *Analytical Support for the Joint Chiefs of Staff: The WSEG Experience, 1948–1976.* Arlington, Va.: Institute for Defense Analyses, 1979.

Potter, E. B. *Admiral Arleigh Burke.* New York: Random House, 1990.

Power, General Thomas S. *Design for Survival.* New York: Coward-McCann, Inc., 1964, 1965.

Prados, John. *The Soviet Threat: U.S. Intelligence Analysis and Russian Military Strength.* New York: Dial Press, 1982.

———. *Keepers of the Keys: A History of the National Security Council from Truman to Bush.* New York: William Morrow and Company, Inc., 1991.

Rearden, Steven L. *The Evolution of American Strategic Doctrine: Paul Nitze and the Soviet Challenge.* Boulder, Colo.: Westview Press, 1984.

Reedy, George E. *The U.S. Senate: Paralysis or a Search for Consensus.* New York: Crown Publishers, Inc., 1986.

Reeves, Thomas C. *Freedom and the Foundation: The Fund for the Republic in the Era of McCarthyism.* New York: Alfred A. Knopf, 1969.

Richelson, Jeffrey. *American Espionage and the Soviet Target*. New York: William Morrow and Company, Inc., 1987.

———. *The U.S. Intelligence Community*. Cambridge, Mass.: Ballinger Publishing Co., 1985.

Roman, Peter J. *Eisenhower and the Missile Gap*. Ithaca, N.Y.: Cornell University Press, 1995.

Rubin, Barry. *Paved with Good Intentions: The American Experience and Iran*. New York: Oxford University Press, 1980.

Schilling, Warner R., Paul Y. Hammond, and Glenn H. Snyder. *Strategy, Politics, and Defense Budgets*. New York: Columbia University Press, 1962.

Schoenebaum, Eleanora W., ed. *Political Profiles: The Eisenhower Years*. New York: Facts on File, Inc., 1977.

———. *Political Profiles: The Truman Years*. New York: Facts on File, Inc., 1978.

Shute, Nevil. *On the Beach*. New York: William Morrow and Company, Inc., 1957.

Sitkoff, Harvard. *The Struggle for Black Equality, 1954–1992*. Revised edition. New York: Hill and Wang, 1981, 1993.

Sloan, John W. *Eisenhower and the Management of Prosperity*. Lawrence: University Press of Kansas, 1991.

Smith, Bruce L. R. *The RAND Corporation: Case Study of a Nonprofit Advisory Corporation*. Cambridge, Mass.: Harvard University Press, 1966.

Spector, Ronald H. *Advice and Support: The Early Years of the United States Army in Vietnam, 1941–1960*. New York: Free Press, 1985.

Talbot, Strobe. *The Master of the Game: Paul Nitze and the Nuclear Peace*. New York: Alfred A. Knopf, 1988.

Teich, Albert H., and Jill H. Pace, eds. *Science and Technology in the USA*. Essex, UK: Longman House, 1986.

Thompson, Kenneth W., ed. *The Eisenhower Presidency: Eleven Intimate Perspectives of Dwight D. Eisenhower*. New York: University Press of America, Inc., 1984.

———, and Steven L. Rearden, eds. *Paul H. Nitze on National Security and Arms Control*. Lanham, Md.: University Press of America, Inc., 1990.

Trachtenberg, Marc. *History and Strategy*. Princeton, N.J.: Princeton University Press, 1991.

Ulam, Adam B. *Expansion and Coexistence: The History of Soviet Foreign Policy, 1917–67*. New York: Frederick A. Praeger, 1968.

Warshaw, Shirley Anne, ed. *Reexamining The Eisenhower Presidency*. Westport, Conn.: Greenwood Press, 1993.

———. *The Eisenhower Legacy: Discussions of Presidential Leadership*. Silver Springs, Md.: Bartleby Press, 1992.

Weinstein, L., *et al. The Evolution of U.S. Strategic Command and Control and Warning, 1945–1972*. Arlington, Va.: Institute for Defense Analyses, 1975.

Whitfield, Stephen J. *The Culture of the Cold War*. Baltimore: Johns Hopkins University Press, 1991.

Wiebe, Robert H. *The Search for Order 1877–1920*. New York: Hill and Wang, 1967.

Williamson, Samuel R., Jr., and Steven L. Rearden. *The Origins of U.S. Nuclear Strategy, 1945–1953*. New York: St. Martin's Press, 1993.

Winkler, Allan A. *Life under a Cloud: American Anxiety about the Atom*. New York: Oxford University Press, 1993.

Wohlstetter, A. J., and F. S. Hoffman, R. J. Lutz, and H. S. Rowen. *R-266: Selection and Use of Strategic Air Bases*. (April 1954). Santa Monica, Calif.: Rand Corporation, 1963.

Wolfe, Alan. *America's Impasse: The Rise and Fall of the Politics of Growth*. New York: Pantheon Books, 1981.

Zimmerman, Carroll L. *Insider at SAC: Operations Analysis under General LeMay*. Manhattan, Kan.: Sunflower University Press, 1988.

Zubok, Vladislav, and Constantine Pleshakov. *Inside the Kremlin's Cold War: From Stalin to Khrushchev*. Cambridge, Mass.: Harvard University Press, 1996.

Articles

Almond, George A. "Public Opinion Polls and the Development of American Public Opinion." *The Public Opinion Quarterly* 24:4 (Winter 1960): 553–72.

Berkner, Lloyd V. "Science and Military Power." *Bulletin of Atomic Scientists* 9:10 (December 1953): 359–65.

Bernstein, Michael A., and Allen Hunter. "The Cold War and Expert Knowledge: New Essays on the History of the National Security State." *Radical History Review* 63 (1995): 1–6.

Biddle, Tami Davis. "Handling the Soviet Threat: 'Project Control' and the Debate on American Strategy in the Early Cold War Years." *Journal of Strategic Studies* 12 (September 1989): 273–302.

Brands, H. W. "The Age of Vulnerability: Eisenhower and the National Insecurity State." *American Historical Review* (1989): 963–989.

Brower, Michael. "Nuclear Strategy of the Kennedy Administration." *Bulletin of the Atomic Scientists* 18:8 (October 1962): 34–41.

Burr, William. "Avoiding the Slippery Slope: The Eisenhower Administration and the Berlin Crisis, November 1958–January 1959." *Diplomatic History* 18:2 (Spring 1994): 177–205.

Cutler, Robert. "The Development of the National Security Council." *Foreign Affairs* 34:3 (April 1956): 441–58.

Daugherty, William, Barbara Levi, and Frank von Hippel. "The Consequences of

'Limited' Nuclear Attacks on the United States." *International Security* 10:4 (Spring 1986): 3–45.

Duchin, Brian L. "'The Most Spectacular Legislative Battle of the Year': President Eisenhower and the 1958 Reorganization of the Department of Defense." *Presidential Studies Quarterly* 24:2 (Spring 1994): 243–62.

Duffield, John S. "The Soviet Military Threat to Western Europe: US Estimates in the 1950s and 1960s." *Journal of Strategic Studies* 15:2 (June 1992): 208–27.

Dulles, John Foster. "Challenge and Response in United States Policy." *Foreign Affairs* 36:1 (October, 1957): 25–43.

Erskine, Hazel Gaudet, ed. "The Polls: Defense, Peace, and Space." *The Public Opinion Quarterly* 25:3 (Fall 1961): 478–89.

Falk, Stanley L. "The National Security Council under Truman, Eisenhower, and Kennedy." *Political Science Quarterly* 79:3 (September 1964): 403–34.

Friedberg, Aaron L. "Science, the Cold War, and the American State." *Diplomatic History* 20:1 (Winter 1996): 107–18.

Garbo, Cynthia M. "The Watch Committee and the National Indications Center: The Evolution of U.S. Strategic Warning 1950–1975." *International Journal of Intelligence and Counterintelligence* 3:3 (Fall 1989): 363–85.

Gaskin, Thomas A. "Senator Lyndon B. Johnson, the Eisenhower Administration, and U.S. Foreign Policy, 1957–60." *Presidential Studies Quarterly* 24:2 (Spring 1994): 341–61.

Goodpaster, Andrew J. "Four Presidents and the Conduct of National Security Affairs—Impressions and Highlights." *Journal of International Relations* 2:1 (Spring 1977): 26–37.

Griffith, Robert W. F. "Dwight D. Eisenhower and the Corporate Commonwealth." *American Historical Review* 87:1 (February 1982): 87–122.

Hall, R. Cargill. "The Eisenhower Administration and the Cold War: Framing American Astronautics to Serve National Security." *Prologue: Quarterly of the National Archives* 27:1 (Spring 1995): 59–72.

Halperin, Morton H. "The Gaither Committee and the Policy Process." *World Politics* 13:3 (April 1961): 360–384.

Handel, Michael I. "Intelligence and the Problem of Strategic Surprise." *Journal of Strategic Studies* 7:3 (September 1984): 229–81.

Hoxie, R. Gordon. "Dwight David Eisenhower: Bicentennial Considerations." *Presidential Studies Quarterly* 20:2 (Spring 1990): 295–313.

Immerman, Richard H. "Confessions of an Eisenhower Revisionist: An Agonizing Reappraisal." *Diplomatic History* 14:3 (Summer 1990): 319–42.

Jackson, Henry M. "Organizing for Security." *Foreign Affairs* 38 (1960): 446–56.

Jervis, Robert. "Deterrence and Perception." *International Security* 7:3 (Winter 1982/1983): 3–30.

Joes, Anthony James. "Eisenhower Revisionism: The Tide Comes In." *Presidential Studies Quarterly* 15:3 (Summer 1985): 561–71.

Kennedy, John F. "A Democrat Looks at Foreign Policy." *Foreign Affairs* 36:1 (October 1957): 44–59.

———. "General Gavin Sounds the Alarm." *The Reporter* 19:7 (October 30, 1958): 35–36.

Killian, James R., Jr., and A. G. Hill. "For a Continental Defense." *Atlantic* 192:5 (November 1953): 37–41.

Kinnard, Douglas. "President Eisenhower and the Defense Budget." *Journal of Politics* 39:3 (August 1977): 596–623.

Kohn, Richard H., and Joseph P. Harahan, eds. "U.S. Strategic Air Power, 1948–1962: Excerpts from an Interview with Generals Curtis E. LeMay, Leon W. Johnson, David A Burchinal, and Jack J. Cotton." *International Security* 12:4 (Spring 1988): 78–95.

Korb, Lawrence J. "The Budget Process in the Department of Defense: 1947–77: The Strengths and Weaknesses of Three Systems." *Public Administration Review* 37:4 (July/August 1977): 334–46.

Larson, Deborah Welch. "Deterrence Theory and the Cold War." *Radical History Review* 63 (1995): 86–109.

Levi, Barbara G., Frank N. von Hippel, and William H. Daugherty. "Civilian Casualties from 'Limited' Nuclear Attacks on the Soviet Union." *International Security* 21:3 (Winter 1987): 168–89.

Lincoln, Colonel G. A. and Lt. Colonel Amos A. Jordan, Jr. "Technology and the Changing Nature of General War." *Military Review* (May 1957): 3–13.

Linklider, Roy E. "The Missile Gap Controversy." *Political Science Quarterly* 85:4 (December 1970): 600–15.

McMahon, Robert J. "Eisenhower and Third World Nationalism: A Critique of the Revisionists." *Political Science Quarterly* 101 (Fall 1986): 453–73.

Metz, Steven. "Eisenhower and the Planning of American Grand Strategy." *Journal of Strategic Studies* 14:1 (March 1991): 49–71.

Murphy, Charles J. V. "The Eisenhower Shift." *Fortune* LIII: 3 (March 1956): 110–112 and 230–238.

Nelson, Anna Kasten. "The 'Top of Policy Hill': President Eisenhower and the National Security Council." *Diplomatic History* 7:4 (Fall 1983): 307–26.

———. "President Truman and the Evolution of the National Security Council." *Journal of American History* 72:2 (September 1985): 360–78.

Newman, Stanley L. "Civil Defense and the Congress: Quiet Reversal." *Bulletin of the Atomic Scientists* 18:9 (November 1962): 33–37.

Nitze, Paul. "Limited Wars or Massive Retaliation?" *The Reporter* 17 (September 5, 1957): 40–42.

————. "Atoms, Strategy and Policy." *Foreign Affairs* 34:2 (January 1956): 187–98.

————. "The Relationship of Strategic and Theatre Nuclear Forces." *International Security* 2:2 (Fall 1977): 122–32.

Patterson, Bradley H., Jr. "Teams and Staff: Dwight Eisenhower's Innovations in the Structure and Operations of the Modern White House." *Presidential Studies Quarterly* 24:2 (Spring 1994): 277–98.

Pickett, William B. "The Eisenhower Solarium Notes." *Society for Historians of American Foreign Relations Newsletter* 16 (June 1985): 1–3.

Roman, Peter J. "Strategic Bombers over the Missile Horizon, 1957–1963." *Journal of Strategic Studies* 18 (March 1995): 200–38.

Rosenberg, David Alan. "The Origins of Overkill: Nuclear Weapons and American Strategy, 1945–1960." *International Security* 7:4 (Spring 1983): 3–71.

————. "A Smoking Radiating Ruin at the End of Two Hours." *International Security* 6:3 (Winter 1981–82): 3–17.

Sloan, John W. "The Management and Decision-Making of President Eisenhower." *Presidential Studies Quarterly* 20:2 (Spring 1990): 295–331.

Smith, Jean Edward. "Kennedy and Defense." *Air University Review* 18:3 (March-April 1967): 38–54.

Suri, Jeremi. "America's Search for a Technological Solution to the Arms Race: The Surprise Attack Conference of 1958 and a Challenge for 'Eisenhower Revisionists.'" *Diplomatic History* 21:3 (Summer 1997): 417–51.

Tobin, James. "Defense, Dollars, and Doctrines." *The Yale Review* XLVII:3 (March 1958): 321–34.

Trachtenberg, Marc. "A 'Wasting Asset': American Strategy and the Shifting Nuclear Balance, 1949–1954." *International Security* 13:2 (Winter 1988/89): 5–49.

Vandercook, Wm. F. "Making the Very Best of the Very Worst: The 'Human Effects of Nuclear Weapons' Report of 1956." *International Security* 11:1 (Summer 1986): 184–195.

Wells, Samuel F. "The Origins of Massive Retaliation." *Political Science Quarterly* 96 (Spring 1981): 31–52.

Welzenbach, Donald. "Din Land: Patriot from Polaroid." *Optics & Photonics* (October 1994): 22–29.

Wohlstetter, Albert. "The Delicate Balance of Terror." *Foreign Affairs* 37:2 (January 1959): 211–34.

————. "Rivals But No 'Race'." *Foreign Policy* 16 (Fall 1974): 48–81.

York, Herbert F., and G. Allen Greb. "Strategic Reconnaissance." *Bulletin of the Atomic Scientists* (April 1977): 33–42.

Unpublished

Chwat, John Steven, "The President's Foreign Intelligence Advisory Board: An Historical and Contemporary Analysis (1955–1975)." Congressional Research Office, 1975.

Hopkins, Robert S., III. "An Expanded Understanding of Eisenhower, American Policy, and Overflights," paper presented at the Society of Historians of American Foreign Relations Annual Conference, Boulder, Colo., June 1995.

Nelson, Anna K. "Before the National Security Advisor: Did the NSC Matter?" Society for Historians of American Foreign Relations Conference, 1988.

Roman, Peter J. "American Strategic Nuclear Force Planning, 1957–1960: The Interaction of Politics and Military Planning." Ph.D. dissertation, University of Wisconsin–Madison, 1982.

Rosenberg, David Alan. "Toward Armageddon: The Foundations of United States Nuclear Strategy, 1945–1961." Ph.D. dissertation, University of Chicago, 1983.

Snead, David L. "Sputnik, the Gaither Committee, and the Escalation of the Cold War," paper presented at the Reconsidering Sputnik: Forty Years Since the Soviet Satellite Conference, Washington, D.C., September 30–October 1, 1997.

———. "Eisenhower, the Gaither Committee, and Intelligence Assessment: The Problem of Equating Capabilities with Intentions," paper presented at the 1996 Annual Meeting of the Society for Military History, Washington, D.C., April 1996.

———. "United States National Security Policy under Presidents Truman and Eisenhower: The Evolving Role of the National Security Council." M.A. thesis, Virginia Polytechnic Institute and State University, 1991.

Transcript of "Project Solarium": A Collective Oral History. John Foster Dulles Centennial Conference, Princeton University, 1988.

Watson, Robert J. "The Eisenhower Administration and the Missile Gap, 1958–1960," paper presented at the 1996 Annual Meeting of the Society for Military History, Washington, D.C., 1996.